From Columbus to ConAgra

Rural America

Hal S. Barron
David L. Brown
Kathleen Neils Conzen
Cornelia Butler Flora
Donald Worster

Series Editors

From Columbus to ConAgra

The Globalization of Agriculture and Food

**Edited by Alessandro Bonanno,
Lawrence Busch, William H. Friedland,
Lourdes Gouveia, and Enzo Mingione**

 University Press of Kansas

Published by the University Press of Kansas (Lawrence, Kansas
66049), which was organized by the Kansas Board of Regents and is
operated and funded by Emporia State University, Fort Hays State
University, Kansas State University, Pittsburg State University,
the University of Kansas, and Wichita State University

Library of Congress Cataloging-in-Publication Data

From Columbus to ConAgra : the globalization of agriculture and food /
    edited by Alessandro Bonanno . . . [et al.].
      p.   cm. — (Rural America)
    Includes index.
    ISBN 0-7006-0660-2 (hard. : alk. paper) — ISBN
0-7006-0661-0 (pbk. : alk. paper)
    1. Food industry and trade—Congresses.   2. Produce trade—
Congresses.   3. Agriculture—Economic aspects—Congresses.
4. International business enterprises—Congresses.   5. International
trade—Congresses.   6. International economic relations—Congresses.
I. Bonanno, Alessandro.   II. Series: Rural America (Lawrence, Kan.)
HD9000.5.F76   1994
338.1—dc20   93-46569

British Library Cataloguing in Publication Data is available.

Printed in the United States of America
10 9 8 7 6 5 4 3 2 1

The paper used in this publication meets the minimum requirements of the
American National Standard for Permanence of Paper for Printed
Library Materials Z39.48-1984.

Contents

Preface

This book is about neither Columbus nor the transnational corporation ConAgra, but about the global agricultural and food sector of which Columbus and ConAgra are two ideal and temporal poles. Columbus symbolizes the era of world explorations during which the global system was established. ConAgra represents the new emerging global actors: transnational corporations (TNCs). Though they are not the only players in the new global economy, TNCs are fundamental actors in the reorganization of the socioeconomic system and are major forces of change. If the era of Columbus is long gone, its legacy remains in the era of ConAgra. The challenge for us, as it was for Columbus, is to understand what lies ahead in a now truly global society.

With the exception of the introduction, the chapters contained in this volume were originally prepared for presentation at an international interdisciplinary conference entitled "The Globalization of the Agricultural and Food Order." The conference, held at the University of Missouri–Columbia in June 1991 and cosponsored by the International Sociological Association Research Committee on Sociology of Agriculture and Food, was designed to attract international scholars conducting cutting-edge research on the globalization of the agro-food sector. Globalization has been a primary agenda for the members of the Research Committee on Sociology of Agriculture and Food, which continues work in this substantive area through a variety of initiatives.

The original papers underwent a peer review process, made possible thanks to the work of many conference participants who carefully and expeditiously reviewed the papers considered for inclusion in this volume. Each of the authors then reviewed the modified drafts and produced the final versions of the chapters. Comments from the reviewers of the University Press of Kansas also guided the final revisions.

The review process was assisted by a number of individuals and organizations. On behalf of all the authors, we would like to acknowledge the contributions of those in the United States and abroad who assisted us in this endeavor. Particular thanks go to the College of Agriculture, Food and Natural Resources of the University of Missouri for its generous assistance in the organization of the conference. We would also like to thank Julie Brandt, Mary Hendrickson, Paula Owsley, and Lynne Moore for their invaluable help in the various phases of the preparation of this volume. Also, thanks go to Michael Schulman and the other, anonymous reviewer for the University Press of Kansas for their constructive suggestions. Finally, our gratitude goes to those who submitted their works for inclusion in the volume. Without their research, this book would have not been possible.

The editors

Introduction

The globalization of the socioeconomic system has become a widely debated issue in recent years. Attention has been given to a number of aspects that form the core characteristics of the phenomenon; however, these aspects have often been viewed along specific disciplinary lines. Economists, for instance, have tended to interpret globalization in terms of the elimination of international barriers to trade, historians and geographers have emphasized the evolution and change of the world system; sociologists have focused their attention on production and consumption processes. Regardless of these disciplinary differences, consensus has emerged in support of the concept that globalization is developing in the context of a new international division of labor.

This new international division of labor mandates a realignment of the relationship among the spheres of production, finances, and socioeconomic control. Indeed, production and capital investments have spread across the globe at a very rapid rate. Firms have shifted an important portion of their operations from core countries to locations that provide more attractive opportunities for the allocation of productive resources, including labor. At the same time capital has been moved at an even faster pace. The redistribution of productive activities and investments across the globe has been paralleled, however, by an increased concentration of the control of financial resources and research capabilities, which remain firmly in the hands of a relatively small number of transnational corporations and advanced nations. More specifically, financial global cities (Sassen 1988; Mingione 1991) use modern communication technology to orchestrate and control worldwide production, while research and development activities follow suit (Busch et al. 1991). Contrary to positions that view the new international division of labor as chaotic, disorganized, or decentered are those that argue for the maintenance of a strong center. This center must be based on the extremely rational control of the most essential fiscal and intellectual resources, which in turn are the keys to exerting command over people and resources that are more widespread than ever before.

The new international division of labor involves a qualitative shift from the past, one that acknowledges that something has been added to the world in the past several decades. Certainly, through the Second World War, despite the growing significance of *inter*national trade, the salient political-

1

economic developments of the past four centuries have been marked by the rise in importance of the nation-state. Thus, one of the first manifestations of change that we regard as crucial in understanding globalization is that the world stands on the brink of a major shift in sociopolitical and economic arrangements in which the nation, previously the critical element in understanding the world, is becoming less significant.

A second manifestation is the emergence of a different distribution of winners and losers. In the past, winners and losers have been conceived, primarily and correctly, in terms of *nations*, more specifically, in terms of a North/South or core/periphery hierarchy, with the United States at its apex. This does not mean, however, that scholars, especially social scientists, were oblivious to the masses of poor populations and regions within the core. Still, the nations of the North invariably fared better on a wide range of socioeconomic indicators than those in the South.

Globalization and the new international division of labor have not drastically altered the main axes of this international hierarchy—at least not yet. But these processes have demoted the nation-state as the defining space for economic activity and, more precisely, for capital accumulation. In this sense, subnational spaces and population groups—regardless of their locations on the world map—are woven into, or excluded from, global production and trade networks and, consequently, turn into new winners or losers. The central defining element behind this configuration of new capital accumulation spaces is the transnational corporation (TNC). In the emergence of the new global system, the distribution of winners and losers will prove to be different. In this book we set out to discover the new principles determining that distribution.

Finally, globalization is a process that permeates major aspects of everyday life. In examining this process, we will be focusing on two of the major elements of the production of everyday life—material production and the ways in which products are distributed, i.e., the market. The basic argument we will be exploring centers on the globalization of production processes and markets.

Previously, the emphasis in the analysis of globalization has been on production. It is now commonly understood, because of the hundreds of studies and thousands of journalistic articles, that automobiles, whether they are assembled in the United States or Japan, have components that are globally sourced. This has long been true: The jute that once provided the insulation for car doors came from India or Africa, just as the rubber for the tires came from Brazil or Malaysia.

Until the 1960s, most automobile components were national in origin. After the 1970s, an increasing volume of parts came from other places in the world. And despite all the hoopla by U.S. automakers about Japanese penetration of the U.S. market and Japan's blockage of U.S. exports, the tendency toward joint ventures between U.S. and Japanese carmakers (as well as the investments that they have in each other's firms) shows that globalization of production is now very advanced. Indeed, Honda is now the fourth largest "American" firm according to Forbes (Flint 1992). Furthermore, "classic" American automobiles such as Ford's Crown Victoria and Chevrolet's Nova are produced in Mexico and Taiwan, respectively.

It is within markets, however, that the globalization process has now become increasingly important. To use the auto industry as an example, Japanese carmakers are able to make cosmetic changes to basic models (as well as more structural changes such as adding catalytic converters) to adapt them for distinct national markets, as well as for niches within national markets. We consider this to be a critical element of the globalization process.

Popular images about globalization, as is already clear from the above examples, come primarily from traditional manufacturing sectors. The focus has long been on linchpin high-tech industries: automobiles, electronics, and, not-so-high-tech but vital, textiles and clothing. Little has entered into the popular literature about the extent of the internationalization of food production (including product recomposition and innovation), consumption (adapting food products to niche markets), and trade (expanding trade and, more profoundly, redefining international markets in food). Yet the internationalization of agriculture and food is bound to make some of the most critical, positive as well as negative, contributions to the reconfiguration of global winners and losers.

The Decline of the Nation-State

The Relevance and Irrelevance of the Nation-State

The main burden of our projections about the future of the nation-state, in this period of accelerated globalization, is that it can be expected to decline, become somewhat irrelevant, but *not* disappear in the foreseeable future. The nation-state can be expected to continue to play an important role in capital accumulation as this process becomes increasingly based on globalization.

The nation-state will continue to protect and legitimate private property rights, including maintaining a monopoly of law and force, domestically and internationally. Similarly, the nation-state will remain an important actor in controlling the movement of goods and, less significantly, of people across geographic boundaries. Regardless of how the world map is redrawn, the nation-state will continue to be, ideologically, a powerful force for mobilizing resources and forging class alliances. What is different, however, is that in the alliances of state, capital, and other domestic classes, the state no longer exercises the hegemonic authority that it once did. Capital—more precisely, global capital—is now in the driver's seat. Thus, there was a time, not so long ago, when a nation-state such as the United States or France controlled how capital and its accumulation process were shaped. Now, as we shall show, TNCs make the accumulation decisions to which nation-states must adapt.

Agencies, such as the TNCs, have become the critical actors in the expansion of the global *economy*, which means that some weak *transnational state forms* can be expected to become increasingly important, though not dominant, in the near future. It also means that, with a vacuum developing because of the inability of the nation-state to resolve the problems of economic organization caused by socioeconomic globalization, we can anticipate that lower levels of political organization (regional and local) will more actively seek control of some of the more difficult adjustment problems created by globalization.

Presently, the major process of globalization is economic. The movement of capital, in its multifarious forms, is probably the most remarkable element of globalization. Studies during the 1970s such as *Global Reach* (Barnet and Mueller 1974) initially recognized this process and correctly recognized the TNCs as the driving force for globalization. There was an accompanying tendency, recognizing how important global capital had become, to denigrate the importance of the nation-state. Some commentators—Borrego (1981), for example—even saw the complete *ir*relevance of the nation-state—its withering away.

Our view is that this perception of the irrelevance of the state gave too much credence to the power of the TNCs. Equally important is the *institutional* power of the nation-state and the psychological attachment that the nation-state (or ethnicity) holds for the majority of its citizens. While the population of most modern capitalist nation-states has become increasingly cosmopolitan, this trend has not manifested itself as much in a psychological detachment from the nation-state as in an increased affinity for transnational forms: the United Nations (UN) and its agencies; the General Agreement on Tariffs and Trade (GATT); as well as regional developments, such as the European Community (EC) and the North American Free Trade Agreement (NAFTA).

In fact, globalization and the decline of traditionally established nation-states are very complex sociocultural phenomena, affected by and affecting the very ways in which individual identities are structured. Human mobility and media communications open sociocultural systems, manifested by a willingness to acknowledge and/or adopt alien customs and traditions—the willingness to eat "strange" foods such as tomatoes and pizza (Levenstein 1985) or Szechuanese food or hamburgers, for example—or new types of social divisions (often based on long-disappeared traditional forms such as Lombardian identity in northern Italy, the revival of Occitanie in southern France or of Catalonia in Spain). The fundamental structure of social identity has remained local and specific (based on family, kin, social, and ethnic groups), but now these forms of identity are decreasingly subsumed by the economic and political imperatives of the nation-state in the industrial age (Tilly 1975). In this context, then, the formation of social identities is freed to regain localistic, familial, and other specific attachments and is increasingly influenced by globalization trends. These processes affect social life in complex ways that are difficult to understand.

The Continuing Significance of the Nation-State

One crucial reason why we do not envision the withering away of the nation-state is related to the continuing demand for the maintenance of regulatory apparatuses. While some TNCs may exercise social responsibility with respect to their labor forces and the environment, the driving force of the TNC is its "bottom line," that is its profits. However, the very size of the large transnationals puts them continuously in public view. At the very least they must maintain an image as a responsible agency. Distancing production from consumption may serve, of course, to conceal attempts to avoid environmental and other regulations. However, all very large corporations are faced with a built-in contradiction between their need for continual cost cutting and their high public profile. Some will be more willing than others to risk their reputations.

But as TNCs move around the globe seeking out new markets and new locations for production, they search for cheap and amenable labor that also, adhering to classic patterns, struggles to organize itself to resolve wage and working-condition problems. Similarly, the economic cost of maintaining a pristine environment is often subversive of the "bottom line." The TNCs resolve such problems by moving to new production locations when the costs of environmental maintenance become too expensive.

In such circumstances, workers and citizens concerned with problems of employment or the environment must turn to the *political* agencies available to them—the nation-state and other forms of governmental organization.

To the extent that the nation-state ignores such demands for action, it becomes vulnerable to criticism for failing to fulfill its legitimation function.

Another reason that the nation-state can be expected to maintain some significance is that it is still the appropriate unit for handling economic development. TNCs pursue their own individual self-interests and cannot plan and manipulate economic development on a basis other than the corporate level. Thus, the role of overall economic development can be expected to remain in the domain of the nation-state.

One element of this sense of identity that many citizens have with their nation-state is that, after several hundred years of cultural development, nation-states still provide the primary cultural identity for hundreds of millions of citizens. While regional dialects may still be important in countries such as Italy, France, or Portugal, and regional cultures flourish (or continue to persist) in Spain and the United Kingdom, national cultural identity is reinforced continuously by national media systems. Germans, given the opportunity to reunite, express preference for their *germanity*, even though slogans appear on West German walls calling for East Germans to "get out." National culture, in a word, continues to carry an enormous burden and responsibility for citizen identity.

But perhaps the most important reason for the refusal of the nation-state to wither away despite its decreasing economic importance is the weaknesses (or, more likely, nonexistence) of alternative political forms. The EC, despite its many difficulties in moving forward to *political* integration, will undoubtedly continue to develop such coordination. As it succeeds, however, it replaces national states with a supranational state, which is still not a political form appropriate for the global political economy. The EC, when it becomes a political community, will still be only a new kind of nation-state, one undoubtedly different from the nation-states that compose it (Bonanno 1992 and Chapter 12, by Bonanno, in this book). And despite the recognition of the theoretical need for a transnational state (Friedland 1991), no clear forms have yet emerged.

The Irrelevance of the Nation-State

While the nation-state cannot be expected to wither away in the immediate future, there can be little doubt about its increased *economic* irrelevance. This irrelevance can be seen most clearly when considering the nation-state from two distinct points of view: regulation on one hand; and production and markets on the other. From the regulation viewpoint—maintaining control over the otherwise uncontrollable economic forces of the TNCs—the nation-state remains the primary control mechanism. Neither regional nor local political bodies, and certainly not the weak international organizations such as the Food and Agriculture Organization (FAO) of the UN or the Organization for Economic Cooperation and Development (OECD), represent viable regulatory agents. By default, then, the nation-state remains the agency to which the citizenry must turn.

At the same time that nation-states must provide legitimation for economic development, however, from the viewpoint of production and the market the nation-state has decreased in significance and can be expected to continue to do so. Our clothing, whether purchased in New York City or Paris or Oslo or Zurich, bears labels now known uniformly throughout the world: Victoria's Secret, Benetton, Calvin Klein, Yves St. Laurent, and so on. The label tells us that this shirt was assembled in Mauritius or the Dominican Republic from cloth manufactured in the United States and cut in Costa Rica. While campaigns are mounted to "Buy American" and "Save the American Farm," the fresh produce in U.S. supermarkets can be found in supermarkets bearing the same name although owned by different corporate groups (Safeway, for example). Or produce may bear different names but come from a variety of production platforms. In the advanced capitalist countries, it is possible to eat grapes from Chile and kiwifruit from New Zealand during the Northern Hemisphere winter and an increasing variety of tropical exotics from the Southern Hemisphere (for example, from Argentina, Brazil, Malaysia, South Africa, as well as from India and Mexico).

Still, the search for new forms of political organization transcending the national level continues. In Europe, the search for a new level of political-economic organization seems relentless. Despite the staggering problems that organizations such as GATT have to confront, the continuing and near-universal ideological hold of the comparative advantage principle must come to grips with traditional national attachments. And the explorations for regional forms of economic organization such as NAFTA, to the extent that they become successful (and this does not just mean the signing of a treaty but the implementation of the treaty at the grassroots level), will continue to erode the significance of the nation-state.

Accompanying this process is the continued growth of localism and regionalism. Organizational forms such as the UN and GATT are too distant for a citizenry to exercise any control over them. As long as the nation-state acts as the crucial intermediary between levels of organization and the citizenry, citizens will seek other forms of political organization to protect themselves. This search accounts, we believe, for the resuscitation of regional identities and political movements. While the Scottish Nationalists may not do very well in British elections, they will not "go away." Bretagne-isme in France waxes and wanes. The rise of the Lombardy League in the

1992 Italian political elections signals the unhappiness of the north with the corruption and inefficiencies of the national government.

Applying this analysis to agriculture, we see the continuing significance of the nation-state as the instrumentality to which agricultural producers will turn to resolve their problems. And the problems will continue—for example, in the United States the continuing decimation of small units of production, the final demise of family-based farming and its replacement by corporate family farms, the continuing cost-price squeeze, and the technological treadmill that drives agricultural producers continually into debt and bankruptcy; and in Europe, the continuous transformation of the nature and economics of family farms toward pluriactivity and part-time farming in order to face increasing competition.

Where should agriculture turn in crisis? Setting aside the fact that the traditional organizational forms in nation-state after nation-state have been geared to national political forms, can one envision a coalition of Belgian, Dutch, French, Italian, U.S., Uruguayan, Brazilian, and New Zealand farmers marching on a GATT meeting in Punta del Este? And what could they demand to benefit them all, since they are all in competition with one another? It is to the traditional loci of legitimation of their own nation-states that agricultural forces, like other economic forces that have not become transnationalized (that is, the local and national bourgeoisie), will have to turn, despite the increased recognition of the continuing irrelevance of those nation-states.

Nor can we expect supernational agencies such as GATT, FAO, or OECD to provide the kind of support and legitimation that has sustained for so long the faith of agricultural producers in the legitimacy of the nation-state. For, despite the willingness of French farmers to gather in front of the agricultural ministry in Paris or of American farmers to organize the occasional tractorcade in Washington or their ability to elect a senator from Minnesota, it is to the nation-state that agricultural producers can be expected to turn for action and for legitimation, not to GATT or the FAO. We are entering a period, then, in which the nation-state will prove to be instrumentally weak, yet the only resource that is historically, culturally, and institutionally available to its citizens. While this experience will be increasingly frustrating, we can expect it to continue.

The Globalization of Production and Consumption: The Case of Agriculture and Food

In turning to the globalization of production and consumption, it is necessary to acknowledge that production and consumption take place in specific geographic locations and that, as a result, some component of *localism* is always involved. That having been said, what is less important than the fixed spatial location of production and consumption is that both now occur on a world-wide basis. This fact was recognized early by economists under the rubric of "trade." But "trade" fails to capture the complexity of the movements of partial and whole commodities as they are circulated around the world for ultimate consumption in markets thousands of miles apart. The profundity of spatial distribution can be understood by examining the components of automobiles or chickens, of cattle or clothing, of kiwifruit or computers. All of these commodities, with some variation of course, are produced in a variety of spatial locations across the globe for distribution and marketing in a similar variety of locations.

The globalization of production is now commonly understood by most citicens, even though a good deal of mystification remains, one result of campaigns to "Buy National." In the automobile industry, for example, the wounded complaints about the Japanese from magnates such as Chrysler Corporation's Lee Iaccoca serve to cover up three critical involvements that Chrysler has in the global production system. The first is the joint arrangements Chrysler has had for years with Japan's Mitsubishi to produce automobiles sold in the United States with Chrysler labels. The second is the fact that Chrysler has been a shareholder in Japanese automobile corporations for some time. And, finally, such complaints overlook the fact that components in Chrysler (and in Ford and General Motors) cars come from many countries outside of the United States. The "Made in America" label has come to mean, in fact, *assembled* in the United States. U.S. car manufacturers have been less than forthcoming in explaining what percentage of labor for each automobile comes from workers outside the United States.

Moreover, automotive corporations such as Ford have developed extensive integration between their factories in the United States, Mexico, Canada, and in different European countries. Such integration was explicitly embodied in Ford's development of its Fiesta model as a "world car": produced in a variety of plants; assembled on a different constellation of assembly lines; and marketed throughout the Western capitalist countries, bearing on the body the flags of the many countries involved in the car's production.

Automobiles are enormously complex, of course, composed of thousands of parts made of different kinds of metal, plastic, fabric, and rubber. Arranging the production of the many components and their delivery to assembly locations involves monumental logistics. In that sense, the transnational character of automobile firms can be easily grasped. But what about quotidian commodities such as chickens, kiwifruit, or orange juice, especially if they are unprocessed and perishable?

Each of these food commodities exposes different aspects of globalization, yet each is much simpler than the automotive system. Chickens, in a large spatial area such as the United States with its enormous market, can be fairly well nationalized. Yet, the globalization of chicken production is well under way, with the production of eggs in one location, the raising of chickens in another, the slaughter in a third, the deboning of the meat (for some markets) in yet another, and finally, the shipment of chicken meat into different markets (Heffernan 1984). These processes increasingly involve production locations such as the United States or Thailand and partial processing in locations such as Mexico for marketing in Japan.

While Sanderson (1986) has defined a "world steer," the global character of the "world chicken" has not yet become as clear. Indeed, to be accurate, we should acknowledge that there is not yet, in fact, a global chicken. Rather, chickens as a commodity, while beginning to become internationalized, are still more of a regional commodity intended for localized markets.

Kiwifruit, in contrast, manifests true globalization. Originally a minor fruit known as the Chinese gooseberry, the kiwifruit became a global phenomenon through an organized campaign by the New Zealanders. Marketing it aggressively in the United States, Western Europe, and Japan, New Zealanders made consumers and pastry bakers everywhere aware of the potential of the fruit. Consumers were intrigued by its fuzzy exterior and bright green and tasty interior. Bakers learned that it could be used instead of strawberries to make colorful fruit tarts and pies and that kiwis, unlike strawberries, had a long shelf life.[1]

But New Zealand's placement of kiwifruit into the consciousness of consumers represented only the beginning of its globalization. As consumption skyrocketed, other national producers clamored to get on the kiwi bandwagon. Thousands of hectares of kiwi vines were planted in Italy, France, Spain, the United States, and Chile. And almost before anyone realized it, kiwifruit was being produced in dozens of locations for distribution in markets all over the Western capitalist world. The result has been the usual case of overproduction.

Whereas the New Zealanders began with a monopoly on the fruit (then available in advanced capitalist societies seasonally), they were quickly joined by producers in other parts of the world. The relatively high storability of kiwifruit, however, soon meant that the "down-under" seasonal availability led to overlaps between Southern Hemisphere and Northern Hemisphere production. In the resultant "kiwi war," California producers claimed that the New Zealanders were dumping fruit in the U.S. market, a claim upheld by the U.S. Trade Commission. Thus, a socially created global *market* was rapidly transformed into a global *production system*.

Finally, the international character of orange juice is often obscured by the minutia of print-cluttered labels. A careful examination of such labels shows that most orange juice, while appearing to be "fresh," has been *reconstituted* from concentrates originating in countries such as the United States, Brazil, Israel, and others. Only the water, added to the concentrate, is "local."

Using computers and electronic equipment as examples, the global character of production and marketing are notable. Whether talking about Apple's Macintosh or IBM's PCs, VCRs, calculators of different kinds, television sets, or electronic calendars, the fact that the label may state "Made in _____" tells only part of the story. The research and development for components may have taken place in the United States or Japan, the fabrication of electronic chips in France or Singapore, and the assembly in Korea or Taiwan. And the markets are *everywhere*, even if the prime markets are in the industrialized, capitalist West. Thus far we have concentrated the discussion on production, with only some mention of marketing/consumption. Let us now address the end-use of globalized commodities more directly.

If Ford produced the first "world car," we should perhaps designate Benetton as the producer of the first "world clothes." Benetton produces clothing in a variety of countries intended for multiple markets. All of Benetton's clothes are initially produced in white and then dyed according to the color preferences of their intended markets. Thus, purple is popular in Europe and easily can be found in Benetton shops there. In contrast, in Columbia, Missouri, for instance, where purple is considered exotic, purple clothes are as scarce as hen's teeth.

What is important about Benetton's marketing strategies is the standardization of production and the coloration for the niche market. And despite the fact that the firm maintains its base in Italy and, indeed, still in a single family, Benetton is globally recognized. Benetton shops, whether in Brighton, England, or Ann Arbor, Michigan, or Florence, Italy, sell a recognized and fundamentally standardized product, just as standardized as a McDonald's hamburger.

As flexible production has become the watchword for the global producers, flexible consumption—the recognition of the existence of a multiplicity of niches—has become the critical element in the globalization of consumption. There are some universally standardized global products (Coca-Cola is a good example), but, increasingly, marketers have discovered that markets should be tailored for distinctive sets of consumers.

What is equally significant, however, to Coca-Cola's global standardization is the recognition that markets change and that they can be very different. In the United States, heightened sensibilities about the relationship between fat and heart attacks has resulted in consumers demanding lean beef. Having spent decades consuming huge "marbled" (that is, fatty) steaks, American consumers now want less beef, and the beef they do want should have less fat marbling. In contrast, the Japanese, not having had a rich beef diet in the past but now having the kind of income that permits the consumption of expensive meats, have demanded marbled beef. In all likelihood, as arteriosclerosis becomes more significant in Japan after some decades of fatty beef consumption, Japanese tastes will change. It will then become necessary for producers to accommodate the changing market. In the meantime, however, beef producers, to be successful, have to learn how to raise some cattle with little fat and others with much fat.

Similar changes are occurring in other food preferences. Iceberg lettuce, long a staple in the United States, was almost unknown in Europe a decade ago. Europeans, in contrast to Americans, thought of "leaf lettuce" when the word lettuce was mentioned. Leaf lettuce in the United States was regarded a decade ago as a kind of aberration, something eaten by eastern intellectuals, academicians, and other elite types. Today, Americans are eating leaf lettuce in increasing quantities, and Europeans have begun their love affair with iceberg lettuce. Lettuce producers, whether in the United States, France, Spain, or Italy, ignore these market trends at their peril.

Thus, there is an ostensible contradiction between the need for mass production and niche marketing that is being resolved by firms that "go global." By standardizing production and making cosmetic changes to their products to fit niches, the firms that do this most effectively become the new winners in the global competition for growth.

Who Benefits from Globalization?
New Winners, New Losers

All societies experiencing stratification (are there any that do not?) have winners and losers. What demarcates capitalist societies from all other societies is that winners and losers change more rapidly. This is not to argue that capitalist societies are continually circulating their elites, but compared with feudal, slave, and other societies, there is greater individual mobility in capitalist societies. The Horatio Alger story may be a myth, but the myth has a strong enough base to sustain a whole host of ideological beliefs.

Globalization, however, introduces a new dimension to the matter of winners and losers. Some general statements can be made about this process: TNCs will, on the whole, get bigger and more powerful; workers historically organized in trade unions will see their gains eroded; medium-sized agricultural production units will continue to be vulnerable, and larger agri-business units will extend their domination of food production; the underclass in the most raucous of the free-enterprise societies (such as the United States) will continue to suffer economic misery while being blamed for their poverty.

Beyond these general statements, however, we also envision a significant reshaping of those who will benefit from the globalization process. There will be new winners and new losers. Some of the previous winners at the nation-state level will become losers as production and markets globalize.

Perhaps the most obvious example of the decline of former winners is the automobile industry. U.S. producers, formerly dominant in production in the United States and globally, have shown a vulnerability in their inability to adapt to flexible production methods *and* flexibility in challenging markets. Grown insufferable by their long-standing dominance of the largest single market, the U.S. automakers never learned to make subcompact automobiles without entering into joint ventures with the Japanese, who directed production of such vehicles. Even the brouhaha about ostensible barriers to the entry of U.S. vehicles into Japan demonstrates this inflexibility; though they complain, U.S. manufacturers have been unwilling to produce cars with right-hand drive to satisfy demands of Japanese consumers.

The downsizing of General Motors in 1992 is being matched by the reorganization of one of the globe's former winners, IBM. Having dominated global production and marketing of large machines, IBM has been largely unsuccessful in dealing with the widespread use of personal computers. For example, IBM, which originally provided McDonald's computerized cash-register and inventory-control system lost the contract to second-ranked Olivetti.

What characterizes these losers, despite their previous status as important global corporations, has been their relative inflexibility and arrogant belief that their control of the U.S. market was untouchable. Yet, what characterizes global production and marketing is the continued expansion of mass production adapted to specialized and niche markets; something to which previous winners at the national level have often been unable to adapt. Considering that technology changes rapidly, that market demands shift continually, what is required by the new globalization of production and marketing are previously unknown levels of flexibility.

Scholars and scientists talk about the new age of production/marketing as being characterized by flexible production. This is, perhaps, a misnomer. Despite the rhetoric about the end of Fordism and the discovery by critical deconstructionists of "post-Fordism," a more accurate designation requires the recognition that we are still living in a Fordist age characterized by two distinct phenomena: (1) mass production, albeit on a new and smaller scale than the mass production of the earlier automobile age; and (2) relatively high incomes for a substantial proportion of the population, which can be translated into higher consumption of the goods being produced.

This new dimension of globalization should not be characterized by the term "Fordism" but rather by "Sloanism," after Alfred P. Sloan[2]. Sloan took five basic models of automobiles and introduced the possibility of an almost unlimited augmentation of accessories. This differentiating of the automotive market into an almost infinite number of segments could, at the same time, force consumers to the very top of their discretionary range in purchasing automobiles (see Chapter 10, by Friedland, in this volume).

Consider, for example, the current move to functional attribute (Moshy 1986), also known as identity-preserved crops (Urban 1991). Under the older Fordist model of agricultural production, what counted was the production of huge quantities of bulk agricultural commodities (wheat, corn, and so on). While there were, and still are, some minor variations in qualities among these commodities, their production still conforms to the Fordist model. In contrast, identity-preserved crops are tailored to specific niche markets. Wheat might be redesigned, using the tools provided by biotechnology, to produce excellent wallpaper paste. Canola has been redesigned to produce lauric acid, a major ingredient in the manufacture of soaps and detergents. Soybeans might be redesigned to produce an analog to cocoa butter. In each case, the transformation of the crop is relatively minor (perhaps a few genes replaced or transformed), but the result is precisely the kind of market segmentation and product differentiation that Sloan had in mind.

This process should be contrasted to the introduction of new crops, an activity that has met with relatively little success in this century. Introduction of large numbers of new crops would truly transform agriculture, while the creation of identity-preserved crops helps save the existing form of social organization surrounding agricultural production from its own excess production. Thus, the changes are not post-fordist as much as they are Sloanist—designed to maintain the existing order, albeit in a new form. It is this shift from Fordism to sloanism that is currently at work in global production systems and markets; systems in which production flexibility meets market flexibility. And those firms, groups, and individuals that can meet these new requirements of flexibility (and can amass the necessary resources) will be the new winners in the global system.

But it will not simply be large TNCs that will be the winners; some, like GM and IBM, have already shown substantial vulnerability, although it is difficult to believe that they will disappear. Other winners besides the Japanese corporate groups (whose domination is also not engraved in stone) show signs of prosperity in meeting the global market with appropriate production. We are especially reminded of the ability of relatively small-scale agricultural producers in Italy's Emilia-Romagna region to develop flexible production, flexible marketing systems, and part-time agriculture in ways that have led them to substantial prosperity, albeit on a much reduced scale and in a dependent position compared with the large TNCs.

The point that must be emphasized is that the traditional winners and losers at the national level will not necessarily be the same as globalization expands. Emilia-Romagna farmers have not always been as prosperous as they have been in the 1980s and 1990s. It has been their ability to develop part-time farming for specialized niche production that has yielded them their winner status, for the moment. Comparing them with another winner, such as ConAgra, demonstrates the meagerness of the Emilia-Romagna status since global food firms such as ConAgra or Ferruzzi or Cargill represent winning on a scale monumentally beyond the gains of part-time farmers. But it would be erroneous to focus exclusively on the large TNCs as the sole winners because, not only are some of them turning into losers, but, just as important, the success of smaller-scale winners gives *them* a stake in the new global organization.

At the same time, it is necessary to emphasize that the expansion of globalization, in production and marketing, is not the product of conspiracy by the TNCs. Globalization, like early capitalism, is simply a process whose time has come. In their struggle to survive, individual corporations and individuals have responded to technological change, to homogenization of demand accompanied by specialized cultural and niche requirements, in the world of competitive capitalism. In this process they have (1) sought cheaper sources of labor and land; (2) captured the benefits of improved technologies of transportation; and (3) whipsawed nation-states and localities into providing tax incentives and benefits, to satisfy their individual "bottom lines"—that is, their profits. In this unceasing search for reduced production costs and expanded markets they have become the driving agents for a qualitative change in the mode of production. In many respects the winners are much like the scientists described by Arthur Koestler (1968): sleepwalkers; simply trying to figure a way out of their immediate problems but stumbling into new forms of social organization.

It is worth examining the issue of winners and losers from the viewpoint of geography, particularly since the imbalance in the North–South distribution of resources has emerged as a critical issue between nation-states in the two halves of the globe. Considering that capitalism emerged in its fullest expression in the Northern Hemisphere, it is not surprising that the Northern Hemisphere has benefited enormously during the stages of development of capitalism up to the present. There are serious grounds for acknowledging the complaints of Southern Hemisphere nations, particularly concerning such issues as germ plasm and biotechnology. The insistence of the North on treating germ plasm as a "common heritage of mankind" while insisting on the patentability of life forms represents an attempt to maintain the pattern of inequality that has been in place for the past three centuries.

This development, however, occurs primarily at the level of the nation-state, and from a national point of view, the solidarity of each hemisphere with respect to the other is understandable. Yet, *within* each nation-state, North or South, there are winners and losers, and sometimes the winners in losing nations or regions have been willing to act as agents, or compradors, for their external exploiters. Yet even these patterns are not engraved in stone; shown the opportunity to develop a competitive advantage, compradors have been known to become independent agents seeking to become bigger winners. This pattern has not yet become significant in southern continents such as Africa, but in other locations—Brazil and Chile in South America for instance—one can already discern new winners beginning to surface, fitting the needs of a globalized economy.

Yet another aspect of the shifting sands of winners and losers can be found in issues of ethnicity and race. In the context of single nations, race and ethnicity are simple: an ostensible central, dominant, homogeneous ethnic/racial group is confronted by some kind of "external other." Whether African-Americans in the United States, Turks in Germany, Finns in Sweden, Filipinos and Somalis in Italy, or Arabs in Spain, each national society historically has attempted to identify a core identity and culture and has sought, at the same time, to distinguish outsiders so as to exploit them to the core group's advantage. This process is not yet at an end, but is becoming increasingly irrelevant.

This is not to say that race or ethnic discrimination has disappeared or will disappear in the future; rather, it is to argue that it will *change*. For one thing, even though labor is much less mobile than capital in the new globalization, it has become immensely more mobile. The Japanese may prefer to remain in Japan, but they require high-level managers and professionals to relocate to the West. As Margaret Thatcher's educational policies devastate British universities, the brain drain of British academicians to other locations can be expected to accelerate as academic labor markets improve.

Of course, the movement of relatively unskilled and uneducated workers can also be expected to continue. Thus, the exhaustion of the labor supply to the U.S. Southwest from Mexico's central highlands has caused a massive population movement from southern Mexico. Mexican Native Americans, in particular Mixtec Indians from Oaxaca, have become a major new factor to feed the demand for agricultural workers in central Mexico and Baja California, as well as across the border in the United States The Mixtecans come from a background in which their corporate identity has been based historically upon the village, the *pueblo*. In their diaspora, following the classical tradition of many immigrant groups, they have learned a new corporate identity, Mixtecan, an identity previously unknown to them. Exploited by Mexicans in Mexico, victimized by all of the institutions of the Mexican political economy and its central political apparatus, the Partido Revolucionario Institucional (PRI), and, of course, by employers in the United States, this new Mixtecan identity has led to experimentation with new forms of political and social organization (Kearney and Nagengast 1989). Can economic organization be far behind?

Freed from the constraints of traditional society, no longer willing to accept their victimization by the central government of Mexico or by the *migra* in the United States, the Mixtecs are experimenting with new forms of organization. Many of the old patriarchal inflexibilities are carried forward, of course, but at the same time, women enter the labor market and begin to question the old ways. The process is very uneven.

Additionally, one must also acknowledge that the present misery of Filipino housemaids in Italy and Mixtecan farmworkers in California is relative. From the point of view of the overall society, these workers are losers. From the viewpoint of the individual actors, they have improved their material situation in the world and often consider themselves to be winners.

Similarly, women as producers and consumers will introduce a new dimension to the issue of winners and losers. As women become the shock troops of production in locations such as Southeast Asia or in the *maquiladoras* on the Mexican side of the U.S.-Mexico border, the degree to which they are winners or losers becomes increasingly problematic. On one hand, their economic status seems to rise with steady employment; on the other, their economic situation remains precarious and their exposure to chemicals and the rigidity of mass production methods makes them physically vulnerable. And this says nothing about the depredations on social organization as women become the economic mainstays of the household.

The situations of women and ethnic groups are also relevant vis-à-vis the process of informalization. Informalization is one of the characteristics of globalization both in terms of the production of goods and services and the use and availability of labor. Informal production strategies and informal use of labor have characterized the creation of production-consumption networks, which have greatly enhanced capital flexibility in recent decades. Women and ethnic groups have been fundamental components of this renewed flexibility, particularly because of their status as weak segments of the labor force. From one point of view they can be considered winners. However, as in the cases discussed earlier, their condition as winners (i.e., people with some form of employment) is increasingly problematic because the conditions of their labor are frequently highly exploitative, often physically dangerous, and recurrently underpaid. From this perspective, the introduction of women and ethnic groups into informal production processes makes them obvious losers.

If we see significant changes in some socioeconomic relations, we do not envision any fundamental restructuring of the capitalist world or of relations between capitalists and the proletariat. But the conditions of each are changing. Capital has become infinitely more mobile and somewhat more cosmopolitan and, despite the continued significance that individuals may place upon their personal cultural identity and/or that of their firm, that sort of identity becomes increasingly irrelevant. It no longer matters that Robert Goizueta, the head of Coca-Cola, is a Cuban; his reward of $82 million for performance in 1991 transcends the cheering stockholders of the corporation who might once (and perhaps even now) have considered him a "greaser" or a "spick." As stockholders and corporate managers become ever more distant from the activities on the shop or office floor, though they may be as racist as ever, the effects of such racism become diluted by their preference for the "bottom line," i.e., profits, to which they will sacrifice much, including their personal predilection for overt racism.

The proletariat has also changed. With the accelerated substitution of labor by capital, the importance of skilled manual workers has dropped, and, instead, the professional-managerial class has emerged as the privileged "working class," a proletariat by classical Marxist standards (since they do not own the means of production even if many of them do have stock options) but one that can no longer recognize its own proletarian status. Just as C. Wright Mills identified the new middle class in *White Collar* in 1953, it is time to recognize that the new proletariat is privileged, highly educated, cosmopolitan, consumption oriented, and bound to the flexibility of the economy. It still takes time to understand that flexibility, but young people in advanced capitalist societies acknowledge it when they refuse to think in terms of lifetime careers but, instead, think in terms of fifteen-year occupational trajectories.

Whither Globalization?

Although there are many arguments about the extent of globalization, most observers of sociopolitical-economic processes agree that globalization is occurring and that it is significant. What is less clear is where the process is headed, how fast it will occur, and the extent of the problems it will cause for nation-states, regions, and localities. We do not consider ourselves sufficiently skilled at prognostication to set out a detailed schema for the future of globalization. We believe it possible, however, to delineate some parameters that will help in the analysis of future developments.

As should probably be clear by now, we consider the critical actors in the near future, during the next several decades at least, to be the transnational corporations. The TNCs have emerged as significant forms of economic organization, knowledgeable about the complexities of production and distribution in many different locations and having developed the skills to handle this complexity. A critical skill in this development has been their ability to understand the variations in regulations of different countries and to adapt to those differences. This capability is not trivial. Yet, it is obvious that many firms have developed these skills as well as the skills of pricing factors of production in differing locations, calculating transportation economies, and comparing advantages of different market locations. This ability has turned out to be the valuable organizational skill of the TNCs and has given them enormous economic power, to the point where the leaders of nation-states often become captive to the TNCs' threats to "leave" to go somewhere else.

The TNCs, while experiencing many constraints, nevertheless have become notable for their increase in degrees of freedom. They can move production almost at will to a new loci or change the venue of managerial direction, and many have become significantly freed from their national origins. Important in this process is their ability to have subsidiary firms in low-tax countries become the units that produce profits while subsidiaries in high-tax countries only break even, or even lose money. It is not inconsequential that, while U.S. automobile corporations such as Ford and GM have sustained significant losses in their operations in recent years, their European divisions have been continually profitable. When GM turns to the head of its European division in the face of unparalleled losses, even if he is an American by citizenship, the bonds of national attachment begin to subtly loosen.

Nor, in this day and age, does the Pax Americana make sense. After the demise of the Pax Britannica that characterized the period of Western imperialism, the Pax Americana made sense in the global political economy of the Cold War. What sense does it make now? Even before the demise of the Soviet Union, the collapse of the Berlin Wall, and the end of the Cold War, it was clear that only a Pax Globalis made sense to the TNCs, so that they could pursue their natural bent to expand and make a profit throughout the world without living under the constant threat of war.

Of course there were national firms linked to, and locked into, war-making production: the Lockheeds, General Dynamics, and other powerful firms that represented, in effect, the nation-state and the still-considerable importance of a national bourgeoisie. While such firms will continue to exercise influence, if only because of their enormous resource base accumulated during forty-five years of Cold War, they will have to look to other forms of production if that influence is to be maintained in the long run. And, in that process, they will in all likelihood follow the patterns of the TNCs, seeking products for a multiplicity of markets (rather than a single national one) and necessarily becoming more willing to shift production to minimize costs and maximize profits. Having swilled so long at troughs sustained by national governments, they will either learn new behaviors or shrink and lose their power.

The current freedom of the TNCs—the freedom to relocate, engage new labor forces, shift capital, and so on—will continue to pose dilemmas for national governments. Any citizenry will create new demands upon national governments when thousands of workers are left bereft of employment or when environmental degradation becomes the price that a community must pay to see people employed. National governments can be expected, therefore, to confront a continuing crisis of legitimation. As well, they will confront increasing fiscal crises as they deal with runaway businesses, permanently unemployed workers, and a shrinking tax base.

This situation represents the *thesis* in the dialectic that we see emerging in the next several decades. The increased significance of financial capital, its incredible mobility, its lack of attachment to national roots, its willingness to move production and markets to wherever its "bottom line" will improve, in a word, its irresponsibility, will create distinct problems for the nation-state and for regional and local political bodies.

The *antithesis* of this development will be increased demands by citizenry for control, for legitimation, for the confrontation with runaway corporations that leave environmental messes and a ruined and unemployable populace behind. The local government of some nation-state somewhere will have to undertake the responsibility for picking up the pieces, for providing relief regardless of its own fiscal crises. Some agencies will have to struggle to provide the basis for social peace. Where will they come from?

The *synthesis* will probably consist of new forms of regulatory behavior, particularly behavior that seeks to establish controls over the mobility of capital and the ability to escape social responsibilities. We do not see this regulation developing at the national level—the nation-state has demonstrated its weakness in coming to grips with transnational capital—but rather at the transnational and regional/local levels.

At the transnational level, we envision new crises within organizations of the UN. The South-North conflict is emblematic of this process, but it is still very attenuated because it is based on nation-state representation. More and more, we believe that the riots, such as those by French farmers at the gates of their Ministry of Agriculture, will shift to Brussels, the "farmgate" of the common agricultural policy. At the same time, someone somewhere is going to discover that the serious decisions, particularly with respect to agriculture, are being made in hidden meetings of "technical experts" in such locations as the FAO, the administrative agency of the Codex Alimentarius (the mechanism for standard setting and monitoring international trade in fresh and processed foods), and the OECD. Will thousands of rioting farmers from the United States, France, Italy, and Japan finally recognize some common interests and be prepared to riot at the Rome headquarters of FAO or the Paris office of OECD when the "experts" meet?

At present, the process is still dominated by the "scientists" and "technical experts" who invoke the names of science and objectivity to justify the political agreements they make among themselves, agreements that hide the interests these "experts" represent. In the process, democratic politics are subverted as the experts take over. In a period of expanding democratization, with citizens uncertain how to organize themselves but mightily unhappy with existing politics, we can expect a resuscitation of demands for democratic participation. How long this will take and what forms it will take remain obscure, but we have confidence that the rule by experts, the technocracy of regulation set in place by the existing international organization, will not be able to withstand the demands for democratic participation.

This volume is divided into three parts. The first discusses selected strategies and patterns that have emerged in the globalization process. Specifically, it addresses empirical dimensions of globalization, its relationship with migratory and productive patterns, and its relationship with trends in the important field of agricultural science.

The first chapter introduces the modus operandi of TNCs at the global level. Heffernan and Constance illustrate that TNCs are the driving force behind the evolution of the global agro-food system. Though other actors are certainly involved in this process, the empirical documentation presented in the chapter underscores the relationship between global action and TNCs' interests in the transnational arena. The authors provide some of the basic data on concentration and transnationalization needed to understand the global food system.

Chapter 2 by Mingione and Pugliese tackles the issue of the expansion of the relative surplus population at the global level through an analysis of selected migratory patterns and the informal sector. The authors discuss some of the consequences that the globalization of agriculture and food has on people whose labor and economic reproduction revolve around agriculture. Specific attention is paid to marginal segments of the labor structure in advanced and developing countries alike. In terms of the overall theme of the volume, this chapter is particularly important because it explores the effects of global production processes on the mobility of marginal labor and on the strategies marginal workers can follow to sustain themselves and their communities.

The last two chapters of Part 1 discuss the relationship between science and technology and the global system in agriculture. In Chapter 3, Lawrence Busch points out that the globalization of the socioeconomic system has changed the categories that scientists use to describe and understand agricultural research. Because these categories are created by humans, a new system should be put in place. Busch recommends a systemic approach that emphasizes human agency as the driving force of the scientific arena, agroecology as the central discipline, and a decentralized model of scientific investigation that pays attention to traditional cultures.

Chapter 4, by Sorj and Wilkinson, analyzes the impact of biotechnology on developing countries. Using a series of interviews with leading private actors in the agro-food biotechnology sector, the authors argue that the picture is more complex than portrayed in previous literature. More specifically, they underscore the significance of quality concerns and cheap labor in influencing innovations in the food industry. Along with Chapter 3, this chapter reveals the centrality of science and technology in the emerging global agricultural and food system.

Part 2 addresses specific local cases and consequences of the globalization of the agro-food sector. Chapter 5, by Marsden, Flynn and Ward, uses the case of Great Britain to discuss the crisis of legitimacy in processes of international and national regulation of food. They argue that the growing internationalization of food systems is reflected in policies and regulations that emerge most forcefully at the local and/or national level. It is at this level, they conclude, that legitimacy crises are eventually mediated, albeit in contradictory terms. This chapter, with Chapter 12 by Bonanno in Part 3, connects the maintenance of forms of consensus (legitimation) and control in a context in which new global arrangements undermine local forms of socioeconomic organization.

Chapter 6, by Lourdes Gouveia, discusses the globalization of the meat-packing industry in the United States. The chapter analyzes the development of this industry and the opportunities that have been made available to firms by the globalization of the sector. The author, however, stresses that firms within the industry are constrained by a complex set of social, economic, and political factors and depend on local political institutions for the resolution of accumulation crises. This contribution further underscores alternative strategies selected by corporations to operate in a transnational socioeconomic system and the relationship between global and local actors in the creation of existing situations.

Chapter 7, by Reed and Marchant, points out that U.S. agro-food firms are much more involved in exporting bulk agricultural commodities than consumer-ready food products. This pattern is significantly different from those of firms located in other advanced nations. U.S. companies prefer horizontal integration and global sourcing through direct investments abroad rather than increasing their share of export of finished food products. The hypothesis stressing the existence of low wages and low costs of production is not considered a valid explanation in this case, because most of the investments take place in Canada and the EC. Conversely, the desire of U.S. companies to avoid potential or real tariff barriers is a more plausible explanation. This analysis of the economic behavior of U.S. agro-food firms further contributes to the elucidation of corporate strategies in the global context.

Using a case study of the fruit-juice industry in Japan, Raymond Jussaume examines the impact of economic liberalism on producers and food-processing and trading companies in Chapter 8. He argues that liberalization has helped giants like Coca-Cola to consolidate their market position while concentration of the food-processing industry escalates. Farmers, on the other hand, might lose out to global sourcing of raw materials and in-house bottling by large firms. He underscores that these changes may have serious consequences for Japanese consumers, producers, and even overseas suppliers. In synthesis, this study represents a clear example of how global restructuring affects actors in the agro-food sector in a developed society like Japan.

In Chapter 9 Luis Llambi shifts attention to Latin America. He points out the limits of the developmental strategies Latin American agricultures are using to enter the global phase of the world economy. The specialized export-oriented patterns selected for the growth of the agro-food sectors depend significantly on unstable consumer markets in affluent societies and speculative strategies in the world financial sector. These strategies have been responsible for an increased dependency on food imports to the disadvantage of a large stratum of the population. The careful analysis of agricultural policies presented in the chapter elucidates the contradictory relationship between the selection of globally open commercial strategies and the maintenance of objectives involving domestic socioeconomic development.

William Friedland, in Chapter 10, discusses the globalization of fresh fruit and vegetable production. He points out that new dietary patterns have stimulated the growth of integrated networks of global agro-food chains that deliver fresh fruits and vegetables to affluent markets. The author discusses the functioning of this global system, provides explanations for its emergence, and explores its relationship with the social stratification of advanced societies. The chapter concludes by indicating that global production of fresh fruits and vegetables creates shortages of staple foods in developing countries, increases environmental problems, and has significant effects on Third World economies, polities, and populations. In essence, Friedland's contribution provides a clear mapping of the globalization of a sector that has traditionally been conceptualized in more geographically restricted terms.

The final chapter of Part 2 employs critical ethnography in the study of the global agro-food system. Ian Cook addresses the symbolic dimension of the manner in which new or "exotic" fruits are introduced to consumers. Using large fruit retailers in Great Britain as an example, the author underscores the fact that production, shipping, and packaging of fruits does not automatically guarantee that they will be purchased. The key issue, then, remains the creation of meanings that translate material production into consumption. The linkage between the material and the symbolic, the author concludes, is negotiated through labor processes.

Part 3 tackles more explicit theoretical issues associated with globalization. It contains works that deal with relevant topics such as the limits of state action and the contradictory nature of global processes. Though located at the end of the volume, these papers complement the theoretical remarks presented in this introduction.

Part 3 opens with a chapter written by Alessandro Bonanno, who illustrates the limits that local political institutions encounter in the new global era. He argues that the increased transnationalization of the economy is paralleled by the existence of political institutions that have a smaller range of operation. He views this disjunction as problematic for the generation of developmental strategies and for the fostering of the interests of dominant and subordinate classes alike.

The last chapter, by Mustafa Koc, examines two seemingly contradictory patterns associated with globalization: The international market has become increasingly fragmented, embodied by the development of trade blocs, while at the same time the global expansion of capital and labor mobility has reached unprecedented levels. Koc analyzes this contradiction in the context of globalization as a discourse.

The editors

Notes

1. In Sweden, for example, when kiwifruit entered the scene, strawberry consumption dropped significantly as bakers replaced them with the equally colorful but longer-lasting kiwis.

2. There is disagreement among the authors of this introduction concerning the use of the terms Sloanism, Fordism, and post-Fordism. Some (e.g., Bonanno 1992, Mingione 1991) have argued that the current conditions contain too many uncertainties to claim that a distinct new stage of capitalism has been consolidated and that all the important elements of the Fordist regime are in permanent eclipse. Nevertheless, they have also maintained that the present conditions are sufficiently different from those characterizing the 1950s and 1960s that the concepts of Fordism and Sloanism do not adequately capture the current status of affairs as much as the concept of post-Fordism.

Bibliography

Barnet, Richard J., and Ronald E. Muller. 1974. *Global Reach: The Power of the Multinational Corporations*. New York: Simon and Schuster.

Bonanno, Alessandro. 1992. "Globalization and the new division of labor in the agricultural and food sector: The crisis of contradictory convergence." Pp. 8–20 in A. Bonanno (ed.), *The Agricultural and Food Sector in the New Global Era*. New Delhi: Concept Publishing Company.

Borrego, John. 1981. "Metanational capitalist accumulation and the emerging paradigm of revolutionist accumulation." *Review 4*, 4 (Spring): 713–777.

Busch, Lawrence, William B. Lacy, Jeffrey Burkhardt, and Laura Lacy. 1991. *Plants, Power, and Profit*. Oxford: Basil Blackwell.

Flint, Jerry. 1992. "Honda: The most efficient 'American' carmaker." *Forbes* 149, 1: 121.

Friedland, William H. 1991. "The transnationalization of agricultural production: Palimpsest of the transnational state." *International Journal of Sociology of Agriculture and Food* 1: 48–58.

Heffernan, William D. 1984. "Constraints in U.S. poultry production." Pp. 237–260 in Harry K. Schwarzweller (ed.), *Research in Rural Sociology and Development: A Research Annual*. Greenwich, Conn.: JAI Press.

Kearney, Michael, and Carole Nagengast. 1989. *Anthropological Perspectives on Transnational Communities*. Davis: California Institute for Rural Studies.

Koestler, Arthur. 1968. *The Sleepwalkers*. New York: Macmillan.

Levenstein, Harvey A. 1985. "The American response to Italian food." *Food and Foodways* 1, 1: 1–23.

Mills, C. Wright. 1953. *White Collar: The American Middle Classes*. New York: Oxford University Press.

Mingione, Enzo. 1991. *Fragmented Societies*. Oxford: Basil Blackwell.

Moshy, Raymond. 1986. "Biotechnology: Its potential impact on traditional food processing." Pp. 1–14 in Susan K. Harlander and Theodore P. Labuza (eds.), *Biotechnology in Food Processing*. Park Ridge, N.J.: Noyes Publications.

Sanderson, Steven E. 1986. "The emergence of the 'world steer': International and foreign domination in Latin American cattle production." Pp. 123–148 in F. Lamond Tullis and W. Ladd Hollist (eds.), *Food, the State, and International Political Economy: Dilemmas of Developing Countries*. Lincoln: University of Nebraska Press.

Sassen, Saskia. 1988. *The Mobility of Labor and Capital*. New York: Cambridge University Press.

Tilly, Charles. 1975. *The Formation of National States in Western Europe*. Princeton, N.J.: Princeton University Press.

Urban, Thomas N. 1991. "Agricultural industrialization: It's inevitable." *Choices* (fourth quarter): 4–6.

Part 1

Global Strategies

1 Transnational Corporations and the Globalization of the Food System

William D. Heffernan and Douglas H. Constance

The purpose of this paper is twofold. First, we raise some issues about the appropriate units of analysis when analyzing the food system. Specifically, this section investigates the utility of different approaches—commodity systems, nation-states, and transnational corporations—as heuristic tools for investigating the restructuring of the global system, in particular the food system. Second, in examining the several approaches, we examine some key players in the global transnational food system, demonstrating the importance of focusing on transnational corporations (TNCs) as the key unit of analysis.

We contend that the unit of analysis to be used depends on the topic being researched. If the research question deals with the dislocation of labor and resulting impact on rural communities, then the appropriate unit of analysis is probably a specific commodity and its related labor process, technological attributes of production, and state policies dealing with labor, trade, and/or environmental issues. The restructuring of the global food system is experienced at the local/regional level as rural peoples either embrace or resist the redefinition of their roles in the global system.

On the other hand, if the research question deals with regulatory issues, particularly of the agricultural and food system, then the appropriate unit of analysis is the nation-state. An example is the deregulation of antitrust policies during the 1980s in the United States in response to the crisis of accumulation and the associated fiscal crisis of the state. Deregulation fostered a general surge of mergers and acquisitions, which had particular consequences in concentrating the food production, processing, and distribution system in the United States. But if the research question is, "What is the driving force behind the restructuring of the global food system?" the unit of analysis has to be the TNC, or group of TNCs, as these units decide what food is grown where, how, and by whom. The TNCs become the concrete instrumentalities implementing the investment decisions of that more abstracted concept, internationalized capital (Sanderson 1985).

This assertion is based on two decades of research during which we have used all three units of analysis. This research suggests that, for the best understanding of the implications of global restructuring of rural areas and food systems, TNCs play a central role as coordinators of the food system because they are dominant actors creating a global agri-food complex based on the concept of global sourcing.

Methodological Approaches

The commodity systems approach was pioneered by Friedland and his associates (1972; 1974; 1975; 1976; 1981; 1984), who have used this approach to study processing tomatoes, lettuce, grapes and wine, and oranges. This approach focuses on the distinct production characteristics of particular commodities. These characteristics include the labor process, technological factors of production, and state policies affecting both the labor process and technological factors. In Friedland's work you can find the importance of (1) the Bracero Program using migrant labor from Mexico in California vegetable production, (2) new forms of mechanical harvesting of commodities that can be used as a threat to migrant labor or labor attempting to organize, and (3) the state policies relating to the Bracero Program as well as state support of mechanization efforts via research at the land grant universities.

Attempts to use this approach have also been made at the global level. Friedmann and McMichael (1989) and Sanderson (1986) pursue this method in dealing with the emerging global nature of the food and agricultural system within a modified world systems framework (Marsden, Lowe, and Whatmore 1990). Friedmann and McMichael (1989) argue that the current food regime is characterized by international commodity complexes, i.e., the intensive meats complex or the fats/oils complex, created by TNCs headquartered in the industrialized countries. Sanderson (1986) argues that a "world steer" agri-food complex has been created by TNCs as they source low-quality beef (often in slash-and-burn rain forest operations) from Brazil, Honduras, and Mexico. According to Buttel and Goodman (1989: 87), the commodity systems approach basically involves the study of the production of agricultural commodities as "a system in which technical and manufactured inputs are incorporated into a labor process in which commodities are produced, processed and marketed in distinctive industrial structures."

The nation-state has long been the most useful unit of analysis for comparative research. Economists employ Ricardo's concept of "comparative advantage" to ascertain what countries should produce which commodities. Modernization theory (Rostow 1960) is based on the development of cash crops in developing countries, which can be used to prime the pump of industrial development. This approach assumes that countries trade with other countries and that the nation-state controls the trading process. The increasingly global nature of the food system calls into question the continuing usefulness of this approach (Constance and Heffernan 1991a, 1991b, Friedmann and McMichael 1989; Heffernan 1990; Sanderson 1985). Rather than countries selling to other countries, it is our contention that the significant forms of trade involve companies selling to other companies. These companies are sourcing inputs and markets while countries are balancing accumulation requirements with legitimation demands.

Sanderson argues that the level-of-analysis problem has retarded understanding of the underlying "dynamics of change at the level of the global system" (1985: 4). Nation-centric models "fail to consider the critical core of the new international division of labor: the transnational organization of the labor process" coordinated by TNCs (1985: 7). Sanderson does not advocate, however, using the firm as the unit of analysis within the traditional industrial organization framework. Rather it is the organization of the labor process, often through production contracts, via vertical and horizontal integration, that is Sanderson's key issue. This vertical integration and coordination of capital across borders, organized by internationalized capital via TNCs, "adversely affects the nation-state's capacity to govern the processes of capital accumulation, let alone to set an agenda on purposive action in food security, employment, or rural development" (1985: 14).

In a similar vein, Friedmann and McMichael argue that in the new global food regime the nation-state no longer serves as the most useful unit of analysis: "Indeed, the restructuring of agriculture in all countries in response to the demand by transnational agro-food corporations for inputs to manufacturing and distribution networks, casts doubt on the very idea of nations as an organizing principle of the world economy. . . . National states are now reinforced by the international payments system and undercut by transnational restructuring of production" (1989: 112). They argue not that the nation-states are powerless but that they are needed by the TNCs in the short term to secure access to markets.

The Development of a Research Project:
From Commodity System to Transnational Corporation

The trajectory of our research has shifted in its methodological focus as the scope of research inevitably led from a consideration of vertical integration in a single commodity to the transnational corporation in global integration. Our research started with an early commodity systems analysis of the structure of production in the poultry industry and the resulting quality of life in rural communities (Constance 1988a, 1988b; Heffernan 1972, 1974, 1984). In the late 1980s we expanded the scope to cover the entire food system in the United States. We call this approach cross commodity conglomerate analysis (Constance and Heffernan 1989a, 1989b; Heffernan 1989). Beginning in 1989 we turned our attention to the emerging global food system (Constance, Gilles and Heffernan 1990; Constance and Heffernan 1991a, 1991b; Heffernan 1990). The research progression will be reviewed in three stages to illustrate the strengths of different units of analysis.

The First Stage: Vertical Integration

Heffernan (1972, 1974, 1984) investigated the implications of the structure of the broiler industry for the quality of life in rural areas dependent on broiler production. Heffernan found that farmers organized as independent producers or contract producers contributed to a higher quality of life in their surrounding communities than those who were hired employees.

The broiler industry became the first livestock commodity to be rationalized and integrated by capital when, during World War II, the U.S. government rationed pork and beef products but not chicken. Federal subsidies were provided to increase the efficiency of broiler production and processing to increase food production, meat in particular. Many of these subsidies were administered through the land-grant experiment stations where research on confinement housing, improved feed conversion ratios, genetic uniformity, and improved health conditions was carried out. With these state subsidies, broiler production was transformed from a sideline operation, mostly carried out independently by women farmers, into integrated operations using confinement production, production contracts, and assembly-line processing (Constance 1988a, 1988b; Heffernan 1974, 1984, 1989).

During World War II the only geographically concentrated location of broiler production in the United States was the Delmarva (Delaware, Maryland, and Virginia) Peninsula. Many independent broiler growers in the area had marketing contracts with the U.S. government. As a result of wartime research, the application of science to broiler production decreased the risks associated with production. Confinement allowed for a controlled environment. Integration of feed production, broiler production, and broiler processing allowed integrating firms to take advantage of economies of scale and reduce costs.

Reduced costs and reduced uncertainty attracted new capital investment. Integration progressed rapidly; by 1960 more than 93 percent of broiler production was contracted. This process was not embraced by the established

Table 1.1. Leading Broiler Firms, 1981 and 1989

1981		1989	
Ranking	Firm	Ranking	Firm
1	Goldkist	1	Tyson Foods
2	Holly Farms	2	ConAgra
3	ConAgra	3	Goldkist
4	Perdue Farms	4	Perdue Farms
5	Country Pride Foods	5	Pilgrim's Pride
6	Lane Processing	6	Continental Grain (Wayne)
7	Tyson Foods	7	Hudson Foods
8	Valmac Industries	8	Foster Farms
9	Central Soya	9	Townsends
10	Pilgrim Industries	10	Seaboard Farms
11	Continental Grain (Wayne)	11	Marshall Durbin
12	Foster Farms	12	Showell Farms
13	Cagle's	13	Fieldale Farms
14	Corbett Enterprises	14	Herider Farms
15	Marshall Durbin	15	Cagle's
16	Cargill	16	Allen Family Foods
17	Showell Farms	17	McCarty Farms
18	Hudson Foods	18	Rockingham Poultry
19	Fieldale Farms	19	Simmons Industries
20	Golden Rod Broilers	20	Sanderson Farms
21	Rockingham Poultry	21	Cargill
22	Campbell Soup	22	Green Acre Farms
23	McCarty Farms	23	Choctaw Maid Farms
24	Sanderson Farms	24	George's, Inc.
25	Empire Kosher Poultry	25	Zacky Foods

Source: *Broiler Industry*, December 1981, pp. 23–24; *Broiler Industry*, December 1989, p. 50.

Delmarva growers. When approached by integrating firms (usually feed companies seeking to add value to their feed by passing it through broilers) to become contract growers, Delmarva producers resisted and refused to be integrated. So the integrating firms moved the broiler industry south where the boll weevil had devastated cotton and desperate southern farmers were willing to embrace broiler contracts as a means to keep their farms. The state stepped in to support the growing industry by providing Farmers Home Administration loans to build growout houses.

In a commodity systems approach we look at an integrated labor process. All the firms producing one commodity, in this case broilers, and the related processes—labor, technology, and state policies—are the components of the approach. By 1990 fewer than sixty integrated broiler firms controlled production, with the top four firms controlling about 45 percent of the industry (Table 1.1). There is a mixture of large TNCs as well as smaller, still independent firms. TNCs such as ConAgra, Cargill, Continental Grain (Wayne), and Central Soya are all on the 1981 list, and the first three are also on the 1989 list; Central Soya sold out of broiler production. Concentration has occurred with both TNC and non-TNC firms. Holly Farms, Lane, and Valmac were incorporated as part of Tyson Foods. Country Pride was absorbed by ConAgra. During late 1989 and early 1990 Tyson and ConAgra became engaged in a bidding war for Holly Farms. Tyson offered $50 million to ConAgra if ConAgra would stop bidding up the price of the stock; ConAgra accepted the offer (Brown 1989). In 1986, the concentration ratio (the market share of the four largest firms) in broilers was 35 percent; by 1989, it had risen to 45 percent.

There has been a steady progression in most food commodities from independent production to a highly integrated system characterized by either contract or corporate production (Table 1.2). In the case of broilers, by 1960 most independent production had ended. The interesting shift in the past two decades is the gradual transition from contract to corporate production. Contract production involves a production contract between the grower and integrating firm. The firm agrees to provide the feed, baby chicks, and veterinary services, while the grower provides the building, labor, and utilities. The firm always maintains title to the birds, but the birds are raised in buildings owned by the grower and on the grower's land. The grower is paid by the pound of gain for the delivered birds. In the corporate system the integrating firm buys land, builds growout houses, and hires labor to oversee the growing of the flocks. The transition of the turkey industry from independent producers in a nonintegrated industry to an almost totally integrated industry from 1960 to 1980 illustrates the shift, which includes an increasing reliance on corporate production. By 1980 62 percent of turkeys were raised under contract and an additional 28 percent were produced in a corporate mode. Only 10 percent of turkeys were raised by independent producers by 1980.

A critical part of the labor process in broilers is the processing workers. Growers are contracted close to processing locations. Poultry processing workers tend to be nonunion, female, and often African American or Asian American. Union attempts to organize the poultry processing workers historically have failed but have recently been renewed (Kwik 1991).

State policies affecting the broiler industry cover several areas. The Farmers Home Administration continues to support some financing of broiler growout housing, and land-grant universities continue broiler production research. The state also subsidizes the promotion of broiler exports through various programs such as the Targeted Export Assistance Program. The state also subsidizes the promotion of the feed and broiler industries in

Table 1.2. Percentage of Commodity Production by Labor Process

Industry		1960	1970	1980
Crops (all)	Independent	82.1	81.6	76.1
	Contract	11.6	12.4	16.7
	Corporate	6.3	7.0	7.2
Feed Grains	Independent	99.5	99.4	92.5
	Contract	.1	.1	7.0
	Corporate	.4	.5	.5
Food Grains	Independent	98.7	97.5	91.5
	Contract	1.0	2.0	8.0
	Corporate	.3	.5	.5
Vegetables	Independent	55.0	49.0	47.0
(fresh)	Contract	20.0	21.0	18.0
	Corporate	25.0	30.0	35.0
Vegetables	Independent	25.0	5.0	1.9
(processed)	Contract	67.0	85.0	83.1
	Corporate	8.0	10.0	15.0
Livestock	Independent	68.9	66.3	62.2
(all)	Contract	27.5	29.2	33.0
	Corporate	3.6	4.5	4.8
Fed Cattle	Independent	83.3	75.3	85.5
	Contract	10.0	18.0	10.0
	Corporate	6.7	6.7	4.5
Hogs	Independent	99.2	98.9	98.4
	Contract	.7	1.0	1.5
	Corporate	.1	.1	.1
Broilers	Independent	1.6	3.0	1.0
	Contract	93.0	90.0	89.0
	Corporate	5.4	7.0	10.0
Turkeys	Independent	66.0	46.0	10.0
	Contract	30.0	42.0	62.0
	Corporate	4.0	12.0	28.0
Eggs	Independent	85.0	60.0	11.0
	Contract	5.0	20.0	45.0
	Corporate	10.0	20.0	44.0
Total farm	Independent	74.6	72.2	69.2
output	Contract	20.6	22.3	24.8
	Corporate	4.8	5.5	6.0

Source: Adapted from Marion 1986: 15.

other countries through tours of U.S. facilities for diplomats and technicians from other countries as well as technical public relations visits to the other countries (Constance and Heffernan 1991a, 1991b).

At the same time, environmental regulation increasingly involves (1) high levels of water usage by processing plants and resulting sewage treatment problems; (2) litter disposal; and (3) health concerns related to salmonella

Table 1.3. Concentration Ratios of U.S. Agricultural Commodities, 1991

Commodity	Year/CR4[a](%)	Year/CR4[a](%)
Broilers	1986/35	1989/45
Turkeys	1986/29	1990/33
Beef slaughter	1972/29	1989/69
Pork slaughter	1977/34	1989/45
Sheep slaughter	1972/55	1990/77
Flour milling	1977/38	1989/61
Soybean crushing	1977/54	1990/76
Wet corn milling	1977/63	1982/74
Dry corn milling	—	1982/57

Source: Heffernan and Constance, 1991b.

[a]CR4 is the market share of the largest four firms.

and other diseases. These issues highlight the conflicting role the state plays in broiler production (Bonanno 1991). Thus, the state supports production while, at the same time, monitoring and regulating an industry that is a major environmental polluter.

Confinement production and assembly-line processing reduce the "natural" aspects of commodity production. Production contracts for growing the birds provide for on-time delivery of chicks to the farmers, feed to the chicks, and broilers to the processing plant. The process is more like that of a factory than a farm. Technology is transferable to any location where adequate feed and low-cost labor exist—taking into account supportive state policies. In addition, the state is active in subsidizing the export of this production system by sponsoring trade missions to other countries (Constance and Heffernan 1991a).

The Second Stage: Conglomerate Integration

In 1986 our research on the rationalization of the U.S. food system expanded to other commodities. We sought to determine which firms were dominant in each major food commodity and their related concentration ratios (Table 1.3). The latter part of the 1980s was a period of merger mania, and we found ourselves tracking the rapid concentration of most food commodity sectors in the United States. We call this method cross commodity conglomerate analysis. The methodology employs an in-depth search of agricultural trade journals. We systematically reviewed trade publications such as *Broiler Industry*, *Turkey World*, *Feedstuffs*, *Hog Farm Management*, *Milling and Baking News*, and *Beef* to track the activities of the dominant firms and establish market shares. U.S. Department of Agriculture bulletins, annual reports of agribusiness firms, and popular press articles were also used as supplements. The results have been presented primarily within the framework of complex organization and industrial organization analysis (Bain 1968; Tausky 1978). The issues of efficiency versus power as industries move from relatively competitive structures to oligopolistic/oligopsonistic structures are the focus of the inquiry. We argue that firms use their economic power to reduce uncertainty as well as to maximize profit (Heffernan 1989).

Agricultural economists such as Marion (1986), Helmuth (1984), Mueller and Rogers (1980), and Connor et al. (1985) have documented the rise in economic concentration in food processing industries. Our contribution to their efforts was primarily to attach the names of the firms to the industries studied (see Table 1.4). Our findings indicated that the same firms, such as ConAgra and Cargill, had dominant market shares across many of the commodity sectors and that the dominant firms tend to operate in concentrated markets (Constance and Heffernan 1989a; Constance et al. 1990; Heffernan 1989; Heffernan and Constance 1991a; and see Tables 1.3 and 1.4).

ConAgra is the largest U.S. turkey processor, sheep slaughterer, flour miller, and seafood processor. It is the second largest broiler processor, beef processor, pork processor, cattle feedlot, and catfish processor. ConAgra is also the fourth largest dry corn miller and the fifth largest multiple elevator company. Cargill is the largest multiple elevator company, second largest soybean processor and wet corn miller, third largest flour miller and pork producer, and fourth largest turkey processor, pork processor, and cattle feedlot.

Archer Daniels Midland (ADM) is the largest soybean processor and wet corn miller, second largest flour miller, third largest dry corn miller, and fourth largest elevator company. Philip Morris is the largest food company in the world with its General Foods and Kraft subsidiaries, the second largest turkey processor with its Louis Rich division, and a top ten pork processor with its Oscar Mayer division. IBP is the largest pork and beef slaughterer.

Tyson is the largest broiler processor, second largest pork producer, and a top twenty-five beef and pork processor. Bunge is the largest dry corn miller, and third largest multiple elevator company and soybean processor. Grand Metropolitan of England is the largest liquor company in the world and, with its Pillsbury division, is the fourth largest flour miller. United Brands, now called Chiquita, is the third largest pork processor.

Ferruzzi of Italy, through its U.S. subsidiary, Central Soya, is the second largest feed processor in the U.S. and the fifth largest soybean processor (Heffernan and Constance 1991b). Many of the same firms control the ma-

Table 1.4. Commodity Rankings of the Dominant Conglomerates

	ConAgra	Cargill	ADM	Philip Morris	IBP	Tyson	Bunge	Grand Met	United Brands	Ferruzzi
Broilers	2	**				1				
Turkeys	1	4								
Beef	2	3		2	1	**				
Pork	2	4		*	1	**			3	
Pork 2		3				2				
Feedlots	2	4								
Sheep	1									
Elevators	5	1	4				3			
Flour	1	3	2					4		
Soybeans		2	1				3			5
Wet Corn		2	1							
Dry Corn	4		3				1			
Catfish	2									
Seafood	1									

Source: Heffernan and Constance, 1991b.

* = Top 10
** = Top 25

Table 1.5. Ownership of Multiple Elevator Facilities

Firm	No. of Facilities	Capacity in Mil. Bushels	Type of Facility* P	R	T	ST	CTY
Cargill	397	440	22	24	25		323
Continental Grain	80	188	11	25	16	18	10
Bunge	55**	164	3	34	8	10	**
ADM	103	135	3	14	36	19	29
ConAgra/Peavey	103	112	5	8	16	28	46
5 Firm Totals	738	1059	44	81	101	75	408
(% of Industry)	46	31	67	34	44	24	11
Top 4 Firm Totals	635	827	39	73	85	47	362
(% of Industry)	39	24	59	30	37	16	10
Top 2 Firm Totals	477	628	33	49	31	18	333
(% of Industry)	25	18	50	20	14	6	9

Source: compiled from *Grain* 89, Milling and *Baking News*, 1988.

*P = port terminal; R = river terminal; T = terminal; ST = subterminal; CTY = country terminal.

**does not include country elevators.

jority of grain elevators in the United States (Table 1.5). Cargill and Continental together control 50 percent of these elevators, which are often key storage units for exporting grains. Only a few firms, most of them large TNCs, control the production, processing, and export of many agricultural commodities in the United States (Tables 1.3, 1.4, 1.5).

The high level of economic concentration associated with the various commodities was largely realized through the merger mania of the 1980s. These mergers were the result of the Reagan administration's deregulation and decreased antitrust enforcement by the U.S. state in response to the accumulation crisis of capital. In short, in the 1980s the U.S. government switched from an economic ideology characterized by the Harvard Business School approach, which advocates high levels of government regulation of business, to the Chicago school of economics, which advocates a climate of deregulation. This switch was triggered by failing U.S. hegemony in global markets. The firms that survived the economic consolidation were large conglomerates diversified enough to adjust to commodity cycles, large enough to take advantage of their economies of scale, and powerful enough to avoid being bought out or driven out of business. Their survival was based on economic and political power rather than economic efficiency.

The agricultural labor process associated with this period saw farmers caught betwixt and between highly concentrated input and product markets (Constance and Heffernan 1989a; Constance et al. 1990; Heffernan 1989; Martinson and Campbell 1980). During this same period, livestock producers were increasingly integrated via production contracts with the large TNCs. In the egg, broiler, and turkey industries corporate farms rose steadily (see Table 1.2). Until 1980 contract production of hogs was low; in the decade that follows, contract production of hogs jumped to about 12 percent. Midwestern hog farmers had traditionally resisted production contracts and resulting corporate integration, but the farm/debt crisis of the 1980s pushed many to take a contract or lose their farm (Rhodes 1990). During this same period, workers in the processing industries, especially beef and pork, experienced a system-wide attack on their unions resulting in wage and benefit concessions. Injuries to processing-line workers rose as line speeds increased in the processing plants (Constance and Heffernan 1989b; Moody 1988; see also Chapter 6, by Gouveia, in this volume).

Using the nation-state as the unit of analysis illuminates more of the picture. From this view we can see that several of the large firms producing broilers are not broiler firms at all, but rather globally integrated TNCs. While not as large and well sourced as ConAgra, Cargill, or Continental Grain, Tyson is still a rapidly growing organization.

This view also shows that contract and corporate integration are progressing in the livestock industries while high levels of economic concentration are uniform in grain processing industries. Firms like ConAgra and Cargill are active in both livestock and grain processing. Livestock farmers have essentially become piece workers for corporate integrators (Breimyer 1965; Davis 1980), and cash grain farmers have been trapped in a cost/price squeeze between oligopolistic input providers and oligopsonistic product markets (Constance, Gilles, and Heffernan 1990; Constance and Heffernan 1989a; Heffernan 1989; Martinson and Campbell 1980). Workers in the processing plants are losing their unions and being maimed because of factory speed-ups (Constance and Heffernan 1989b; Moody 1988). The state is loosening its antitrust policies to attract capital investment and accumulation.

The Third Stage: Global Integration

While documenting the dominance of a handful of conglomerates in the U.S. food system, we constantly encountered international activities of the same firms. As a result, we set out to catalog the concentration levels of the commodities we researched in the United States for other countries. We instantly encountered numerous difficulties. First, reliable information on market shares by country was scarce and/or unavailable. Second, reliable and systematic information about the activities of the agribusiness TNCs was also difficult or impossible to obtain, partly because of the difficulty in

Table 1.6. Summary of Major Trading Firms' Activities by Country

Poultry	
Tyson	Mexico, Canada
ConAgra	Puerto Rico, Portugal, Spain, J/V Soviet Union
Cargill	Argentina, Brazil, England, Thailand
Mitsui and Co.	Malaysia
C. Itoh	Mexico
Mitsubishi	Brazil
Ajinomoto	Brazil
Nippon Meat Packers	Thailand
Feed	
Tyson	Japan, Canada
ConAgra	Portugal, Spain, J/V Soviet Union
Cargill	Canada, Brazil, Japan, Spain, Malaysia, Taiwan, South Korea, Thailand, Philippines, J/V China
Ferruzzi/Central Soya	France, Netherlands, Taiwan, Portugal, Puerto Rico, Thailand, J/V Yugoslavia, J/V USSR, J/V Hungary, J/V Poland, J/V China

Source: Constance and Heffernan, 1991a.

J/V = Joint Venture

ascertaining whether commodity production and processing were carried out by independent domestic firms, state owned enterprises, or subsidiaries of TNCs. In light of the barriers encountered with this method, i.e., country-specific information on commodity markets, we switched our unit of analysis to the activities of the TNCs.

About this same time, the literature on the globalization of the agricultural and food system was growing. A paper by Friedmann and McMichael (1989) provided us with a useful framework for our empirical investigations. Friedmann and McMichael use Aglietta's (1979) concept of historically contextualized food regimes, combined with Sanderson's (1985) concept of global sourcing, to argue that TNCs, mostly U.S. based, are creating a new food regime, which they label a global agri-food complex based on global sourcing. A food regime refers to different international divisions of labor linked to different periods of capitalist accumulation creating an international food production and consumption system. Global sourcing refers to the ability of TNCs both to obtain inputs and to market outputs at various sites around the globe, thereby reducing the uncertainty of commodity procurement and product sales, as well as to their ability to play different nation-states against one another to obtain maximum profits.

The firms that dominate the U.S. poultry industry and the U.S. food industries are also the most active in global poultry production (Table 1.6). Other major firms such as Ferruzzi/Central Soya have major international feed operations. At one time Central Soya was a major U.S. broiler firm (see Table 1.1). The presence of Japanese firms trading in poultry and feed is also notable. Table 1.7 shows the connections, via joint ventures, of various TNCs and the export designations of some of their commodities. Notice that Tyson Foods has a joint venture agreement with C. Itoh of Japan to produce broilers in Mexico for consumption in domestic markets and for export to Japan. Tyson also ships leg quarters from chickens grown in the United States to Mexico for further processing for Japanese markets. Breast meat is removed for use in the U.S. fast-food industry, then the remaining leg quarters are deboned in Mexico where labor is cheaper (about $4/day versus $40/day).

Cargill has a joint venture with Nippon Meat Packers, Japan's largest meat packer, to produce and process broilers in Thailand for export to Japan. In this arrangement, Cargill provides vertically integrated production and Nippon provides access to Japanese markets. Mitsubishi has an operation in Brazil for export to Japan, and Mitsui has a similar operation in Malaysia, as does Ajinomoto in Brazil.

By attaching the names of firms to their specific activities, a clearer picture emerges. In the case of poultry, most international production for export is targeted for Japanese consumption and is coordinated by Japanese and U.S. firms (Constance and Heffernan 1991a). A study we conducted later focuses on TNC joint ventures in the Soviet Union, Eastern Europe, and the People's Republic of China. That study showed the same firms active in the food production and processing industries. The evidence supported the hypothesis that the TNCs are creating a global agro-food complex based on global sourcing of input sites and output markets (Constance and Heffernan 1991b).

Large Global Food TNCs

Cumulatively, the data show that the TNCs have a more global vision of food-system coordination than any given nation-state and are the active actors, whereas the nation-states are much more passive "receivers" of commodities produced through global production systems. It is the ability of the TNC to gather and utilize information that gives it primacy as the global actor. Information dictates where different kinds of production will occur and by whom.

Obviously there are local, regional, and national attempts to resist the global roles assigned based on the comparative advantage of the TNCs; large nation-states are concretized institutions that will not willingly wither

Table 1.7. Summary of Major International Trading Firms' Activities for Export by Country and Destination

TNC	Joint Venture Partner, Countries Involved
Tyson	J/V C. Itoh, Trasgo in Mexico to Japan
Cargill	J/V Nippon Meat Packers in Thailand to Japan
Mitsubishi	J/V Perdigao in Brazil to Japan
Mitsui	J/V Malayan Flour Co. in Malaysia to Japan
Ajinomoto	J/V d'Osato Ajinomoto Alimentos S.A. in Brazil to Japan
Nippon Meat Packers	J/V Cargill in Thailand to Japan

Source: Constance and Heffernan, 1991a.

J/V = Joint venture.

away. In addition, the TNCs need nation-state apparati to assist in resource extraction and market penetration, even though nation-state regulatory policies hinder TNCs in their search for barrier-free inputs and market sources (Bonanno 1991). Still, investigation of the driving force behind the global food-system restructuring is served by focusing on the activity of the TNCs in the global food system. These TNCs are the "going concerns," with vested interests all over the globe.

Cargill

Headquartered in Minneapolis, Minnesota, Cargill is a firm most people have heard about. It is the largest grain trading firm in the world. Cargill operations cover forty-nine countries with more than 800 offices and/or plants employing more than 55,000 people (Table 1.8). Cargill functions primarily in the supply of bulk commodities and service, being active in trading in at least 103 commodities ranging from apple juice to wool. Also included are "ordinary" foods such as corn, oats, and rice; food constituents such as sunflower meal, citrus pulp, and cocoa butter; minerals such as ferrous metals, gold, platinum, and salt; fuels such as fuel oil, gas oil, and gasoline; gases such as nitrogen; and other activities such as ocean freight, financial instruments, and investor services.

In 1990, among its other activities, Cargill acquired United Agricultural Merchants from Unilever; created, with Nippon Meat Packers of Japan, Sun Valley Thailand as a joint venture; built a $1.25 million molasses plant in the United States; bought Alexander, a New York feedmill, from Continental Grain; agreed to buy for its subsidiary, Excel, Emge Packing of Indiana; announced plans to open offices in Moscow and Warsaw; expanded its corn milling plants in Tennessee; and planned an $8.3 million expansion of its poultry processing facility in Florida (Constance and Heffernan 1991b).

Table 1.8. Cargill Operations by Country, 1988

Country	Number of Operations	Country	Number of Operations
Argentina	5	Malaysia	2
Australia	10	Mexico	6
Belgium	3	Netherlands	10
Bermuda	1	New Zealand	2
Brazil	20	Nigeria	1
Canada	21	Pakistan	1
Chile	1	Panama	1
Colombia	3	Paraguay	1
Dominican Republic	1	Peru	2
Ecuador	1	Philippines	2
El Salvador	2	Portugal	3
England	17	Scotland	2
Ethiopia	1	Singapore	1
France	14	South Africa	1
Guatemala	1	Spain	21
Honduras	3	Switzerland	4
Hong Kong	1	Taiwan	4
India	1	Tanzania	2
Indonesia	1	Thailand	5
Italy	3	Turkey	2
Ivory Coast	1	United States	638
Japan	4	Venezuela	3
Kenya	2	West Germany	4
Korea	3	West Indies	1
Malawi	2	Total (49 countries)	841

Source: Cargill 1988, *Cargill 1988 Directory*.

Kneen (1990) provides useful insight into Cargill's successful attempt to restructure Canadian agriculture.

ConAgra

Headquartered in Omaha, Nebraska, ConAgra is relatively new to the international arena but has expanded rapidly through acquisitions during the past ten years to own fifty-six companies and employ more than 58,000 people (ConAgra 1990). ConAgra operates in twenty-six countries in a variety of commodities that are almost exclusively agricultural. Brand names such as Armour, Swift, and Banquet are produced by ConAgra. ConAgra recently acquired Beatrice, including Swift Butterball Turkeys, Eckrich Meats, Hunts, Wesson, and Orville Redenbacher, for about $1.3 billion. Its recent acquisition of Elders of Australia provides ConAgra with a major global beef and sheep exporter with linkages to the Pacific Rim and increased its size to the third largest food processing firm in the world (*Milling and Baking News* 1990: 34).

In addition to facilities in the United States, Canada, and Australia, ConAgra has processing facilities in Europe, the Far East, and Latin America. It maintains pulse bean and dry fruit operations in Chile; is a leading processor and international marketer of Canadian sulphur; has a joint venture to process beef and mutton in Australia for local and export markets; owns firms in Spain and Portugal that produce and process animal feed, hogs, and broilers; owns 50 percent of Gelazar, a leading European seafood distributor; owns a majority interest in Société Anonyme Méditerranéenne de Salaisons of France, a distributor of processed meats; has a joint venture in flour milling and owns an oat mill in Chile; is active in Puerto Rico in poultry products, processed corn products, formula feeds, and grocery products; and is a leading worldwide marketer of fertilizers (ConAgra 1990).

During 1990, ConAgra's activities included buying Méditerranéenne in France; arranging a fifty–fifty partnership with D. R. Johnson of Australia to export beef and lamb; creating, with an 80 percent share of ownership, Superior Barge Lines; working out a joint venture with Esso on nitrogen distribution in the United States; forming, with Compania Molinera San Cristobal of Chile, a new firm, Conasan, to engage in oat processing; arranging a joint venture with the Soviet Union for feed conversion operations in poultry and swine production; buying Beatrice (United States) from Kohlberg, Kravis, and Roberts (KKR) for $1.34 billion; bought 50 percent of meat operations of Elders (Australia) as well as its brewing division and international wool operations (Constance and Heffernan 1991b).

Gruppo Ferruzzi

Headquartered in Ravenna, Italy, Ferruzzi is a very large conglomerate employing more than 80,000 people in some twenty-three nations (Ferruzzi 1989). The agricultural sector, of which Central Soya is a part, represents less than 30 percent of Ferruzzi assets. Its primary activities are in chemicals, construction, engineering, and insurance (Ferruzzi 1989). During 1990, the following were some of Ferruzzi activities: It formed the Mississippi River Grain Company in the United States; its subsidiary Central Soya and Agard (Hungary) formed a joint venture, Agrokomplex, for animal feed products; it arranged an agreement with the Yugoslav government to form a new firm in a joint venture to produce soy protein concentrates; it announced a restructuring merger with Italy's Montedison; it bought, through one of its subsidiaries, Unilever's oilseed plant in Mannheim, Germany, and a 3 percent interest in Finanziaria Centro Nord of Italy; it bought, through another

Table 1.9. Numbers of Ferruzzi/Central Soya Plants by Country

Country	Number	Country	Number
Canada	4	Ireland	1
United States	55	United Kingdom	4
Mexico	1	Denmark	1
Caribbean	3	Belgium	3
Peru	1	Holland	4
Brazil	8	Portugal	3
Paraguay	2	Spain	16
Uruguay	1	France	25
Argentina	4	Germany	5
Italy	358	Thailand	1
Japan	2	Taiwan	1
Indonesia	1		

Source: "Ferruzzi and the global market," 1989.

subsidiary, a 25 percent interest in Indiana Packing (a joint venture with Mitsubishi to produce and process hogs); it obtained authorization for the construction of a new company to process sugar beet juice in Fenara, Italy; it organized a new company, Comagri, with the Italian government and beet growers, owning 27 percent of the new firm; its subsidiary Central Soya completed a sow breeding operation in Indiana; it arranged through Central Soya a joint venture with Universal Edible Oils, part of the Birla group in India; and it worked out another joint venture with the Birla group for soy processing and vegetable oil operations (Constance and Heffernan 1991b).

Japanese Food TNCs

The Japanese firms mentioned earlier have a corporate structure more like Ferruzzi's. Food and agriculture are usually a small part of the very large Japanese TNCs. Several of the Japanese TNCs have a business structure whereby they own small parts (5–10 percent) of each other (Floyd 1991). The relationship of some of the Japanese firms is exemplified by two firms, C. Itoh and Nippon Meat Packers.

C. Itoh is one of Japan's larger trading houses with 692 affiliated companies operating in eighty-seven countries. With about 10,000 employees, C. Itoh has assets of $30 billion. Among other things, C. Itoh owns Kokusai Soso Kigyo, a globally integrated subsidiary; the Consolidated Barge and Grain Co. of St. Louis, Missouri; thirty-eight grain facilities on the Mississippi River shipping grain, to Eastern Europe and elsewhere; Riverport Steel in Louisville, Kentucky, and Ravel, engaged in the precious metals trade, in

Clearwater, Florida. It is also engaged in forestry operations in Chile and Brazil and, of course, has extensive investments in Japan (C. Itoh 1991).

Nippon Meat Packers, the number one food company in Japan, operates in thirteen countries with 13,232 employees. It imports meat from the United States, Canada, the U.K., Russia, Brazil, Mexico, Australia, New Zealand, Thailand, Singapore, China, Sweden, and Denmark. Besides owning Day Lee Meats in Los Angeles, it has subsidiaries in Australia, the U.K., and Canada (Nippon Meat Packers 1991).

The point we are making here is that the food industry is increasingly intersectoral. Cargill is also a major salt and steel manufacturer. It trades in commodities such as gold and silver as well as providing financial services. Ferruzzi is a major industrial concern, with its food sector an important but minority division. Food is a minority division in most of the large Japanese firms.

Conclusion

We argue that TNCs have a vision of the global economic system, including a global food system. Their unique access to information gives them the power to influence the domestic affairs of nation-states. The effects of TNC restructuring of the global food system have only just begun to be documented; their activities in different nation-states often create significant social shocks (see, for example, Barkin 1985; Constance, Gilles, and Heffernan 1990; Kneene 1990; Lawrence 1990; Rama 1985; Sanderson 1985; Teubal 1987). If there is to be a clear conceptualization of the emerging global order, a careful and detailed analysis of the varying effects of TNC restructuring will be necessary.

Perhaps this phase of global economic development should be referred to as the "new globalization" because, while there have been earlier global arrangements (see Friedmann and McMichael 1989; see also Chapter 13, by Koc, in this volume), they were qualitatively and quantitatively different from the emergent food regime. The TNCs are quantitatively different because the previous system has reached the edges of the earth's production systems, i.e., there are few frontiers left (aquaculture). The size of firms has already passed the limit where technical economies of scale, accrue. Pecuniary economies of scale, such as access to large amounts of capital and credit and increased numbers of strategic options due to more and deeper pockets, do continue to accrue. In sum, the new TNCs are huge with many deep pockets, i.e., many sourcing options. The TNCs are qualitatively different because of the impact of information technology and their decreasing attachment to their parent nation-states. Many TNCs have information systems for weather forecasting and electronic mail for instant information exchange beyond the capabilities of most nation-state satellites. Instant-info technology is their primary source of advantage, which they use to reduce uncertainty related to obtaining inputs and marketing outputs. Nations-states depend on the TNCs for information related to agricultural production and trade (Morgan 1980).

According to Barnet and Mueller, the men who operate the TNCs see themselves as "world managers" because they are the first in history "to make a credible try at managing the world as an integrated unit" (Morgan 1980: 275). As multinational corporations cut their apron strings with their parent nation-states and become transnational, the locus of control of the TNC becomes problematic. Cargill has its subsidiary Tradax in Geneva, Switzerland, and could operate its business from there if it needed to do so (Morgan 1980). Corporate accountability becomes increasingly difficult without the clout of the nation-state to enforce environmental or worker safety guidelines. If the nation-state makes it too expensive to do business, then business will be done where regulations and protections are not as powerful. Who or what will regulate the TNCs and hold them accountable for their actions?

Other serious questions need to be addressed. Given that the TNCs increasingly source their products from "have-not" nations and sell the products to "have" nations, will this trend in global food concentration just continue the long-term inequalities in relationships between rich and poor nations? As TNCs avoid countries with stringent environmental regulations, will environmental degradation increase in "have-not" nations that depend on foreign direct investment? What are the long-term implications of decreased fossil fuel availability for an emerging food system that requires the worldwide movement of food? Finally, if part of a nation's mandate is to provide food security for its people, then is it wise for nations, both rich and poor, to become dependent on the TNCs for food?

Alternatives remain, however, for local organization of food production in the increasingly bipolar food system. This bipolarity consists, on the one hand, of the mass system of mega supermarkets hooked to TNCs, and, on the other hand, of local and regional organic markets, local farmers' markets, community supported/shared agriculture, and other nonintegrated niches. Several authors have called for the development of a global political organization to regulate the activities of the TNCs (Bonanno 1991; Borrego 1981; Friedland 1991; Friedmann and McMichael 1989). While the growth of the European Community, the North American Free Trade Agreement, and the organization of the Japanese/Pacific Rim benefit the TNCs by creating larger venues within which the TNCs can operate under standardized trade regulations, the issue of legitimation remains problematic. As the new world order emerges, the negotiations between old nation states, new regional states, TNCs, and social movements will continue to make the new global landscape a contested terrain.

Bibliography

Aglietta, M. 1979. *A Theory of Capitalist Regulation*. London: New Left Books.

Bain, Joe. 1968. *Industrial Organization*. New York: Wiley.

Barkin, David. 1985. "Global proletarianization." Pp. 26–45 in S. Sanderson (ed.), *The Americas in the New International Division of Labor*. New York: Holmes and Meier.

Bonanno, Alessandro. 1991. "The globalization of the agricultural and food sector and theories of the state." *International Journal of Sociology of Agriculture and Food*, 1: 15–30.

Borrego, John. 1981. "Metanational capitalist accumulation and the emerging paradigm of revolutionist accumulation." *Review* 4, 4 (Spring): 713–777.

Breimyer, Harold. 1965. *Individual Freedom and the Economic Organization of Agriculture*. Urbana: University of Illinois Press.

Broiler Industry. 1981. "Top 50 Companies." December 1981, pp. 23–24.

———. 1989. "Top 50 Companies." December 1989, p. 50.

Brown, Robert H. 1989. "Tyson, Holly could be operating in month." *Feedstuffs* 61, 27: 1, 27.

Buttel, Frederick, and David Goodman. 1989. "Class, state, technology, and international food regimes." *Sociologia Ruralis* 14, 2: 86–93.

C. Itoh. 1991. *Annual Report*.

Cargill. 1990. "Cargill Company Profile."

———. 1988. "Cargill 1988 Directory."

Connor, John, Richard T. Rogers, Bruce W. Marion, and Willard F. Mueller. 1985. *The Food Manufacturing Industries: Structure, Strategies, Performance, and Policies*. Lexington, Mass.: Lexington Books.

Constance, Douglas. 1988a. "The State and Structure of the Broiler Industry: Missouri and the US." Master's thesis, University of Missouri, Columbia.

———. 1988b. "Obstacles or Detours: The Broiler Industry Revisited." Paper presented at the annual meeting of the Rural Sociological Society, Athens, Ga.

Constance, Douglas, Jere Gilles, and William D. Heffernan. 1990. "Agrarian policies and agricultural systems in the United States." Pp. 9–75 in A. Bonanno (ed.), *Agrarian Policies and Agricultural Systems*. Boulder, Colo.: Westview Press.

Constance, Douglas H., and William D. Heffernan. 1989a. "The Rise of Oligopoly in Agricultural Markets: The Demise of the Family Farm." Paper presented at the Agriculture, Food, and Human Values Society meeting, Little Rock, Ark., November.

———. 1989b. "IBP's Rise to Dominance in the US Meatpacking Industry: Boxed Beef and Busted Unions." Paper presented at the Agriculture, Food, and Human Values Society meeting, Little Rock, Ark., November.

———. 1991a. "The global poultry agro/food complex." *International Journal of the Sociology of Food and Agriculture*, 1: 126–142.

_____. 1991b. "The Global Food System: Joint Ventures in the USSR, Eastern Europe, and the People's Republic of China." Paper presented at the annual meeting of the Midwest Sociological Society, Des Moines, Iowa, April.

Davis, John E. 1980. "Capitalist agricultural development and the exploitation of the propertied laborer." Pp. 133–154 in Frederick H. Buttel and Howard Newby (eds.), *The Rural Sociology of the Advanced Societies: Critical Perspectives.* Montclair, N.J.: Allanheld, Osmun.

Ferruzzi. 1989. "Ferruzzi and the Global Market."

Floyd, Rob. 1991. "Assessment of global agribusiness." Technical paper, Department of Rural Sociology, University of Missouri, Columbia.

Friedland, William H. 1984. "Commodity systems analysis: An approach to the sociology of agriculture." Pp. 221–235 in Harry K. Schwarzweller (ed.), *Research in Rural Sociology and Development: A Research Annual.* Greenwich, Conn.: JAI Press.

_____. 1991. "The transnationalization of agricultural production: Palimpsest of the transnational state." *International Journal of Sociology of Agriculture and Food*, 1: 48–58.

Friedland, William H., and Amy E. Barton. 1975. *Destalking the Wily Tomato: A Case Study in Social Consequences in California Agricultural Research.* Research Monograph No. 15. Davis: College of Agriculture and Environmental Studies, University of California, Davis.

_____. 1976. "Tomato technology." *Society* 13 (September/October): 35–42.

Friedland, William H., A. E. Barton, and R. J. Thomas. 1981. *Manufacturing Green Gold.* New York: Cambridge University Press.

Friedland, William H., and Dorothy Nellcon. 1972. "Changing perspectives on the organization of migrant farm workers in the eastern United States." *Social Problems* 19, 4 (Spring): 509–521.

Friedland, William H., and Robert J. Thomas. 1974. "Paradoxes of agricultural unionism in California." *Society* 11 (May/June): 54–62.

Friedmann, Harriet, and Philip McMichael. 1989. "Agriculture and the state system: The rise and decline of national agricultures, 1870 to the present." *Sociologia Ruralis* 39, 2: 93–117.

Heffernan, William D. 1972. "Sociological dimensions of agriculture structures in the United States." *Sociologia Ruralis* 22, 3/4: 481–499.

_____. 1974. "Social Consequences of Vertical Integration: A Case Study in the Poultry Industry." Paper presented at the annual convention of the Association of Agricultural Scientists, Memphis, Tenn., February.

_____. 1984. "Constraints in the US poultry industry." Pp. 237–260 in Harry Schwarzweller (ed.), *Research in Rural Sociology and Development.* Greenwich, Conn.: JAI Press.

_____. 1989. "Confidence and courage in the next fifty years." *Rural Sociology* 2: 149–168.

_____. 1990. "The Internationalization of the Poultry Industry." Paper presented at World Congress of the International Sociological Society, Madrid, Spain, July.

Heffernan, William, and Douglas H. Constance. 1991a. "Concentration in the Food System: The Case of Catfish Production." Paper presented at the annual meeting of the Southern Rural Sociological Society, Fort Worth, Tex.

_____. 1991b. "Concentration of Agricultural Markets: Jan. 1991." Technical paper, Department of Rural Sociology, University of Missouri, Columbia.

Helmuth, J. W. 1984. "Update on Cattle and Hog Slaughter Data." Memorandum to Congressman Neal Smith, U.S. House of Representatives, June 12.

Kneen, Brewster. 1990 . *Trading Up: How Cargill, the World's Largest Grain Company, Is Changing Canadian Agriculture*. Toronto: NC Press.

Kwik, Phill. 1991. "Poultry workers trapped in a modern jungle." *Labor Notes* 146 (May): 1, 14–15.

Lawrence, Geoffrey. 1990. "Agricultural restructuring and rural social change in Australia." Pp. 101–128 in Terry Marsden, Philip Lowe, and Sarah Whatmore (eds.), *Rural Restructuring: Global Processes and Their Responses*. London: David Fulton Publishers.

Marion, B. W. 1986. *The Organization and Performance of the U.S. Food System*. NC117 Committee. Toronto: Lexington Books.

Marsden, Terry, Philip Lowe, and Sarah Whatmore (eds.). 1990. *Rural Restructuring: Global Processes and Their Responses*. London: David Fulton Publishers.

Martinson, Oscar B., and Gerald R. Campbell. 1980. "Betwixt and between: Farmers and the marketing of agricultural inputs and outputs." Pp. 215–253 in Frederick H. Buttel and Howard Newby (eds.), *The Rural Sociology of the Advanced Societies: Critical Perspectives*. Montclair, N.J.: Allanheld, Osmun.

Mueller, W. F., and Richard Rogers. 1980. "The role of advertising in changing concentration of manufacturing industries." *Review of Economics and Statistics* 62: 89–96.

Milling and Baking News. 1988. *1989 Grain Guide: North American Grain Yearbook*. Shawnee Mission, Kan.: Sosland Companies.

———. 1990. "World's largest food processors." 25 Dec.: 34.

Moody, Kim. 1988. *An Injury to All*. London: New Left Books.

Morgan, Dan. 1980. *Merchants of Grain*. Middlesex, Eng.: Penguin Books.

Nippon Meat Packers. 1991. *Annual Report*.

Rama, Ruth. 1985. "Some effects of the internationalization of agriculture on the Mexican agricultural crisis." Pp. 9–94 in S. Sanderson (ed.), *The Americas in the New International Division of Labor*. New York: Holmes and Meier.

Rhodes, V. James. 1990. "US Contract Hog Production." University of Missouri Agricultural Economics Report.

Rostow, W. W. 1960. *The Stages of Economic Growth*. London: Cambridge University Press.

Sanderson, Steven. 1985. "A critical approach of the Americas in the new international division of labor." Pp. 26–45 in S. Sanderson (ed.), *The Americas in the New International Division of Labor*. New York: Holmes and Meier.

———. 1986. "The emergence of the 'world steer': Internationalization and foreign domination in Latin American cattle production." Pp. 123–148 in F. L. Tullis and W. L. Hollist (eds.), *Food, the State, and International Political Economy*. Lincoln: University of Nebraska Press.

Tausky, Curt. 1978. *Work Organizations Major Theoretical Perspectives*. Itasca, Ill.: F. E. Peacock Publishers.

Teubal, Miguel. 1987. "Internationalization of capital and agroindustrial complexes: Their impact on Latin American agriculture." *Latin American Perspectives* 54, 14, 3 (Summer): 315–364.

2 Rural Subsistence, Migration, Urbanization, and the New Global Food Regime

Enzo Mingione and Enrico Pugliese

Same Words, Different Meanings; Different Words, Same Meanings

Any phenomenon observed empirically can be named in different ways, according to one's point of view, disciplinary perspective, or ideological, political, or cultural orientation. The impoverishment of self-employed workers, artisans, or peasants when capitalist production becomes generalized, for example, can be understood as a phenomenon of proletarianization or as the diffusion and generalization of poverty. Proletarians generally are poor. But the poor are not always proletarian. The different concepts—proletarian and poor—take into account different aspects, different questions, and different phenomena. Proletarianization refers to people's location in social relations of production, with the need to sell one's labor power in order to survive. Poverty, in contrast, has to do with living conditions and is generally associated with positions at the bottom of the economic structure, in conditions of economic marginality. Although it is not always the case, those using the term "poverty" seldom refer to relations of production. There is nothing wrong with this as long as it is recognized that the use of different terminology refers to different dimensions of the two phenomena.

At the same time, different dimensions of a given phenomenon can become more or less relevant at different times in history. Scholars in various disciplines may become alerted to and develop new interests when these dimensions become relevant to their fields of study. To give an example, poor people in a large American city can be studied as part of the secondary labor market. Once they start organizing themselves as welfare recipients, especially if they are successful, they attract the attention of analysts of social movements. If they are expelled from their areas of residence, they engender the interest of yet other scholars, who call them "homeless." In the last two cases, these same people will be seen as poor in the socioeconomic structure, not as persons acting in the labor market.

Similarly, the impoverishment of peasants may lead to their transformation into the proletariat (as happened in Europe throughout the last century). This process is generally accompanied by migration, particularly when there is a corresponding pull effect, a demand for labor in other places. There is a sequence in which the peasant initially becomes part of the relative surplus population, i.e., unemployed (or more correctly underemployed), then a migrant, and finally a proletarian, the classic outcome of the process of proletarianization. At the same time, it is also historically known that the population is, at almost any time, larger than can be absorbed by capitalist production (which is the Marxian concept of relative surplus population). It is only when possibilities for mobility exist that we can study migration and proletarianization. When mobility channels are blocked, the focus of research interest, if there is any, is on the poverty of those who cannot migrate. These underemployed potential migrants are still relative surplus population, but since mobility channels are blocked, they remain peasants—poor, often hungry, but still peasants.

And here again, approaches to their study may vary significantly. Some scholars may be concerned with the problem of hunger. Their approach will often focus on individual needs, whose satisfaction is seen as independent from production and distribution of resources, but rather as a problem to be solved through international food aid. Others may be concerned with conditions of hunger as an effect of rural poverty and will analyze the social and economic situation of the poor, attempting to specify the mechanisms causing rural poverty.

Globalization is one such mechanism and, indeed, in the current context may have become the most important one. This means that, just as we must study poverty from a multiplicity of perspectives, when we study globalization we have to be concerned with poverty. And poverty has to be understood not just in vague terms such as "low per capita income" but also in terms of its causes. Poverty, in this context, has to be understood as the inability of a society to produce sufficient food to feed its population, in particular, its rural peasant population. Rural poverty is not mainly a question of the quantity of goods produced; in underdeveloped, agriculture-centered countries, poverty can be observed as a situation of overproduction. In some countries, the "Green Revolution" has caused hunger and surplus production. In fact, the actual demand for food on the commodity market was too low because the hungry population (starved by the progressive limitation of their previous survival self-provisioning arrangements) had no buying capacities (Myrdal 1968; Sen 1981). This has been recently aggravated in the new agricultural countries (NACs) by the effects of overspecialization of exports.

As we shall see, it is the peasant population, based on the land and in agriculture, that paradoxically is most exposed to hunger in such situations. The origins of this paradox can be found in the globalization of the food order. The coexistence of globalization and world peasant poverty is not by itself indicative of a causal nexus between the two. But we are convinced that the two are linked (Myrdal 1956, 1968; Sen 1981).

In this chapter we seek to clarify the expansion of the relative surplus population on a global scale, something that hitherto has occurred on a regional or national scale, while analyzing migrations and the informal sector. If one dislikes Marxian terminology, e.g., "relative surplus population," we can refer to "excess population" (Lewis 1954), population that is influential for the level of food production within the food and agricultural world order. This chapter sets out some of the consequences of the new global food order. We will analyze the situation of those people expelled from agricultural production. This means not that these people leave agriculture or the rural areas (although this is most often the case), but that such people must try to find alternative arrangements to sustain their existence.

Migration is one such alternative. Other alternatives may involve accepting a downgrading of the rural subsistence economy or the need to enter the urban informal sector. In the latter cases, seemingly similar arrangements may come to have widely different meanings. People working in craft production or small trade or in small service activities can be defined as being in the *informal* sector provided that a *formal* sector exists. Before an economy is fully penetrated by capitalism and international capitalist trade, it makes little sense to define such activities as "informal." In such cases it is more appropriate to define such activities as being in the *subsistence* economy. Once an economy has been penetrated by capitalist social relations, from a strictly phenomenological point of view the same people may be doing the same jobs (tilling the soil or making handicrafts) but are now in different social circumstances; they are much more at the mercy of the market. The globalization of the agricultural and food order changes the character of the livelihoods in Third World countries from subsistence activities, relatively protected from market pressures, to the more vulnerable forms of subsistence of the urban informal economy.

Traditional and Current Transformations of Rural Subsistence

Capitalism and industrial development as a world order began centuries ago. Since its inception, one of the crucial aspects of the process has been the subversion of rural subsistence. Overly simplified, more than two hundred years of socioeconomic history of the Third World can be reduced to the following stereotypical progression: from rural subsistence to plantations to various forms of extensive and large capitalist agriculture. This stereotype is basically accurate, but it is necessary to correct the substantive and methodological confusion and imprecision it can create.

Micro-Social Change

The beginning and end points of agrarian capitalist transformations in the Third World are characterized by highly variable social conditions. Thus, no single model describes the passage from preindustrial subsistence to underdeveloped agrarian-dependent capitalism. It is inappropriate to simply analyze the process "from the top," i.e., in terms of the structuring of an agribusiness corporate global order at the center versus a fully and homogeneously proletarian and impoverished population in the periphery. The long and complicated transformation has been one in which local social conditions have adapted in varying degrees in time and space. In contrast to what occurred in Europe, in the Third World proletarianization was limited, particularly during the colonial-imperial phase (Myrdal 1956; Wallerstein 1974). This was reflected in very low income levels that had to be supplemented with impressive forms of local survival adaptation accompanied by a radical downgrading of the traditional systems of entitlement that increasingly exposed the population to famine and natural catastrophe (Sen 1981: 1–4).

There have been two basic models for the attack on rural subsistence arrangements. One, typical of the colonial period but extending beyond that period, did not substantially move the rural population from the countryside but dramatically changed its entitlement systems. The second and more recent model saw the dramatic shift of the rural population out of the countryside. Both waves transformed rural subsistence but did not terminate it. To understand the conditions of survival in the Third World it is necessary to study the local adaptations of rural subsistence to these two long waves of capitalist attack. This perspective alerts us that rural subsistence was destroyed not once, but twice in the history of global capitalism.

The Political Base for Transformation

Although rarely noticed, the recurrent and persistent importance of various arrangements of rural subsistence played a crucial role in restructuring the various forms of colonial and postcolonial regimes, particularly land tenure conflicts, which continue in many Third World countries. The postcolonial civil or military dictatorships have been actively sustained by agrarian coalitions fiercely opposed to agrarian reform. Even the populist or democratic regimes have experienced enormous difficulties in redistributing land to farmers/peasants when this process damages the interests of large landed estates. The recent examples of reestablished democracies in Brazil and the Philippines confirm the persistence of this issue, even when weakened by urbanization and dependent industrial development.

It is also becoming clear that the weakening of agrarian controversy is accompanied by transformations of the global agri-food order. The NACs (Bessis 1991; Friedmann and McMichael 1988) have increased export production to repay huge foreign debts. This strategy has not proven to be particularly successful because of both the increasing dependence on imports of other agricultural commodities to sustain a growing urban population and the need for technology imports to continue the agricultural transformation. The NACs and, to some extent, many African countries have kept the agrarian/land tenure controversy at the top of their political agendas and missed the opportunity to upgrade small intensive farm units oriented to self-provisioning and production of food for local urban consumption.

Furthermore, the expulsion rate from agriculture has been kept at very high levels. This situation is fragile and tense because it promotes the importance of fragmented urban populist movements as is abundantly clear in the case of Brazil (Ruellan and Ruellan 1989). The new political scenario decreases the chance of agrarian revolutionary confrontations; it is difficult, however, to know how it affects the development of political perspectives or how current NAC strategies or the current African agrarian disasters can be reversed toward agrarian import substitution strategies and new labor-intensive, locally oriented, productive arrangements. It is also difficult to see what social and political coalitions might support such a radical change or how such coalitions can hold at bay the powerful transnational interests, large corporative farmers, and the international business elite.

The Persistence of Subsistence Arrangements

An overview of the capitalist history of agricultural social relations in peripheral countries should focus on two different transformations (Kahn and Llobera 1981). The first is basically constituted by one of two principles of the colonial and postcolonial formations. On the one hand, there was extensive agricultural production for international trade, which often, but not always, took the form of plantation systems. On the other hand, there was the adaptation of rural subsistence economies, leading not to the expulsion of populations but rather to dependence on local resources augmented by various forms of wage labor (and exploitation) in extensive capitalist agricultural systems. The second and more recent transformation has been constituted by the Fordist and post-Fordist impact of the agri-food order leading to a wave of expulsion of the population from the rural sector through out-migration and urbanization.

Both transformations radically modified the entitlement systems through partial proletarianization. The latter transformation refers to partial dependence on monetary income through various forms of wage labor, although acceptable standards of living are seldom fully achieved. In both transformations the reproduction patterns of the rural population (and this is also true of the urban population) remain rooted in the subsistence economy through high rates of self-provisioning. However variably structured the different sociohistorical contexts may be, rural self-provisioning remains central to the production of food for direct consumption.

The importance of food self-provisioning has been extensively confirmed (Bronson 1972; Epstein 1962; Firth and Yamey 1964; Gregory and Altman 1989; Jerome, Kandel, and Pelto 1980; Miller 1987; Myrdal 1968; Scott 1985). The recurrent vulnerability of rural populations to famine and food shortages confirms not only the importance of Sen's (1981) "entitlement" approach but also that the peripheral rural population does not have access to food imports, nor to the increasing volume of food production globally. Limiting self-provisioning agrarian systems to the worst land and to decreasing per capita parcels and the chronic lack of investment resources to maintain and/or increase productivity for self-provisioning result in famine and food shortage rather than the disappearance of self-provisioning itself.

This process is confirmed by two additional arguments. First, the data on the food trade demonstrate that the increase in food exports from peripheral countries is not connected to the transformations of local agricultural systems but rather to urbanization and urban growth (Abu-Lughod and Hay 1977). Second, because of the extremely low level of monetary income, the survival of agricultural workers, peasants, and small farmers in developing countries can be explained only by assuming that it is supplemented by self-provisioning.

The character of the second transformation is particularly relevant, yet difficult to synthesize and generalize. Different historical and geographical social formations produce different syndromes. However, all are the result of the global division of labor and the international economic order that developed during the Fordist and post-Fordist periods. The combined pressures of high demographic increase and the rationalization of agricultural production for international trade constitute the main attack on rural subsistence.

Different from the first transformation, the second is characterized by waves of expulsion of the rural population through out-migration, urbanization, and urban growth. Subsistence food arrangements not only are downgraded and impoverished but are substantially transformed as the urban population can no longer count on food self-provisioning while, at the same time, local agriculture is decreasingly able to feed them. Agricultural rationalization is thus connected with increased dependence on food imports and with local integration into the international agri-food order and food regime.

Acceleration of agricultural rationalization, which took place in recent decades in NACs such as Brazil, Mexico, Argentina, and the Philippines, produced negative consequences through an increase in food dependence and the destruction of local dietary habits. Agricultural exports increase in parallel with increased food imports and worsening trade balances; in many African countries, for example, agricultural per capita production decreases and overall agricultural dependence and trade deficits increase. The least worst-off are some Asian countries (South Korea, Taiwan, India, and China) where various small farm arrangements partially absorb rationalization pressures and maintain a partial capacity to feed local urban populations. In South Korea, Taiwan, and several other countries the milder effects of the vicious circle experienced elsewhere can be explained by lesser urbanization and demographic pressures.

In conclusion, if these transformations cannot be held to be immediately responsible for the mortal starvation of a significant proportion of the rural population, they may well produce such catastrophic effects in the long run. Moreover, the downgrading of the entitlement systems of the rural population produces not only famine and food shortages in the countryside but a chain of perverse sociocultural effects on the social assets of the peripheral countries. The general outcome of this process is twofold. First, it reflects the search for new economic and social arrangements for survival in urban settings. Second, it strengthens the push effect, which eventually leads to international migrations.

Migrations

Understanding migration as a general social phenomenon implies a multidisciplinary or transdisciplinary approach. Sociological variables are inadequate to understand the basic and original issues: Why do people move? When do they move? Where do they go when they move?

Most causal analysis in migration studies looks at push and pull forces.

The first has to do with the sending conditions, i.e., the causes that make people's lives difficult or impossible. But push effects only explain at best migratory potential, not actual migration. People move only when there is a corresponding pull effect (higher wages, job opportunities, general life chances) in some potential area of in-migration and when institutional barriers don't hinder potential flow (Boehning 1984).

Potential migratory flow and actual migration are related by a complex set of variables among which the institutional ones (i.e., people's freedom and possibilities to move from one location to another) are critical (Martin 1989). Demographers measure potential migrations on the basis of comparative demographic trends. The variables they take into account provide insights on both push and pull effects. Recent demographic studies show dramatic increases in excess population in Third World countries. These scholars can evaluate the demographic situation in comparative terms, emphasizing the differences between countries or groups of countries. They may also relate demographic variables with other variables, generally economic. Thus, we learn that given current demographic trends, for a country merely to hold the existing rate of unemployment constant (i.e., not increase it), the number of new jobs that will have to be created is, usually, astonishing.

The term "population explosion" has become commonplace in discussions of migrations in the Third World, and, in fact, a demographic explosion is taking place in Third World countries. Also, studies show that the contributions of Europe and North America to global population are decreasing and that this trend is accelerating (Golini and Bonifazi 1989; United Nations 1986). In 1960, for example, according to United Nations data, Europe and North America accounted for 20.7 percent of the total world population. This figure dropped to 16.8 percent in 1985 and is expected to drop to 13.3 percent by 2000.

Another aspect of the demographic explosion is the imbalance between population and resources. Here, one of the limits of demographic analysis can be found because it does not generally take into account what is happening to resources, particularly agricultural resources. The imbalance between resources and population in any given country becomes greater when the resource potential diminishes or when it is not properly utilized. This is a matter of national and international economic policy, and consequently it concerns international trade. Attention to processes of globalization of the agricultural and food order could place migration studies on a more solid foundation.

The internationalization of the labor market has accelerated in the past two decades. And, notwithstanding severe limitations on the admission of

Third World people (which started in Europe in the early 1970s and was fostered and generalized during the 1980s), Third World people are now integral to this new process of migration (Sassen 1988). Third World migration to core countries is not new but in the past was more limited to border countries (e.g., Mexico and the United States) or to colonial and postcolonial movement from colony to metropole. Patterns have changed sharply in recent years. Trans-Pacific migratory flow toward the United States has become more pronounced, and the Rio Grande border is now crossed by substantial numbers of non-Mexicans.

The most impressive aspect of this new trend is the shifting role of countries that have become migrant-receivers after having played the sender role for a century or longer. Italy is one specific case, but Spain, Portugal, and Greece have now joined this trend. Thus, it is appropriate to group these Mediterranean countries together for analytical and political purposes. Italian political leaders, as well as some scholarly apologists, have taken immigration as an indicator of the new powerful role of Italy in the world economy. The war over economic indicators between recent Italian governments and Thatcher's Britain concerning the ranking of the two countries in the top economic powers is well known. But the power of the Italian economy, apart from the high rate of unemployment in some regions, does not explain the new immigration flow to Spain, Portugal, and Greece.

Different and more complex explanations of the phenomenon have to be found. Contemporary acceleration of internationalization and segmentation of the labor market is one explanation. But the causes of these processes need to be explained. What causes the internationalization of the labor market? Unprecedented push effects, which are strongly though not exclusively related to the new food and agricultural order, can be identified as one basic cause of a more internationalized labor market. People find jobs and incomes at the cost of a difficult and sometimes dangerous migration. On the other hand—and this has to do with segmentation processes—the new international labor supply fits particularly well with some segments of labor demand, with immigrant workers filling low-wage "dirty" jobs that "native workers" are reluctant to fill at those wages.

The number of countries that have entered the new international migration picture has increased significantly in recent times. Hunger and rural poverty are not the only push factors; nor are the poorest countries necessarily those that contribute most to migration. In some more successful countries, emigration has been stimulated by general social change and modernization processes in which higher economic and social expectations have been frustrated.

Among the pull factors are many sociocultural elements; the attractions of the modern, rich, inviting "North" certainly stimulate migrations. But it is obvious that structural and economic push factors are the crucial ones. The evolution of migration is complex. Push factors cause actual migration only of some segments of Third World populations and, in general, only after some intermediate steps. The first response to agricultural crisis, to rural impoverishment and hunger in the Third World, is urbanization and *over*urbanization. Overurbanization is the first obvious effect of the new food and agricultural order. Research on immigration carried out recently in Italy has shown that the majority of immigrants, particularly those of the first wave, came from urban areas (Macioti and Pugliese 1991; Melotti 1988).

One important aspect of international migration that has not been adequately analyzed is differential flows. South–North migration is important, but certainly not the most important from a quantitative point of view. There are also North–North flows to which we will not give any attention. But there are, as well, South–South flows, that is, migrations between Third World countries. Although a large part of this flow is generated by political disasters and wars, some flows are clearly economic. The explanations of South–South migrations are, of course, variable, but certainly a very important one is the impossibility or difficulty of migrating to richer countries.

This leads to the important issue of explaining the direction of the flows (Salt 1989; Zolberg 1989). In criticizing orthodox push-pull and supply-demand theories of migration, Portes and Borocz comment, "If push-pull theories of the causes of migration were to be taken seriously, the most vigorous outflows to the advanced West should originate in equatorial Africa and similarly impoverished countries; within such countries, migration should come from the poorest regions. Similarly, if we were to take supply-demand models at face value, migration should follow, with some lag, the economic cycle declining or stopping altogether during downturns" (1989: 625).

It is well known that the different character of the main flows has been affected by economic, historic, and social relations. Countries that are near to each other may or may not have had strong migratory flows and interflows. In the same way, countries at enormous geographic distances to each other may register significant population flows. Recent Italian immigration provides a good example. One of Italy's present-day "tributary" countries (feeding population to Italy) is the Philippines, separated from Italy by thousands of miles and no historic interconnections. Geography does not explain this flow, nor do standard economic variables. It is impossible to understand this migration without understanding the role of Catholic religious organizations and the place of young Philippine women in the Italian occupational structure. Most of the women are housemaids, a role that tends to disappear in advanced labor markets. Conservative and religious upper- and middle-class families, aided by the Catholic church, began this new international trade.

However, this story is even more complex. The young women of the first wave were rarely as pious as their Catholic employers; they simply wanted to leave the Philippines. Some, as we have gathered from our interviews (Calvanese and Pugliese 1991; Macioti and Pugliese 1991), intended to use Italy as the first stage of migration, because it was not as closed as other Western democracies with more restrictive migratory policies. Once in Italy, they were unable to pursue their planned migration to a second stage. In the meantime, however, new immigrants, with lesser abilities and lower expectations, arrived. They now occupy an important place in the Italian occupational structure. They are *colf* ("domestic cooperators"), for all practical purposes, servants. Some, speaking English, undoubtedly would have preferred to go to the United States but, as is known, the United States has stricter immigration rules. Restrictive migratory legislation may be more or less enforced, and many governments may allow nonofficial immigration in order to fill secondary labor market jobs. From this point of view, Italy has been one of the most permissive countries during the 1980s.

This case is emblematic of a more general question, which concerns new immigration countries such as Italy. Many current immigrants to Italy have chosen it as a first choice—and this is particularly true of immigrants from Morocco, Tunisia, and other impoverished Arab countries. For many others, however, Italy is simply a transition point en route to North America or other countries presenting better opportunities. People are not allowed to go where they like; free trade for commodities does not mean free movement for all people.

Developed countries have established barriers against immigration. U.S. immigration policies have been very selective for the past seventy years. Exclusionary and selective policies were initiated in Western Europe in the early 1970s. These policies have both reduced immigration and changed its character. Illegal immigration from the Third World has become the prevailing form of immigration. Although illegal immigration in Europe has not reached the impressive levels in the United States, it has become distinctly noticeable. Institutional factors hinder the pull effect, with the result that people keep moving within the Third World (i.e., South–South migrations).

One consequence of hunger and the agricultural crisis (the main aspect of the new global order for the Third World) is that people are pushed out of their original area of work and life. They move to cities or to countries where in-migration is possible. Very seldom are they allowed into the richer countries of the West. This does not mean, however, that advanced countries are always and consistently against immigration. Each individual country has its own conflicting interests. Capitalists, of course, want a large and flexible labor supply. Labor unions usually greet migration with no enthusiasm, regarding immigrants as a new, potentially competing army of labor. State policy mediates between conflicting interests to find solutions that guarantee the highest level of social stability. Of course this tripartite schema is very simplistic, but it is complicated by the dualistic and segmented nature of labor markets in which workers' positions in particular economic sectors (i.e., particularly in the "core" sector) are not threatened by the newcomers.

Not all national labor markets, however, are segmented in the same way. In the United States, segmentation remains very high, leaving open large areas of secondary sectors that are underpaid and unprotected, attracting new waves of illegal migrants. In other countries, labor markets are less dualistic, labor demand is different, and illegal migration is less profound. In any case, even if *minimal* legal and larger but still very modest illegal migrations are allowed, South–North migrations are hindered by legislation and guarded frontiers. Thus, migration to rich countries is only theoretical. The push effect is strong, but there is no pull factor of corresponding strength. The food order is the main cause.

The Urban Informal Sector, Dependent Food Regimes, and New Forms of Urban Poverty

The largest part of the world's population, tending toward becoming an absolute majority, is composed of low-income populations residing in Third World cities. Only the demographic importance of China, which still has a different distribution and social composition of its population, reduces the importance of this question at the global level. The way of life and the typical socioeconomic contexts of these low-income populations are now often defined by the expression "urban informal sector." This formulation has become so widespread that it would be difficult to avoid even if it is inaccurate and confusing.

The reality defined by this expression is anything but a "sector," a set of homogeneously delimited socioeconomic relations. On the contrary, the "urban informal sector" is heterogeneous and includes a vast range of economic and social activities. It may be intended as a sector (and there is considerable controversy in its physical sense) referring to portions of cities where low-income groups are densely segregated. Moreover, not all the socioeconomic activities included in the expression are, in fact, "informal," i.e., unrecorded, unregulated, or violating or evading various legal regulations. In fact many of the socioeconomic relations of the "sector" are recorded, legal, and regulated, including a range of low-income "formal" wage work and self-employment. Thus, the "urban informal sector" is usually meant to convey a set of physically delimited social arrangements of livelihood that allow survival with low and theoretically insufficient (relative to the cost of urban life) monetary income. Basically it is a set of urban variations of rural subsistence economies and arrangements (Bhaduri 1989; Lomnitz 1977).

These sorts of subsistence arrangements vary considerably within different sociocultural traditions; thus, any generalizations about the urban informal sector should be particularly cautious. For reasons of space we shall limit consideration to arguments directly or indirectly relevant to the food regime of the urban poor in peripheral countries and, consequently, to the meaning of its relative and absolute growth in the new international food order.

The expansion of the urban informal sector is the most important consequence of the agrarian transformation. In fact, the impact of social change in the countryside has led to the urbanization of peasants and agricultural workers who can no longer find practical rural subsistence because of the demographic increase in the rural population. Survival in cities reflects poor employment structures and labor markets in which the number of jobs with sufficient income to survive in relatively costly urban social contexts is extremely limited. Nevertheless, subsistence means, as it also does in the countryside, ways of coping with very low *monetary* income. But, in contrast to the countryside, depleted finances cannot be supplemented through self-provisioning of food. Direct agricultural production for self-consumption contributes very little to the diet of the urban population; a very high proportion of income (from 40 percent of the less poor to practically all of the income of the very poor) is spent on purchased food (Gregory and Altman 1989).

The savings of the urban poor traditionally take place through cheap housing, resource pooling, low-cost community services, and solidarity. Housing is so important that it is often included in the definition of the urban informal sector, particularly in Latin America. Squatting on public or private land and constructing put-together shelters without formal or legal permission has been the common way of circumventing the highest single cost of survival in the city (Gilbert and Gugler 1982; Perlman 1976; Safa 1982). Construction of housing in an urban milieu serves as a functional equivalent of self-provisioning of food through small-scale production in the rural sector, because housing is the principal survival cost in an urban context.

Merging various contributions from part-time employment, barter, and presents from the networks of family, friends, and neighbors is the second most important factor in urban survival (Hart 1973; Lomnitz 1977). Finally—and here the concept of the informal sector becomes most plausible—communities develop systems of services alternative to the expensive, formal, private ones and extremely poor or nonexistent public ones, ranging from transport, repairs, sales of used goods, to babysitting and elementary forms of education and health care. If we use Sen's entitlement approach, we arrive at a picture in which the maximization and pooling of very small amounts of resources, complemented by the radical savings in housing and services, makes it possible to buy what cannot be obtained otherwise, including food (the most inelastic of expenses), durables, fuel, tools, raw materials, as well as some services unavailable within the informal sector.

While this picture of the urban informal sector is clear, it raises important questions that we can answer only tentatively: What kind of food do the urban poor buy and how is their food consumption affected by the globalization of the agri-food order? Answers to these questions are bound to be impressionistic because of the relative lack of data. The widespread presence of street vendors and informal food stalls does not necessarily mean that traditional diets persist. Persistence of traditional diets depends on a set of conditions: the availability of traditional foodstuffs at reasonable costs; the impact of urban multicultural and multiregional contexts and their effects on dense and crowded urban life; the change in time budgets and household organization in urban life; and the cultural competition that exposes urban dwellers to imported cultural models through the aggressive marketing strategies for manufactured food produced by multinational corporations.

These considerations suggest that low-income urban groups in peripheral countries are particularly subject to dramatic changes in their dietary habits and to increasing economic and cultural dependence on imported dietary models. This is particularly true in large NACs such as Brazil and Mexico and, as well, in countries subject to large waves of out-migration. In the first case, increasing specialization of local agriculture toward export production diminishes the production of local foodstuffs and causes an increase in food imports, a process fully confirmed by recent international trade data (Bessis 1991; Lecaillon et al. 1987; OCDE 1984). Moreover, in large countries this tendency is accelerated by the regional and multiethnic urban mix that makes the preservation of unique regional habits extremely difficult. In the latter case, as powerful agents of cultural change, migrants produce a deep transformation of dietary traditions in adapting to the new economy and sociocultural context.

The most recent wave of deruralization in the Third World has produced a drastic transformation of diets toward higher caloric intake that is very uneven, with the very poor spending all their money on food while remaining malnourished and dependent on imports and foreign eating habits. In those contexts where locally produced cheap food is no longer or decreasingly available, low-income urban groups become increasingly exposed to standardized cheap imported food. This suggests that, in parallel with the decentralization of Fordist labor processes profiting from the exploitation of low-paid workers (often under semiauthoritarian regimes preventing the consolidation of trade unions or progressive political parties) there is also the diffusion of a degraded standardized version of a Fordist diet.

This process accentuates the polarization between the dietary habits of the wealthy and the poor on a global scale. The wealthy are increasingly attentive to qualitative, multicultural habits involving organic agriculture, ecological, and health concerns. Furthermore, they are affected by the diffusion of foreign and cosmopolitan habits (though adapted to local tastes and consequently bastardized with respect to their original cultural contents) and by the introduction of new foods, often produced locally in artificial climatic conditions, which further weakens the competitiveness of original producers. The poor are exposed to standardized imported mass-produced food, alien to their cultural traditions, a situation that contributes to a worsening trade balance of payments, even in those countries where agricultural transformation has led to increasing agricultural exports. In conclusion, even if the highest costs are immediately paid by the low-income groups in Third World cities, this transformation constitutes a dangerous sociocultural loss for humanity in general.

Bibliography

Abu-Lughod, Janet, and Richard Hay, (eds.). 1977. *Third World Urbanization*. Chicago: Maaraufa Press.

Bessis, Sophie. 1991. *La faim dans le monde*. Paris: Editions la Découverte.

Bhaduri, Amit. 1989. "Employment and livelihood." *International Labour Review* 128: 685–700.

Boehning, Rochelle Lloyd. 1984. *Studies in International Labour Migrations*. London: Macmillan.

Bronson, Bennet. 1972. "Farm labour and the evolution of food production," in B. Spooner (ed.), *Population Growth: Anthropological Implications*. Cambridge, Mass.: MIT Press.

Calvanese, Francesco, and Enrico Pugliese. 1991. *La presenza straniera in Italia: Il caso della campania*. Milano: Angeli.

Epstein, Trude S. 1962. *Economic Development and Social Change in South India*. Manchester: Manchester University Press.

Firth, Raymond, and Basil Yamey (eds.). 1964. *Capital, Saving and Credit in Peasant Societies*. London: Allen and Unwin.

Friedmann, Harriet, and Philip McMichael. 1988. *The World-Historical Develop-*

ment of Agriculture: Western Agriculture in Comparative Perspective. Sociology of Agriculture Working Paper Series. London: Rural Studies Research Center.

Gilbert, Alan, and Joset Gugler. 1982. *Cities, Poverty and Development.* Oxford: Oxford University Press.

Golini, Antonio, and Corrado Bonifazi. 1989. "Recenti tendenze e prospettive in tema di evoluzione demografica." Pp. 87–112 in *Abitare il Pianeta.* Torino: Fondazione Giovanni Agnelli.

Gregory, Chris A., and Jon C. Altman. 1989. *Observing the Economy.* London and New York: Routledge.

Hart, Keith. 1973. "Informal income opportunities and urban employment in Ghana." *Journal of Modern African Studies* 11: 61–89.

Jerome, Norge, Randy F. Kandel, and Gretel Pelto (eds.). 1980. *Nutritional Anthropology: Contemporary Approaches to Diet and Culture.* New York: Redgrave Publishing.

Kahn, Joel, and Josep Llobera (eds.). 1981. *The Anthropology of Pre-capitalist Societies.* London: Macmillan.

Lecaillon, Jacques, C. Morrison, H. Schneider, and E. Thorbecue. 1987. *Politiques économiques et performances agricoles dans les pays à faible revenu.* Paris: OCDE.

Lewis, William A. 1954. "Economic development with unlimited supply of labour." *Manchester School* May: 27–41.

Lomnitz, Larissa. 1977. *Networks and Marginality: Life in a Mexican Shantytown.* New York: Academic Press.

Macioti, Maria Immacolata, and Enrico Pugliese. 1991. *Gli immigrati in Italia.* Bari, Italy: Laterza.

Martin, David. 1989. "Effects of international law on migration policy and practice: The use of hypocrisy." *International Migration Review* 23, 3: 547–578.

Melotti, Umberto (ed.). 1988. *Dal terzo mondo in Italia.* Milano: Centro Studi Terzo Mondo.

Miller, Daniel. 1987. *Material Culture and Mass Consumption.* Oxford: Blackwell.

Myrdal, Gunnar. 1956. *An International Economy.* New York: Harper and Row.

———. 1968. *Asian Drama: An Inquiry into the Poverty of Nations.* New York: Twentieth Century Fund.

OCDE. 1984. *Echanges agricoles avec les pays en développement.* Paris: OCDE.

Perlman, Janet. 1976. *The Myth of Marginality.* Berkeley and Los Angeles: University of California Press.

Portes, Alejandro, and Jósef Borocz. 1989. "Contemporary immigration: Theoretical perspectives on its determinants and modes of incorporation." *International Migration Review* 23, 3: 606–637.

Ruellan, A., and D. Ruellan. 1989. *Le Brésil.* Paris: Karthala.

Safa, Helen (ed.). 1982. *Towards a Political Economy of Urbanization in Third World Countries.* Delhi: Oxford University Press.

Salt, John. 1989. "A comparative overview of international trends and types, 1950–1980." *International Migration Review* 23, 3: 431–456.

Sassen, Saskia. 1988. *Mobility of Labor and Capital.* Cambridge: Cambridge University Press.

Scott, James C. 1985. *Weapons of the Weak: Everyday Forms of Peasant Resistance.* New Haven, Conn.: Yale University Press.

Sen, Amartya. 1981. *Poverty and Famines: An Essay on Entitlement and Deprivation.* Oxford: Clarendon Press.

United Nations. 1986. *World Population Prospects: Estimates and Projections as Assessed in 1984*. New York: United Nations.

Wallerstein, Immanuel. 1974. *The Modern World System*. New York: Academic Press.

Zolberg, Aristide R. 1989. "The next waves: Migration theory for a changing world." *International Migration Review* 23, 3: 403–430.

3 The State of Agricultural Science and the Agricultural Science of the State

Lawrence Busch

Once upon a time everyone knew that science and technology were the hallmarks of progress, that modernization was good for you, that economic growth was unending, that cities were dependent upon their rural hinterlands, that nature could be tamed. Today, we are not so sure of these and other "truths." The world has changed; we have changed; our language has changed. The categories that we use to describe and understand agricultural research (among many other things) are shifting. Where we once were able to make certain clear distinctions, we now see only fuzzy borders, or worse, no borders at all. But lest the reader think that I write from an idealist point of view, in which the categories of experience are their determinants, let me emphasize that it is not so much that the categories have shifted as it is that their grounds are no longer as apparently solid as they once were. To put it another way, it is the social world that has shifted, leaving us with antinomies that no longer serve to divide the world as they once appeared to do.

Because what I have to say is somewhat speculative, I offer a series of ten related theses, each of which I attempt to defend within the space allotted. I conclude by offering some observations on what needs to be done to confront the emerging global agricultural and food order.

1. *All technical changes are social changes.* This is not to say that technical change causes social change. Far from it. What I mean by this is simply that technical change is the obverse of social change; every time scientists create technical changes, they also create social changes (Latour 1987). At the very least, their fellow scientists are confronted with new literature to read. More than likely, a new gadget or process must be reckoned with. And certainly farmers, agribusiness, consumers, are affected by this change. The very fact of its existence is sufficient for it to be a social change.

But it is also a social change at a deeper level. Every new technology or technique increases the range of choices that might be made. It also restructures the distribution of income, wealth, and power within agricultural subsectors as well as within particular portions of a subsector. Farmers are now aware of this as they never were before. In a world of rapidly growing population with rapidly growing purchasing power, such distributive effects were far less likely to be noticed. However, as the number of farmers has declined, and as demand for food has become more and more inelastic, the distributive consequences of technical change have become painfully apparent. The recent turmoil produced among farmers over bGH (Bovine Growth Hormone) in the two dairy states of Wisconsin and Minnesota is strong evidence to support this view. Moreover, it appears that farmers are no longer content to sit and watch these changes occur as if they were the result of some mysterious, immutable force.

One consequence of this sea change in our understanding of technical change is that the fundamental assumptions of the diffusion model (e.g., Rogers 1983) are undermined. Proponents of that model assumed a relative equality among farmers with respect to technical change. Moreover, they confined the model almost entirely to farm-level changes, rarely asking about either upstream or downstream changes. The early proponents mistook the peculiar circumstances in some areas for those of the world as a whole. In short, the world is not limited to any specific agricultural region.

2. *Scientists make the world as much as they discover it.* Anyone who has entered a scientific laboratory knows that it is filled to overflowing with equipment, tools, and instruments. As Bachelard (1934: 16; my translation) noted some years ago, "The phenomenon must be selected, filtered, purified, poured into the mould of the instruments, produced according to the plan of the instruments." It is through the instruments that scientists are able to make—through work—the world that they claim to discover. Of course, in one sense the world was there before they "discovered" it, so one might argue that I have exaggerated the point. Similarly, sculptors might argue poetically that a block of marble contained a particular statue and that their role was simply to reveal it. The same poesis occurs in the case of science. As Heidegger (1977) argued, scientists make nature reveal itself through instruments. They reorganize it such that certain of its infinite features are amplified and others are reduced (Idhe 1990). We are usually so impressed by this amplification that we call the end result a "discovery." Yet, the very construction of the word indicates the point that I wish to make: To *dis*cover is also to *un*cover, that is, to reveal. And, as Bacon rightly noted, nature does not yield her secrets[1] without considerable effort. Descartes may have been a better scientist than Bacon, but his armchair methodology proved less than satisfactory.

The active making in science has been increased in recent years by the finalization process (Schafer 1983). Wolf Schafer and his colleagues argue that sciences reach a postparadigmatic phase in which the central problems are no longer determined by what is possible but by what is socially desirable. They use agricultural chemistry as one of their cases in point. The analogy with agricultural research today is straightforward: Scientists in most situations now face a myriad of choices. Two hundred years ago, scientists were few and research opportunities were even fewer. Today, the number of potential research projects far exceeds the scientific personnel available to accomplish the task. And every project breeds more unanswered questions. Thus, under the conditions of finalization, the making of nature becomes more evident.

Finally, the entry of new scientific actors into the world of science has challenged the orthodoxy that suggests that Western science has all the answers. Ethnobotany, which began largely as a way of dealing with the "inferior" knowledge systems of non-Western peoples (Barreau 1971), has now developed a serious challenge to Western approaches under such new names as indigenous or local knowledge (e.g., Biggelaar 1991).

3. *All those who study the natural world are social scientists.* Put another way, to understand the natural world requires that one change it. However, since all technical changes are also social changes, those whom we usually refer to as natural scientists are really charged with changing the *social* world. In contrast, those whom we usually refer to as social scientists rarely if ever change society. More likely, as ethnographers, they describe the social world in much the way that natural historians of the eighteenth century did. This is not to say that they develop these new varieties of crops and animals out of whole cloth. To the contrary, they only do it through negotiations with nature, through struggle, through hard work (Bird 1987). Occasionally nature refuses to accept the metaphors and theories that we thrust upon it. In those cases, the products of our scientific labor are stillborn or they yield unpleasant surprises in the form of unexpected consequences.

To pursue this point further, what I am arguing is that the agricultural scientists who develop new varieties of crops and animals change the structure of social life as well. It is not merely machines that enter into our world as new possibilities for social relations; it is also new living creatures. This occurs because there is no way to restructure nature according to our wants without simultaneously restructuring society. The plant breeder who develops a new wheat variety alters the behavior of the farmer who adopts, the baker who bakes, the miller who mills, perhaps even the consumer who eats it. Were this not to occur, we would say that no technical change at all had taken place.

4. *In creating "objective" knowledge of the world, scientists further certain values.* Until recently, scientists hid behind the shroud of objectivity when questioned about their work. Many still do. However, we are about to enter a new age in which, in part as a result of the finalization process described above and in part because of our new understandings of science, the values that scientists hold will become as important as the facts they construct.

In the most obvious sense, scientists are proponents for such values as objectivity, quantification, replicability, and so on. But in addition, scientists are actively engaged in furthering other values including productivity, efficiency, speed, effectiveness, and standardization. Such values are the values of a capitalist world (Busch and Marcotte 1987) as much as they are the values of science itself. Thus, as Veblen (1932: 17) noted more than half a century ago when speaking of a scientist: "His inquiry is as 'idle' as that of the Pueblo myth-maker. But the canons of validity under whose guidance he works are those imposed by the modern technology, through habituation to its requirements; and therefore his results are available for the technological purpose."

Moreover, as knowledge is power, the apparent power over nature that science and technology provide is *at the same time* power over other people, power that is hardly distributed randomly or equally. Since it is scientists who are the creators of this power, in whose service they work is an issue of more than trivial importance.

Moreover, as science is more and more often "finalized" (Schafer 1983), so the value questions in science become both more complex and more visible. Consider the new biotechnologies. The new instrumentation that they provide opens a wide range of opportunities for research and technical change. It also opens the door for capital investment and economic growth. However, time, cost, and availability of trained scientists put severe limits on the use of these new tools. How they are to be used will depend on the values that scientists and others hold dear (Busch et al. 1991).

5. *Knowledge is now a commodity of considerable importance.* Until recently, there was general agreement that technology was private and subject to the rules of the marketplace while science was public and therefore subject only to the relatively unregulated "marketplace of ideas." The distinc-

tion, with a longstanding foundation in law in most Western nations, rested upon the seemingly obvious observation that science had knowledge of nature as its goal while technology focused on practical implications. This separation between the pursuit of knowledge "for its own sake" and the pursuit of profit through technical change appeared easy to make. It formed the basis for the division of labor within agricultural research between the public sector, which emphasized the biological, and the private sector, which emphasized the chemical and physical aspects of research. New agrichemicals and new machines were clearly the products of human endeavor while plants, animals, and other living creatures were part of nature and, hence, were to remain outside the realm of private profit.

The development of hybrid corn marked the first steps in blurring the distinction between the natural and human-made worlds by virtue of its being claimed as a contribution to genetics and commercial profit at the same time (but see Berlan and Lewontin 1986). The creation of plant patents for vegetatively propagated plants in the 1930s (35 U.S.C. 161–164), followed by the passage of the Plant Variety Protection Act in 1970 (7 U.S.C. 2321 et seq.) and the establishment of international conventions through the Union pour la Protection des Obtentions Végétales (UPOV)[2] have continued the trend set by hybridization. The more recent 1980 Chakrabarty decision of the U.S. Supreme Court extended the *utility* patent to microorganisms. The Patent Office responded by opening the door to patents on plants and animals soon after. In so doing the Court and Patent Office changed the grounds upon which distinctions between public and private science and technology were made.[3] Instead of the older distinction based on "products of nature" vs. "products of human ingenuity," the new distinction within agricultural research was to be profitable vs. not profitable. The public sector would henceforth only engage in those types of research that could not be financed by the corporate sector because they took too long, required too much capital, and most importantly, did not lead immediately to the production of a product for sale. In contrast, the private sector would take on all those forms of research that led clearly to profits.

The new regime in knowledge acquisition and transfer turns scientific knowledge into intellectual commodities to be bought and sold as are other commodities (Nelkin 1984). The consequences for public research as well as for the international agricultural research centers remain to be seen, though some of the problems described by Nelkin, including illegitimate use of graduate assistants, lack of access to data sources, and secrecy about unpatented research results, have already reached the public agricultural research establishment. However, early indications are that the new regime will place restrictions on what can be published, where it can be published, and what use may be made of the published information (Blumenthal et al. 1986a, 1986b; Kenney 1986).

6. *The state is no longer the major actor in agricultural research.* Until very recently, agricultural research was nearly entirely the province of the state. We may date the entry of the state into agricultural research with the Columbian exchange of 1492. This period marks the first major commitment of state resources to the promotion of what was the Big Science (Price 1963) of the day: economic botany. As Brockway (1979) and Crosby (1986) have argued, the valorization of the rapidly growing colonial empires necessitated the exchange of plants and animals that could be used to establish plantations and increase the exports of raw materials from the colonies. Surely, the first truly globally traded commodities were the spices—sugar, pepper, cinnamon, etc.—and the new beverages—coffee, tea, and cocoa— that were grown on large plantations in the colonial empires. Only in the late nineteenth century would one of the staple crops, wheat, be traded on such a grand scale (Friedmann 1978). Thus, we might well say that the Columbian exchange, whose five hundreth anniversary was celebrated by some and denounced by others, marked the beginning of state intervention in agricultural research. For most of those five hundred years, the state has been far and away the dominant actor in agricultural research.

However, the advent of plant variety protection, the new biotechnologies, changes in the tax laws, and the purchase of the seed companies by the agrichemical and pharmaceutical companies has transformed the nature of research (Busch et al. 1991). No longer does the public sector set the agenda, either domestically or internationally. Estimates of domestic agricultural research expenditures as little as a score of years ago suggested an equal state and private investment. More recent estimates suggest that the private sector now accounts for more than two-thirds of all research investment (Ruttan 1982). Moreover, the nature of public research has begun to shift away from its traditional concerns.

Critiques of U.S. public agricultural research during the last several decades have hardly been lacking (e.g., Hightower 1973; National Research Council 1972; OTA 1981), but it was only with the publication of the Winrock report in 1982 (Rockefeller Foundation 1982) that support began to emerge for new directions in U.S. agricultural research. Soon afterward, Buttel (1984: 3) noted that "the Winrock conferees placed major stress on public agricultural researchers increasing their emphasis on basic biology for one specific purpose: to enable the rapid transfer of basic or fundamental biological knowledge to the private sector for commercial exploitation."

The National Research Council of the National Academy of Sciences issued a report in 1989 calling for a new initiative along the lines originally suggested by the Winrock report. This finally culminated in what has become known as the National Research Initiative (NRI).

As proposed to Congress by the Bush administration, the NRI would eventually set aside $500 million in new money for agricultural research. The plan has been enthusiastically embraced by hard-pressed experiment station directors in their strategic plan for the 1990s (ESCOP 1990).[4] However, the NRI differs from previous programs in several respects. First, the funds are to be distributed to scientists based on competitive grants for which any scientist (in or outside of the land-grant system) may apply. Second, the research conducted under the new legislation is supposed to be interdisciplinary in character and address fundamental systemic issues affecting American agriculture. However, despite the congressional caveats, the program description (USDA 1991) tends to emphasize single-investigator disciplinary research. Moreover, it tends overwhelmingly to emphasize the more fundamental (read reductionist) aspects of research as opposed to those issues of more direct concern to constituent groups.

In response to similar desires for privatization, public-sector agricultural research in Great Britain has been drastically shrunk by the Thatcher government, culminating in the sale of the Plant Breeding Institute at Cambridge. In France, the Institut Nationale de la Recherche Agronomique (INRA) has continued to see its budget increase, but it has focused more and more on "basic" research further removed from farm production. In developing nations much of the advance in developing effective research systems made during the 1970s was lost in the 1980s, leaving a void and declining yields (Pardey 1989). The result of this rather rapid transformation has not been a shift to local companies but to new global actors only some of which are private in the classical sense of the term.

7. *The major actors in global agriculture, input supply, commodity trading, and agricultural research are not states but multinational organizations and companies.* In the last century there were already huge companies, such as McCormick, that engaged in agricultural research. Their work was largely confined to the provision of mechanical and later chemical inputs. Similarly, there were few large food companies with the exception of those directly connected to plantation crops in the tropics. More importantly, most of these companies were local in scope. They rarely transcended the boundaries of the nation-state. Moreover, virtually no supranational quasi-governmental organizations existed.

Today, the situation has changed markedly. Chemical, pharmaceutical, machinery, and seed companies are increasingly transnational in scope. For example, Pioneer Seed is the largest supplier of hybrid maize in France. Monsanto is a large producer and supplier of agricultural chemicals in Brazil. The "merchants of grain" control world grain trade virtually in its entirety (Morgan 1979). Similarly, the large food companies now transcend national boundaries either by selling products under their brand names worldwide (e.g., Kellogg's breakfast cereals) or by interlocking directorates that link European and American firms.[5]

However, far less noticed has been the emergence of other supernational entities, usually of a quasipublic sort, in agriculture and agricultural research. These newer supernational entities usually have as their members nation-states, though they are hardly responsible to nations in the way that democratic states claim to be responsible to their citizens.

The Organization for Economic Cooperation and Development (OECD) has been active in sponsoring economic research on agriculture. More importantly, OECD has set in place standards for the marketing of fruits and vegetables (OECD 1983). These standards pertain to cosmetic qualities of the fresh produce as well as to packaging requirements. They are essential for the creation of a global market in fresh produce for they permit for those commodities what has been the case for bulk commodities such as wheat for a century. OECD has also sponsored a series of highly uncritical studies of the new biotechnologies in an attempt to encourage restructuring of research, regulation, and standards to encourage their widespread use (Beier, Crespi, and Straus 1985).

Similarly, the Food and Agriculture Organization of the United Nations (FAO) maintains the *Codex Alimentarius*, which permits the development of international standards for food processing and production. The World Intellectual Property Organization (WIPO) helps to coordinate the patent and copyright laws of its member nations. These include administration of the plant variety protection laws (through its subsidiary, UPOV) and the encouragement of similar legislation in developing nations. Finally, the Consultative Group on International Agricultural Research (CGIAR) has encouraged the development and growth of a system of international agricultural research centers (IARCs) that promote (certain kinds of) agricultural research in the developing nations of the world.

Many, though not all, of these organizations have as one of their goals the "harmonization" of national norms on all sorts of things. (The problems of "harmonization" reach their zenith in the General Agreement on Tariffs and Trade [GATT] negotiations, though the debates within the European Community [EC] on the subject have not been without cries of foul play.[6]) Without a doubt, many differences in legal regimes constrain trade, create enormous amounts of red tape, and increase the cost of imported goods to consumers. However, the creation of global norms for agricultural products *in particular* raises thorny questions regarding biodiversity and local autonomy. What some see as a health hazard others see as a trade barrier.[7] What some see as an unnecessary environmental risk others see as a desirable policy for keeping costs down. What some see as cruelty to animals others see as efficient agricultural production.[8]

I should note that my purpose here is not so much to critique these diverse organizations as it is to note their growth and importance. Taken together these transnational corporations and supernational organizations are eroding the established role of the nation-state in both agriculture and agricultural research. This erosion has both its positive and negative aspects. Nevertheless, as relatively centralized international bodies, subject to little if any democratic control, they cannot help but to produce a kind of agriculture and a kind of research that is standardizing in its character, that glosses over small regional differences in agriculture, and that ignores or overlooks local problems and concerns.

8. *The very success of agricultural research in fostering accumulation is undermining its legitimacy.* In the public sector, the very success of research in reducing the size of the farm population through massive gains in labor productivity has eroded the public support for it. Whereas farmers once were the majority of the population, in most developed nations they are now just another special-interest group. Moreover, the trend of research has been to remove value-added from the farm and put it in the input and output industries. This change has increased the power of the input and output industries, which have demanded a retreat from direct service to farmers. Yet, succumbing to those demands, as enticing as they may be, will undermine the public research enterprise still further. Only by rebuilding the client base, by broadening it to include environmental and consumer interests, will public research be able to recapture its legitimacy with the public.

The private sector, too, now has reason to be concerned about legitimacy in its research endeavors. Fifty years ago, the private sector performed little research and company size was small. The public was virtually unaware of errors of judgment. Today, the large companies that do the research that formerly took place in the public sector are in the foreground. Their role is quickly seen as illegitimate when they trample strongly held values, even if inadvertently. The current problems associated with bGH are an excellent case in point. The companies involved are now as much concerned about their image as they are with the research products that have engendered the controversy (Busch 1991). They are also grudgingly being forced to develop positions on environmental and sustainability issues. As the private sector continues to develop new products (e.g., herbicide-tolerant crops), we can expect further crises of legitimacy to occur. Thus, both the public and private sector need to rethink the balance they must strike between accumulation and legitimation.

9. *Increased production is not and should not be the central goal for agricultural research*. It has been well known for some time that increasing agricultural production is of little value in resolving the problems of world agriculture. The developed world is already drowning in a sea of farm commodities, yet the homeless and hungry are still among us. In contrast, the underdeveloped world is suffering from shortfalls in large part because the prices of imported food from the West are simultaneously so low that local producers cannot compete and so high that urban consumers cannot afford to buy them. Only by increasing household incomes of the poor in developed and developing nations will access to food be improved. Merely increasing the volume of food produced will not resolve the problems of the hungry.

At the same time research oriented toward increasing productivity, if defined in the usual sense that economists use, is desirable because it makes the best use of scarce resources. However, there is a catch. The pricing system does not necessarily provide an adequate guide to what is the most efficient use of resources. This is true for several reasons: First, "green" issues of the 1980s and 1990s are just barely represented in the pricing system. On the one hand, the use of nonrenewable resources receives no special weight in the pricing system. On the other hand, the innumerable externalities—ranging from water and soil pollution to the loss of biological diversity—are ignored by the price system. Conceivably, such information could be included in prices, but I for one doubt that it will occur in the near future. Nor would its inclusion resolve the problem (Sagoff 1988). Second, the statistical collection system upon which all sorts of policies are built is itself suffering from severe burdens that make it highly suspect.

10. *The national and international systems of agricultural statistics are becoming less and less useful for understanding agricultural markets and trade*. Statistics have their origin with the state (Lazarsfeld 1961). The conventional wisdom has it that agricultural statistics reflect the nature of world

agriculture. Using statistics, social scientists can come to grips with some of the theoretical issues reflected in those numbers. Yet, looked at from another point of view, statistics only reflect that which they were designed to measure. Even if the "object" to be measured is not present, or is inadequately summarized by the numerical index, the statistical system will provide data to fill in the table. Consider the review of Indian land tenure statistics by Hindess (1973). He notes that the categories of the data hardly reflected the reality of the Indian agricultural situation. Yet, nothing whatever prohibited the census takers from gathering the numbers.[9] As Hindess (1973: 41) remarks, "There is no correct and unique distribution that exists independently of its means of production, no distribution that is independent, in particular, of the system of categories into which the population is to be distributed." In short, just as natural scientists make nature as much as they discover it, so social statistics make what they purport to describe.

From still another point of view, it is possible to argue that statistics make possible certain kinds of actions with respect to social relations (Latour 1987; Tufte 1983; Yates 1989). In particular, as Latour has suggested, they permit action at a distance. For example, the data collected on yield trends allow us to determine if investment in agricultural research has been sufficient to keep up with population growth.

Yet, we are now suffering from a gradual disconnection between the data gathered and the concepts they claim to measure. As the agricultural economy has become more and more global in character, two interrelated trends have become apparent. On the one hand, prices often reflect the peculiarities of market structure. The price of grain bought and sold by the large international grain traders reflects the differences in tax laws among nations as well as the various embargoes that may be in effect. Moreover, for many goods, prices are now set by contracts with growers rather than in the market. Thus, for example, the average price of milk sold to processors may reflect the residual rather than the average price received. Moreover, the development of functional attribute crops (Moshy 1986) makes things once summable into incommensurables. Thus, wheats specially designed for use in making wallpaper paste or certain types of pastries may be developed. These new crops will tend to fragment the broad-based commodity markets such that commodity prices reflect only those uses that are not contracted.

On the other hand, changes in processing are increasing the substitutability (Goodman, Sorj, and Wilkinson 1987) of various agricultural products and turning them into "raw materials" to be transformed into industrial products. Already, the markets for various edible oils have been virtually merged. Bread manufacturers can now use any of more than half a dozen oils in various blends as the market price dictates. This increases the volatility of markets and makes forecasting increasingly difficult.

Moreover, even in cases where the phenomenon appears adequately represented by the statistics, prices may be artifacts of the price system in ways that are at considerable variance with economic theory. The nature of the tax structure, machinations by multinational corporations to raise or lower prices of a given commodity in order to escape high taxes or other national legal restrictions, subsidies for agricultural research (Pineiro, Trigo, and Fiorentino 1979), and the complex structures by which agriculture is subsidized (Charvet 1988) may have more to do with the nature of price data than any notion of supply or demand. Recently, Federal Reserve Board Chairman Alan Greenspan was quoted as saying that "the economy has been changing faster than our ability to measure it" (quoted in Gleckman with Carey 1991: 112). However, it is worth emphasizing that these issues cannot be resolved by merely improving the quality of the data collection system; they suggest a shift in the nature of the underlying phenomena that the statistics purport to measure. The very fact of globalization, high-speed capital transfers, keeping of multiple sets of books by multinational corporations in order to minimize national taxes, the increase in the role of services in the economy, new linkages between sectors of the economy, and new kinds of cross-elasticities—not to mention the decline in federal financing for collection of statistics—all contribute to the increasing disparity between the world as described by statistics and the world experienced daily.

In short, the world of agricultural research can no longer be thought of in merely national terms. Research is now a global activity involving not only nation-states but large transnational actors. Moreover, research is a fundamentally value-laden enterprise—an enterprise that will in large part determine the future of world agriculture. Most seriously, the very data upon which we have relied for some time to inform us of changes is no longer as valid as it once was. Thus, we face a future full of both opportunities and pitfalls. It is only fitting to ask what should be done now.

It is all too typical of papers like this one to close by calling for more research. Clearly, that is needed. But what is needed even more is debate and dialogue on the future of agricultural research and world agriculture. To date, nearly all the dialogue that has occurred has been confined to transnational actors and bureaucratic representatives of nation-states. Within the scientific community there has been little but bandwagon support for biotechnology (as if all biotechnologies were likely to have the same effects on agriculture). Even in the most democratic societies there has been little or no legislative direction given.

Let me take a few moments, then, to sketch out what an alternative to the current system of agricultural research might look like. First, it would feature agroecology as the central discipline. This would be based on the realization that agriculture is a form of ecosystem management. What is often called sustainable agriculture would simply be the management of agroecosystems in ways that ensure their continuance. Second, the human sciences would play a central role in the new agricultural research system, by virtue of the realization that it is humankind that maintains, changes, and is the pivotal actor in all agroecosystems. Third, the new system would employ a systems perspective as its central theoretical framework. This is not to say that reductionist research would be abandoned, but that it would be employed in such a manner that it fit into a larger, more holistic systems approach. Fourth, the new system would develop technologies that were decentralizing in nature and that conserved traditional cultures—both human and nonhuman. Finally, the new system would include the study and understanding of values as part of the training and activities of scientists in all fields. This would be necessary since it is biologists, chemists, engineers, and others who actively change society through technology.

This is clearly another path that might be taken. It is one that I frankly doubt we will take unless many more voices demand it than is now the case. But this is why I feel it necessary to close by arguing for democracy. Expert knowledge has its place, but it must be in the service of democratic ideals, rather than the other way around. Thus, the proper place to discuss the globalization of agriculture is not only among academics, but also among legislators. While our current system of democracy is hardly perfect, it is far better than nondemocratic systems. We need to use that democracy as the arbiter among competing visions of world agriculture. We need to use democratic procedures to determine just what kind of nature we want.

Notes

1. Whether nature should be seen as masculine, feminine, or neuter is a topic of hot debate in some circles. I only report here Bacon's view on the subject. But see Keller (1985) for a study of sexual imagery in Bacon.

2. UPOV was founded in 1962, several years before the United States approved the Plant Variety Protection Act and joined the organization.

3. The situation in Europe is complicated by the fact that Napoleonic code, the basis for most continental law, requires explicit amendments in order to include plants and animals in patent law. For a review of some of the issues see ICDA (1989) and Edelman and Hermitte (1988).

4. It is worth noting that the Cooperative Extension Service has taken a considerably different approach in its strategic plan (ECOP, 1991). The extension plan is considerably broader in scope and includes areas hardly mentioned in the ESCOP plan.

5. Wimberley (1991) has noted a disturbing negative relationship between the presence of these entities in Third World nations and per capita calorie and protein consumption.

6. For example, the use of the term "marmalade" connotes a quince-based jam in Great Britain while it has the broad meaning of anything mixed together in Portugal.

7. The recent debate over the importation of meat from the United States by the EEC nations is a case in point. The United States uses antibiotics in feed while the Europeans do not.

8. Currently, Sweden prohibits the confinement raising of hogs while Switzerland prohibits the confinement of chickens.

9. Cicourel (1974) goes even further in arguing that statistics are inherently useless if not grossly misleading. However, Cicourel appears to miss the point. The issue is one of formation of cases; if the cases are well conceived they may still provide an adequate indicator (Boldrini, 1972).

Bibliography

Bachelard, Gaston. 1934. *Le nouvel esprit scientifique*. Paris: Presses Universitaires de France.

Barreau, Jacques. 1971. "L'Ethnobotanique au carrefour des sciences naturelles et des sciences humaines." *Bulletin de la Société Botanique de France* 118 3/4: 237–248.

Beier, F. K., R. S. Crespi, and J. Straus. 1985. *Biotechnology and Patent Protection: An International Review*. Paris: OECD.

Berlan, Jean-Pierre, and Richard Lewontin. 1986. "Breeders' rights and patenting life forms." *Nature* 322 (28 August): 785–788.

Biggelaar, Christoffel den. 1991. "Farming systems development: Synthesizing indigenous and scientific knowledge systems." *Agriculture and Human Values* 8, 1: 25–36.

Bird, Elizabeth. 1987. "The social construction of nature: Theoretical approaches to the history of environmental problems." *Environmental History* 11, 4: 255–264.

Blumenthal, David, Michael Gluck, Karen Seashore Louis, Michael A. Stoto, and David Wise. 1986a. "University-industry research relationships in biotechnology: Implications for the university." *Science* 232 (13 June): 1361–1366.

Blumenthal, David, Michael Gluck, Karen S. Louis, and David Wise. 1986b. "Industrial support of university research in biotechnology." *Science* 231 (17 January): 242–246.

Boldrini, Marcello. 1972. *Scientific Truth and Statistical Method*. New York: Hafner.

Brockway, Lucille H. 1979. *Science and Colonial Expansion: The Role of the British Royal Botanic Gardens*. New York: Academic Press.

Busch, L. 1991. "Risk, values, and food biotechnology." *Food Technology* 45 (April): 96, 98, 100–101.

Busch, Lawrence, and Paul Marcotte. 1987. "Instruments and Values in Science." Paper presented at the annual meeting of the Society for Social Studies of Science, Worcester, Mass., November.

Busch, Lawrence, William B. Lacy, Jeffrey Burkhardt, and Laura R. Lacy. 1991. *Plants, Power, and Profit: Social, Economic, and Ethical Consequences of the New Biotechnologies*. Cambridge, Mass.: Basil Blackwell.

Buttel, Frederick H. 1984. *Biotechnology and Agricultural Research Policy: Emergent Issues*. Bulletin no. 140. Ithaca, N.Y.: Cornell University, Department of Rural Sociology.

Charvet, Jean-Paul. 1988. *La guerre du blé: Bases et stratégies des grands exportateurs*. Paris: Economica.

Cicourel, Aaron. 1974. *Theory and Method in Study of Argentine Fertility*. New York: John Wiley.

Crosby, Alfred W. 1986. *Ecological Imperialism*. Cambridge: Cambridge University Press.

Edelman, Bernard, and Marie Angèle-Hermitte (eds.). 1988. *L'Homme, la nature, et le droit*. Paris: Christian Bourgeois.

Experiment Station Committee on Organization and Policy, Subcommittee on Budget and Planning. 1990. *Research Agenda for the 1990s*. ESCOP 90-1. College Station: Texas Agricultural Experiment Station.

Extension Committee on Organization and Policy (ECOP). 1991. *Patterns of Change: A Report of the Cooperative Extension System Strategic Planning Council*. Washington, D.C.: Extension Service, U.S. Department of Agriculture.

Friedmann, Harriet. 1978. "World market, state, and family farm: Social bases of household production in the era of wage labor." *Comparative Studies in Society and History* 20, 4: 545–586.

Gleckman, Howard, and John Carey. 1991. "Washington's misleading maps of the economy." *Business Week* 3216 (3 June): 112–113.

Goodman, David, Bernado Sorj, and John Wilkinson. 1987. *From Farming to Biotechnology: A Theory of Agro-Industrial Development*. Oxford: Basil Blackwell.

Heidegger, Martin. 1977. *The Question Concerning Technology and Other Essays*. New York: Harper and Row.

Hightower, Jim. 1973. *Hard Tomatoes, Hard Times*. Cambridge: Schenckman.

Hindess, Barry. 1973. *The Use of Official Statistics in Sociology*. London: Macmillan.

Idhe, Don. 1990. *Technology and the Lifeworld: From Garden to Earth*. Bloomington: Indiana University Press.

International Coalition for Development Action (ed.) 1989. *Patenting Life Forms in Europe*. Proceedings of a conference at the European Parliament, Brussels.

Keller, Evelyn Fox. 1985. *Reflections on Gender and Science*. New Haven, Conn.: Yale University Press.

Kenney, Martin. 1986. *Biotechnology: The University-Industrial Complex*. New Haven, Conn.: Yale University Press.

Latour, Bruno. 1987. *Science in Action: How to Follow Scientists and Engineers through Society*. Milton Keynes, Eng.: Open University Press.

Lazarsfeld, Paul F. 1961. "Notes on the history of quantification in sociology: Trends, sources, and problems." Pp. 147–203 in Harry Woolf (ed.), *Quantification*. Indianapolis, Ind.: Bobbs-Merrill.

Morgan, Dan. 1979. *Merchants of Grain*. New York: Viking Press.

Moshy, Raymond. 1986. "Biotechnology: Its potential impact on traditional food processing." Pp. 1–14 in Susan K. Harlander and Theodore P. Labuza (eds.), *Biotechnology in Food Processing*. Park Ridge, N.J.: Noyes Publications.

National Research Council. 1972. *Report of the Committee on Research Advisory to the U.S. Department of Agriculture*. Washington, D.C.: NTIS, PB 213 338.

Nelkin, Dorothy. 1984. *Science as Intellectual Property*. New York: Macmillan.

Office of Technology Assessment. 1981. *An Assessment of the United States Food and Agricultural Research System*. Washington, D.C.: OTA.

Organisation for Economic Cooperation and Development. 1983. *The OCDE Scheme for the Application of International Standards for Fruit and Vegetables*. Paris: OECD.

Pardey, Philip G. 1989. *ISNAR Agricultural Research Indicator Series: A Global Data Base on National Agricultural Research Systems*. New York: Cambridge University Press.

Pineiro, Martin, Eduardo Trigo, and Raul Fiorentino. 1979. "Technical change in Latin American agriculture." *Food Policy* 4, 3: 169–177.

Price, Derek J. de Solla. 1963. *Little Science, Big Science*. New York: Columbia University Press.

Rockefeller Foundation. 1982. *Science for Agriculture*. Report of a workshop on Critical Issues in American Agricultural Research, Winrock International Conference Center, Morrilton, Ark., June 14–15. Washington, D.C.: Rockefeller Foundation.

Rogers, Everett M. 1983. *Diffusion of Innovations*. 3d. ed. New York: Free Press.

Ruttan, Vernon W. 1982. *Agricultural Research Policy*. Minneapolis: University of Minnesota Press.

Sagoff, Mark. 1988. *The Economy of the Earth: Philosophy, Law and the Environment*. Cambridge: Cambridge University Press.

Schafer, Wolf (ed.). 1983. *Finalization in Science: The Social Orientation of Scientific Progress*. Dordrecht: D. Reidel Publishing Co.

Tufte, Edward R. 1983. *The Visual Display of Quantitative Information*. Cheshire, Conn.: Graphics Press.

United States Department of Agriculture. 1991. *National Research Initiative, Competitive Grants Program*. Program Description. Washington, D.C.: Cooperative State Research Service, USDA.

Veblen, Thorstein. 1932. *The Place of Science in Modern Civilization and Other Essays*. New York: Viking Press.

Wimberley, Dale W. 1991. "Transnational corporate investment and food consumption in the Third World: A cross-national analysis." *Rural Sociology* 56, 3: 406–431.

Yates, JoAnne. 1989. *Control through Communication: The Rise of System in American Management*. Baltimore: Johns Hopkins University Press.

4 Biotechnologies, Multinationals, and the Agrofood Systems of Developing Countries

Bernardo Sorj and John Wilkinson

There is probably already as much anticipatory literature on the impacts of biotechnology on developing countries as retrospective literature analyzing the consequences of the Green Revolution. In fact, biotechnology, along with microelectronics, has been in the forefront of prospective technology studies. In addition, the wealth of analysis of the Green Revolution served as a point of comparison and contrast, facilitating identification of the issues at stake (Buttel, Kenney, and Kloppenburg 1985).[1]

Prospective studies by their nature incorporate a large element of speculation. At the same time they have a mobilizing effect that may influence patterns of innovation and diffusion as the relevant actors assimilate the probable impacts of different strategies.[2] This may be particularly true for biotechnologies; early catastrophic projections of their impact on developing countries have had a notable influence at least on the public relations postures of leading actors. This can be clearly seen in the case of the leading agriculture and food multinationals whose biotechnology strategies for developing countries we analyze in this chapter.[3]

A Review of the Literature

The tone of early prospective studies of biotechnology and developing-country agrofood systems, emerging toward the end of the seventies and continuing until the mid-eighties, was influenced by two factors. On the one hand, emphasis was placed on the revolutionary character of biotechnologies, particularly the ability to manipulate genetic inheritance beyond the obstacles of sexual reproduction and classical breeding. At the same time, the radical potential of the new biotechnologies, particularly for developing countries, was apparently confirmed by the enzymatic transformation of maize, and potentially other carbohydrate substrates, producing a sweetener (high-fructose corn syrup) able to compete with sugarcane and sugar beet. As a result, this early literature concentrated on the radical substitution potential of the new biotechnologies and predicted sweeping changes in international trade to the detriment of developing countries and widespread rural unemployment. The strategic priority within this scenario was agricultural reconversion.[4]

An optimistic variant of this perspective was premised on the emergent character of the new biotechnologies on a world scale. It was argued that, while developing countries had lost out on the microelectronic revolution, the new biotechnologies could provide a niche-based opportunity for participating in the new high-technology world division of labor. The new biotechnologies, in addition to being largely scale neutral, were well placed to benefit from the potential comparative advantage of developing country biomass. At the same time, the comparatively low costs of developing specific scientific and technological competence in this area would permit the development of autonomous strategies (Bifani 1984).

Social research directed at the institutional context in which the new biotechnologies were developing arrived at a less optimistic evaluation. In this literature the increasing privatization of biotechnological innovation and diffusion was seen to be the most decisive characteristic. Again, using the Green Revolution as a point of comparison, it was argued that the "gene revolution" would not be mediated by the public international agricultural research network. Instead, innovation and diffusion would be controlled by the leading multinationals active in agrofood markets, to which public research institutes were also increasingly subordinated (Kenney 1986; Otero 1989).

Two basic conclusions drawn from this analysis could be seen to reinforce the "substitutionist" thesis. Privatization of biotechnology research and development and the institutionalization of diffusion through systems of intellectual property rights were seen to be factors inhibiting the conditions for technology transfer to developing countries. At the same time, control over the innovation process by multinationals situated in the industrialized countries would lead to innovation directed to enhancing the competitiveness of developed-country agrofood systems. To the extent that transfer occurred the dynamic would be to reinforce the large-scale agricultural model implanted in the wake of the Green Revolution, accelerating even further the marginalization of the peasant economy. In this process the potential for the new biotechnologies to address problems specific to developing countries would be substantially undermined.

Recent analyses of these issues have tended to be more nuanced. The longer-than-expected lead times governing innovation and diffusion, together with the costs and technological problems associated with industrial upscaling, have led to greater caution about both the speed and the extent of substitution impacts on developing countries.

On the other hand, the dominant position of the major agrichemical and pharmaceutical groups in biotechnology innovation would suggest a trajectory in which the new biotechnologies are integrated into existing Green Revolution models rather than providing a basis for a rupture in the pattern of agroindustrial development. Within this perspective, biotechnologies can be seen as reinforcing the existing model, particularly through increasing the size and scope of agrichemical markets, or at most mitigating some of their more problematic technical features, such as problems of salinity in irrigated agriculture (Buttel 1989). In short, as biotechnology has come closer to being marketable, radical perspectives have given way to more pragmatic appreciations of its impact for developing countries. At the same time, there has been a shift from a focus on scientific potential and public policy to a more detailed examination of markets and the leading private actors, particularly the multinationals involved in food and agriculture.

Multinationals in Agrofood

This section is based on a series of interviews with leading private actors in agrofood in the context of a broader focus on biotechnology strategies. Three factors influenced the interview selection. First, a peculiarity of the agrofood sector is its low level of endogenous innovation combined with a marked capacity for the internalization of innovations generated outside the sector. This has allowed for the maintenance of average rates of industrial productivity growth. Therefore, we focus here on multinationals involved in agrofood rather than simply agrofood multinationals. Specialist agri-biotechnology firms were also included since they have been and continue to be important sources of innovation. Second, the agrofood system historically has been organized around successive distinct stages in the technical and economic manipulation of specific raw materials. This has led to an industrial structure characterized by a high level of market and technological heterogeneity, as well as an equally high level of interdependence, which has been responsible for the emergence of analytical concepts such as the "agrofood production chain." Third, historically the agrofood system of a country has been heavily influenced by the structure of its agriculture and the accompanying institutions and regulations. Therefore, current patterns of globalization of markets and investments must be evaluated against the respective agricultural environments in which the leading actors operate.

In the light of these considerations we chose an interview sample to ensure representativeness both in terms of the different markets that make up the agrofood system and the major agroindustrial blocs on a world scale. Hence,

Table 4.1. Firms Interviewed

Agricultural Genetics Company	Gist-Brocades	Plantech-Mitsubishi
Agrigenetics	ICI	Rhône Poulenc
Amylum	Kyowa Hakko	Sanofi
Animal Biotechnology Cambridge	Limagrain	Shell
Calgene	Monsanto	SME
Ciba Giegy	Native Plants	Snow Brand
Dalgety	Nestlé	Suntory
Dekalb	Pioneer	Unilever
Ferruzzi	Plant Genetics	

leading firms in seeds, agrichemicals, primary processing, biological intermediates, and final foods were selected with a view also to establishing a balance among the three major blocs: Europe, the United States, and Japan. Logistical and cooperation problems led to some gaps, affecting partly agrichemicals and primary processing, but a considerable measure of representativeness was achieved (see Tables 4.1 and 4.2). The interviews covered the same ground for purposes of comparative evaluation but were open-ended to permit an appreciation of the specific strategies of each of the leading actors. Given the importance of institutional issues determining innovation patterns, additional interviews were also conducted within the public sector. In the case of Japan, particularly, this led to a series of interviews with the different relevant ministries and agricultural and food research institutes.

Contextualizing Biotechnology Innovation

Two basic assumptions underlie the substitution prognoses with respect to the impact of biotechnology on developing country raw materials: The first of these would be a protectionist drive in the industrialized countries to pro-

Table 4.2. Leading Firms Interviewed According to Type and Location

Type/Location	Europe	United States	Japan	Total
Seeds	1	2	1	4
Agrichemicals	4	1	0	5
Primary processing	2	0	0	2
Intermediates	2	0	1	3
Final foods	3	0	2	5
Specialist Biotech	2	3	0	5
Total	14	6	4	24

vide new markets for stagnant domestic agricultures. The promotion of oil crops in Europe is a major example of this tendency, although the limits of such a policy are now becoming clear as crop subsidies are being cut. Isoglucose in the United States would be the paradigm for this type of substitution. The second assumption would be competitive advantages deriving from industrial substitution. From this point of view stagnant food consumption in the industrialized markets serves as a stimulus to cost-cutting competitive strategies.

However, a large measure of consensus has now emerged in the literature, and was amply confirmed in our interviews, that direct industrial bioreactor substitution is and will remain uncompetitive for commodity crops. Substitution among agricultural crops, therefore, with or without the aid of industrial amino acid supplements, would be a stronger tendency. Cost pressures of this type are apparent in the animal feeds sector, where the incorporation of specific amino acids either by plant biotechnology or in the form of industrially fermented additives may allow greater use of cheaper cereals.

Biotechnology therefore is being harnessed to both protectionist and cost reduction strategies. However, the scope for protectionist measures is being increasingly limited as agricultural policies based on subsidies are subject to more stringent limits. In addition, protectionism is more likely to be adopted by local, regional, or national interests, particularly farmer or primary processing groups. Thus, it is not a general tendency characterizing the leading actors in the industrialized countries.

In contrast, the leading firms interviewed emphasized the global context of their strategies. Within this global perspective, the saturation of industrialized-country markets pointed not to the need for protectionist domestic substitution policies but rather to the strategic medium-term role of developing-country markets for global agrofood industry expansion. We return to the specific implications of this perspective below.

In addition, while cost cutting represented an important goal in certain sectors, particularly animal feeds, the strategic response to market saturation in the industrialized countries is not primarily price-cutting competition, but market segmentation exploiting the potential for quality products instead. It is the potential for redefining agrofood markets according to quality criteria that has the larger impact both on raw material and investment strategies, and it is in this context that the potential (or risk) of the new biotechnologies is largely situated.

Whether for protectionist, cost, or quality strategies, the importance of the new biotechnologies lies in the increased capacity that they offer for manipulation of raw materials and biological agents. This in its turn has led to new strategies for agricultural research and development (R&D). Whereas

Table 4.3. Leading Seed Companies

Company	Nationality	1989 Seed Sales (US$m)
Pioneer	United States	840
Sandoz	Switzerland	480
Limagrain	France	360
ICI	United Kingdom	280
Upjohn	United States	270
Cargill	United States	240
Dekalb	United States	205
Takil	Japan	200
Sakata	Japan	160
KWS	Germany	150
Ciba-Geigy	Switzerland	150

Source: Financial Times, 15 November 1990.

Note: Limagrain and ICI figures include sales of seed companies acquired in 1990.

previously agronomic criteria prevailed in the R&D programs of plant and animal breeding, the latter are now increasingly geared to processing and end-user priorities. This has led to a greater integration of upstream and downstream activities involving the biotechnologies and has particularly led to a greater investment in plant biotechnology R&D by food companies. However, in spite of these higher levels of interaction, the market segmentation within the vertical organization of the agrofood system still offers a useful analytical point of departure for capturing the differential dynamics of biotechnology innovation.

Biotechnology Upstream in Agrofood

Perhaps the most important industrial restructuring within the agrofood system has been the widely documented entry of agrichemicals into seeds (Table 4.3). If expenditures on advanced plant biotechnology research were to be taken as the criterion, the composition and order of the leading players would be as shown in Table 4.4. At the other end of the agrofood system, Nestlé can now be included as a player in plant biotechnology R&D and Unilever can be seen in terms of both seed markets and R&D.

Two contrasting positions emerged from the interviews with regard to the potential of developing-country seed markets. First, major new actors in seeds insisted on the strategic significance of global seed markets. To sustain this position they pointed to the slowdown in agricultural productivity from classical breeding and the long lead time for yield results from conventional plant biotechnology. Given world population trends and patterns of proba-

Table 4.4. Chemicals Firms and Plant Biotechnology

Company	Nationality	Plant Biotech. R&D (US$m)
Dupont	United States	20
ICI	United Kingdom	17
Ciba Geigy	Swiss	17
Sandoz	Swiss	16
Monsanto	United States	15
Enimont	Italian	15
Pioneer	United States	7
Dekalb	United States	6
KWS	German	5
Upjohn	United States	3

Source: Adapted from *Biofutur*, May 1990.

ble future demand for cereals and oils, a major expansion of these crops in developing countries will be needed. In the words of one interviewee, new "breadbaskets" would have to be created, particularly for the markets in the East. Therefore, market expansion would be fueled in the medium term by the incorporation of local and farmer-supplied markets into the global agrofood system. The decisive role of the new biotechnologies would be as tools to accelerate the development of varieties and expand the potential for hybrid markets.

Second, the current strategy of seed firms in the industrialized countries and the realities of seed markets in the developing countries would tend toward a qualification of this perspective. The major seed markets in the industrialized countries, particularly cereals, are now mature both in the sense that self supply by farmers is negligible and planted area is now stagnant. Hence, competitive strategy has focused on the agronomic segmentation of these markets with the substitution of broad spectrum for more ecospecific hybrids and varieties. For example, in the United States individual farmers will now use a range of different hybrids for the same crop. The leading seed firm in the United States now offers more than a hundred cultivars of the same crop.

In developing countries price and a variety of risk factors have led both to slow diffusion of existing varieties and a tendency toward the use of less sophisticated broad-range hybrids. This has limited the presence of the multinationals to the most modernized segments of developing-country markets. The costs of plant biotechnology research indicate that applications will be primarily directed to premium markets and may even lead to a decline in the presence of the multinationals in developing-country seed markets. One leading seed firm interviewed has since announced its withdrawal from the Brazilian seed market arguing that the latter is not able to absorb the quality products of the new plant biotechnology. Such a tendency may be reinforced by the growing importance of patent legislation as a precondition for investments in developing countries. Interviewees emphasized the importance of institutional as well as market factors as determinants of investment policy. Of these, inflation levels, strength of the local currency, and intellectual property legislation and practice were singled out as the most important investment determinants.

Current advances in hybrid technology may also have a negative impact on developing countries. The production of maize hybrids has traditionally involved heavy labor demands for "detassling." The difficulty of mobilizing rural labor in the developed countries has led to much relocation of hybrid multiplication to developing countries. Advanced techniques for achieving male sterility through genetic manipulation can now eliminate the labor-intensive "detassling" stage, which could lead to a substantial relocation of such activity to the developed countries. Such a move would be attractive to seed companies because it would allow for greater control over elite germplasm, which has had a tendency to "migrate" from developing countries where controls are less strict into the hands of competitors.

In addition to strategies based specifically on the potential of biotechnology for seed markets, two alternative or complementary priorities can be detected among the leading agrichemical groups involved in seeds. The first of these and the most widely discussed is the use of plant biotechnology to defend agrichemical markets, either enhancing the use of existing products or permitting the application of more specific-action chemicals involving lower dosage with positive cost and environmental implications. The second strategy is that of gene package supplier to the seed industry, offering desirable agronomic or quality traits. In this latter case, in principle, there would be no preference in terms of crops or varieties.

While the structure of the seed industry in developing countries may inhibit biotechnology investment directed specifically to seeds, this would not necessarily be the case for biotechnology firms looking more to agrichemical markets or to the sale of biotechnology packages. Indeed, the greater uniformity of seed markets using broad spectrum hybrids may make diffusion of modified varieties incorporating new traits or resistant to pests and herbicides an attractive proposition.

Technology Transfer

Much of the critical literature on increasing privatization of plant biotechnology research has been associated with limitations on the transfer of technology to developing countries. This is in contrast to the role of the public international agricultural research centers in the transfer of Green Revolution technology. However, a number of factors would point to a more favorable climate for the transfer of biotechnology expertise or biotechnology processes and products.

The increasingly global scale of multinational strategy means that sourcing and investments are less constrained by domestic market interests. Indeed, the success of globalization strategies depends on the degree to which the leading private actors can distance themselves from the policies of specific geographical interest groups and policies. Thus, in our interviews, the leading players showed great concern for their image in developing countries. At the same time the interviewees were unanimous in identifying the critical importance of winning the image battle with respect to the new biotechnologies.

While cutting-edge research may be centralized in the developed countries, the representatives of the leading firms interviewed wanted very much to be identified with projects that had a positive image in relation to developing-country problems. This is particularly true of the biotechnology firms specializing in the production of gene technology packages. One firm indicated its willingness to participate in such cooperative projects on a strict cost recovery basis, while others drew attention to their research competence in typical developing-country "orphan" crops such as cassava.

Potential for R&D cooperation with the specialized biotechnology firms was also evident. These firms have reached a level of maturity in their scientific and technological expertise but at the same time are under heavy financial pressure as the "burn-rate" of investment capital accelerates ahead of marketable products. Major agroindustrial complexes and cooperatives as well as national and regional governments in developing countries would be in a position to fund cooperative R&D initiatives drawing on the expertise of the specialist biotechnology firms.

This suggests that the shift of frontier biotechnology competence to the private sector does not automatically constitute a barrier to technology transfer. Rather it demands the elaboration of new institutional mechanisms that facilitate collaboration between these private actors and the traditional public national and international networks of technology transfer. More than this, it demands strategies of institutional innovation able to exploit disparate competencies between public and private, and national and international actors. At the same time, the price for technology transfer will be closer harmonization with the regulatory structures prevailing in the industrialized economies.

Tissue Culture

Plant tissue culture is being developed by both public institutions and the major multinationals active in cash crop production in developing countries. Specialized biotechnology firms have also been involved in large-scale joint ventures involving tissue culture technology transfer. This has become a major area of research for multinationals involved in tree crops, from coffee to bananas and oils. However, earlier expectations with regard to productivity have not always been borne out, and one large-scale application of such technology to oil crop plantations is now in question.

It is in the horticulture market, primarily for orchids, that the impact of tissue culture is strongest in developing countries, particularly in Southeast Asia. The diffusion of expertise in tissue culture and the strategic importance of cheap labor for the labor-intensive multiplication phase have provided developing countries with a competitive niche. As a result there has been a considerable, though partial, relocation of the industry out of the industrialized countries.

Animal Biotechnology

Mention should be made here of animal biotechnology and specifically of bovine somatotropin (bST). There has been considerable opposition to the introduction of this product in the industrialized countries. On the one hand, appeals to the advantages of quantity improvements and lower costs make little headway where milk surpluses and subsidies are the norm. In addition bST has been widely associated with the separate problem of hormone levels in food. Moreover, it has also been argued that the benefits of bST are limited to highly modernized temperate-climate intensive livestock conditions. From this perspective the potential of bST would not be realized in typical developing-country conditions where output improvements are most urgent. However, one of the leading manufacturers of bST would contest such an interpretation. They argued that trials in a traditional African livestock context had shown significantly increased yields when applied without changes in feeding patterns. The problem is the delivery system, which requires daily injections. The leading firms in this market are working to reduce the rate of injections to once every two weeks or even once per month. In such an event it is thought that bST may have a wider applicability to developing-country conditions than originally thought.

Additives and Ingredients

A major tendency in agrofood during the twentieth century has been the substitution of chemical for agricultural inputs in the case of different quality components of food (Wilkinson 1987). Chemical-based colors and flavors increasingly compensated for the loss of these qualities as a result of industrial processing. A wide range of functional elements also became incorporated into food products. One of the major consumer preoccupations in the seventies was directed to the health implications of chemical additives. Accommodation to consumer demands led to a renewed interest in agricultural sources for these products, opening up the potential of new markets, particularly in developing countries. Furthermore, it was argued that advanced biotechnology techniques, particularly plant cell culture, would allow for a continuation of the secular trend toward the use of industrial substitutes for agricultural inputs. However, biological rather than chemical inputs would now be the basis of such substitution.

None of the interviewees attached much credibility to large-scale plant cell culture substitution. They believed this would only be feasible, if at all, for very high value, low quantity products, which was not the case for the vast majority of food additives and ingredients. In addition, it was pointed out that many of the products that would be hypothetical targets for plant cell culture are currently farmed on a very rudimentary basis. Competition from industrial processes could therefore be offset by more conventional farm modernization or field productivity increases based on plant biotechnology and a readiness to accept lower prices.

A major European player in flavors, textures, colors, and a variety of functional ingredients for food products argued that the consolidation of these activities has led to wide-ranging direct investment upstream in the different raw-material sources. This, in turn, has led to a significant increase in marine and agricultural involvement in developing countries. Direct investment becomes increasingly important to the extent that attention is now directed to nontraditional raw materials or to nontraditional characteristics of these raw materials. This productive investment is accompanied by a decentralization of research in those developing countries that constitute a market for the resulting ingredients. Therefore, the move to more "natural" ingredients leads to an increasing segmentation of markets as catering to locally specific tastes assumes priority.

Algaculture emerges as an important area of investment as a source of alginates and carrageenans in addition to its protein value, particularly for animal feed. The nutritional potential of algae for developing countries has long been recognized. Investment in production and research in this area by major multinationals opens the opportunity for a broader integration of algaculture into the agrofood systems of developing countries.

Primary Processing and Agricultural Commodities

A wealth of literature already exists on the increasing interchangeability of carbohydrate and saccharose feedstocks in the sweetener market. In addition, alternative sweeteners, particularly aspartame, are expanding the range of their food industry applications. This originally corresponded to a defensive strategy on the part of a primary processing sector facing a saturation of its traditional outlets. However, the shift away from saccharose and high calorie sweeteners has been further advanced by dietary and health considerations.

The fundamental importance of these latter issues emerged more clearly from the interviews in the case of edible oils. During the 1980s palm oil emerged as a dynamic competitor to soybeans with the rapid development of modern plantations in Malaysia and more recently in Colombia stimulated by multinational investments. Modern palm oil production competed with other traditional oil producing centers in developing countries, particularly Africa. The rapid success of these modern plantations was attributed in part to the application of tissue culture and micropropagation techniques. In short, biotechnology was not employed for substitution purposes but as a means to increase competitiveness within the different supply centers of developing countries.

Thus, in this case multinationals can be seen to employ biotechnology to stimulate competitive oil sourcing in developing countries primarily on cost criteria. This competitiveness has proved vulnerable to the health preoccupations of current patterns of food consumption. Soybean interests have taken advantage of concern over saturated fats to campaign successfully for the exclusion of coconut and palm oil from food industry products in the United States. At the same time, tissue culture technology has proved less than successful, compromising productivity and quality.

The issue of quality, whether for industrial or final food use, poses a permanent threat to commodity crops. An important emerging tendency in the developed economies is the segmentation of commodity markets with the development of specialty crops tailored to industrial or final consumer demand. This is particularly notable in the case of edible oils where premium markets are being developed by the new biotechnology companies. Therefore, to the extent that basic commodities are not directly undermined by nutritional or related quality criteria, price levels will be affected by the consolidation of a premium edible oils market.

A reverse tendency can be noted in the case of cocoa butter. Here, a rapid expansion of demand in foods, and particularly in the cosmetics market, is leading to substitution efforts based on the enzymatic upgrading of cheaper oils. However, it remains to be seen whether such products will be vulnerable to competition with the "original" products.

Of course, market segmentation along quality lines is a very general tendency and relates to a multiplicity of factors ranging, in the case of agrofood, from farming practices to toxic compound levels and processing and packaging practices. Pressures exerted by these tendencies are already evident in the case of developing-country exports and are claimed often to constitute no more than a convenient nontariff trade barrier. Specifically biotechnology-based segmentation, however, is now a relevant consideration, as is clear from the above examples, and begins to extend to other key crops. Decaffeinated coffee is now an important market achieved on the basis of different processing techniques. Recently, however, success in the genetic modification of coffee beans has been announced. Thus, depending on consumer acceptance, decaffeinated coffee plantations may be a further factor in market segmentation.

In an earlier study we showed how the special characteristics of biotechnology allow for very different competitive applications depending on the agrofood sectors involved (Wilkinson 1987). Substitution tendencies were primarily identified with the defensive strategies of major cereal processing interests in the United States and policy making in the European Community. On the other hand, Japan has a directly opposite policy of promoting agricultural commodity supply bases outside its domestic territory. Such "out-sourcing" would extend from cereal and oils to milk, meat products, and grapes for winemaking. Even the production of bulk amino acids is now being stimulated in areas producing cheaper raw materials. In the Japanese context, biotechnologies would be harnessed instead to the development of a high value-added domestic agricultural economy. A similar policy strategy has been adopted in a number of European Commission biotechnology programs (e.g., ECLAIR, FLAIR). This policy strategy would point to a quite different division of labor between developed and developing countries. Substitutionist threats would be replaced by a polarization of bulk agricultural commodity production in developing countries as against an agriculture dedicated to high value-added products in the industrialized countries.

The Final Food Products Sector

Developing-country markets were said to be strategic to the medium- and long-term growth strategies of the final food sector as demographic and per capita consumption trends stagnate in the industrialized countries. Therefore, among these companies, there was great concern that the image of the firm not be associated with biotechnology innovations that might have a negative impact on developing-country terms of trade.

More than this, it was suggested that lowering raw material prices may not necessarily be in the interests of firms involved in processed foods. It is a peculiarity of the food system that fresh products continue to compete with their industrialized equivalents. A lowering of raw material prices may favor the fresh product since costs for the industrialized alternative are more rigid.

Two interrelated preoccupations influence the final food sector's perception of biotechnology: concern for consumer reaction and concern for quality. The former inclines such firms to adopt a cautious strategy; indeed, it is unlikely that the traditional final food producers will lead innovation in this field. It is not surprising that the principal innovations have come either from firms in the primary processing sector looking for new outlets or from agrichemical firms exploiting spin-offs from scientific research. However, the second of these concerns is leading to a more direct involvement with the quality of the raw material. In-house agricultural research or the financing of such research is therefore an increasing priority. At the same time the seed sector is actively engaged in involving the final food products sector in the development of new markets.

Radically new biotechnology innovations should not be expected to emerge from the final food sector. Nevertheless, such actors will be an important vehicle for the diffusion of accepted biotechnology practices in developing countries to the extent that new markets are opened up and domestic resources increasingly mobilized. According to one leading firm, hard currency constraints and changes in agricultural policy were tending to increase the use of domestic raw materials for local food production in developing countries. This would point to the possibility of developing new biotechnologies specifically suited to developing-country crops.

Conclusions

Radical conjectures on the probable impact of biotechnologies for developing countries tend to ignore the complexity of the market forces influencing innovation and diffusion. Product substitution predictions were premised on the defensive strategies of primary processing interests; the technology push of specialized biotechnology firms; and the predominance of cost-cutting priorities.

While not denying the importance of these pressures, our interviews would give greater emphasis to quality factors as influencing innovation in the food industry. The concern for quality has led to a greater preoccupation with the ingredients and raw materials of final food products. Biotechnologies that limit the use of chemicals, increase toxicological controls, and lower disease incidence would be favored in this context. Furthermore, quality is also identified with concepts of "naturalness," and it is here that doubts over consumer acceptance of genetically modified food ingredients persist. Since raw materials in the food industry cannot be reduced to functional inputs but must also be consumed along with the final product, innovations at any point in the agrofood chain must be acceptable to all the relevant actors.

The current restraint found in biotechnology impact analysis can be related to these two phenomena. Concern over consumer response has shifted innovative effort from cost cutting to quality promotion. At the same time, however, uncertainty remains as to the consumer's willingness to assimilate genetically modified ingredients. Therefore, biotechnology diffusion to developing countries has primarily involved intermediary rather than frontier technology, particularly plant tissue culture and micropropagation. Here, cheap labor provides a distinct advantage to developing countries, leading to a significant decentralization of industry from the industrialized countries. Moreover, the advantages of cheap labor are coupled with scientific competence acquired either in the universities of the industrialized world, the international public research network, or in collaboration with the private sector. While the research agenda has shifted to the private sector, the public sector remains an important vehicle for technology transfer. At the same time, as we have seen above, in addition to their direct R&D investment leading firms showed themselves open to collaboration involving technology transfer to developing countries. The impediments to such transfer were primarily institutional, relating to intellectual property and royalties.

As opposed to those concerned about major substitutions, the interviews pointed instead to a renewed interest in developing country raw materials as natural products to replace chemical additives and in exotic foods to open important avenues for market growth. Bioreactor substitution is unlikely to be a major factor here. Depletion of poorly developed resources is a larger threat, which may be offset by the modernization of agricultural and marine production systems, stimulated by direct investment by leading firms.

The issue of quality is beginning to have an important impact on developing-country raw materials. On the one hand, these materials are being directly challenged on health grounds, as in the case of vegetable oils. Equally important, however, is the segmentation effect of quality markets. As the segmentation of previous commodity markets advances, primarily in the industrialized countries, basic commodity exports from the developing countries may face increasingly depressed market conditions. At the same time quality criteria may serve as a mechanism for the implementation of non-tariff trade barriers. On the other hand, the importance of biotechnology for cost cutting was seen to be particularly important in the area of animal feed. At the same time animal biotechnology is increasing the potential for accelerating reproduction cycles and productivity levels. These two areas could become important priorities for developing countries to the extent that economic development must also confront the challenges of a transition to an animal protein diet.

Notes

1. For a comprehensive state of the art review of current biotechnology activity in developing countries see Sasson (1990). A global appreciation of biotechnology's impact on developing country agriculture can be found in Persley (1990).
2. The biotechnology studies of the FAST (Forecasting and Assessment in Science and Technology) program of the European Commission (DG XII) provided an important stimulus to prospective studies on this issue.
3. This work is part of a larger research project on the biotechnology strategies of leading firms in agriculture and food. See Sorj and Wilkinson (1990). For a more general appreciation of long term socioeconomic impacts see Goodman et al. (1987).
4. Important studies on the trade impacts of biotechnology were conducted under the coordination of Bijman et al. (1986).

Bibliography

Bifani, P. 1984. *Biotechnology for Agricultural and Food Production in Africa*. New York: United Nations Science and Technology for Development.

Bijman, Jos, Kees van den Doel, and Gerd Junne. 1986. *The Impact of Biotechnology on Living and Working Conditions in Western Europe and the Third World*. Dublin: European Foundation for the Improvement of Living and Working Conditions.

Buttel, Frederick. 1989. "How epoch making are high technologies? The case of biotechnology." *Sociological Forum* 4, 2: 247–261.

Buttel, Frederick, Martin Kenney, and Jack Kloppenburg, Jr. 1985. "From Green Revolution to biorevolution: Some observations on the changing technological bases of economic transformation in the Third World." *Economic Development and Cultural Change* 34, 1: 31–55.

Goodman, David, Bernardo Sorj, and John Wilkinson. 1987. *From Farming to Biotechnology: A Theory of Agro-Industrial Development*. Oxford: Basil Blackwell.

Kenney, Martin. 1986. *Biotechnology: The University-Industry Complex*. New Haven, Conn.: Yale University Press.

Otero, Gerardo. 1989. *Industry-University Relationships and Biotechnology in the Dairy and Sugar Industries*. Geneva: International Labor Office.

Persley, Gabriel. 1990. *Agricultural Biotechnology: Opportunities for International Development*. Wallingford, Eng.: CAB International.

Sasson, Albert. 1990. *Les biotechnologies dans les pays en développement: Les an-nees 80*. Paris: UNESCO.

Sorj, Bernardo, and John Wilkinson. 1990. "The Biotechnology Strategies of Lead-ing Firms in Agrofood." Report presented to the Organisation for Economic Co-operation and Development, Science and Technology Policy Division.

Wilkinson, John. 1987. *Europe within the World Food System: Biotechnologies and New Strategic Options*. Brussels: Commission of European Communities.

Part 2

Globalization of Agriculture and Food and Local Consequences

5 Food Regulation in Britain: A National System in an International Context

Terry Marsden, Andrew Flynn, and Neil Ward

Agriculture and food have been far from immune from the radical shifts in the accumulation and regulation "regimes" operating at the international level. Although some writers have suggested the demise of the "Fordist" mode of regulation, which was typified by American hegemony and the internationalized mass production and consumption of food, it has been difficult to identify any similar coherence concerning a post-Fordist stage. Commentators have pointed to increasing market instabilities and international sourcing by the transnational food manufacturers and retailers, as well as variable technological innovation within the food system.

These emergent tendencies have important implications, not only for the distribution of food production and consumption, but also in fostering "crises of legitimacy" in both the international and national regulation of food. It is our contention that as these tendencies become more pronounced so the potential for crises in the legitimacy of food itself develops. We argue that, in this sense, the growing transnationalization of food systems is being incorporated into the policy and institutional frameworks of nations and regions, promoting broader crises of legitimacy in institutional and political structures.

We aim in this paper to examine the current legitimation crises in the regulation of food by focusing on the nature of a national food system within the changing context of international forces. We argue that it is at the national level that legitimation crises are most acutely expressed and mediated. This does not deny the potency of international restructuring. Rather, it focuses attention on its progressive incorporation into the polity and economies of different national regulatory structures. The evidence and analysis here, focusing specifically on food hygiene, suggest that we have some considerable way to go before we can effectively identify new and sustainable modes of social regulation (at national levels) that can effectively generate a new, dominant transnational accumulation system that is reproducible in the medium term,[1] as occurred with the productivist Keynesian, Fordist mode in the postwar period. In this sense, new systems of accumulation in the international food order have yet, we would argue, to properly define and establish new sustainable modes of regulation.[2]

Global Disorder and the National Food Economy

Political economy approaches have been most useful in portraying the broad historical sweep of change within the food system. At their core is a conjunction between the growth of Fordist industrial employment (i.e., an accumulation system) and the necessity to provide wage and salary earners with an enhanced range of readily available food products (i.e., part of a compatible mode of social regulation). Among the advanced economies, a combination of farm subsidization and technology push ensured adequate food supplies both for home consumers and as a valuable export. Both new industrializing countries and new agricultural countries became increasingly dependent on manufactured food products supplied by the West. By the early 1980s, two-thirds of agricultural exports came from advanced nations (the countries of the Organization for Economic Co-operation and Development), while "developing" countries accounted for approximately one-half of the world's agricultural imports.

Despite the entrenchment of ties of dependency throughout much of the 1980s, slower rates of economic growth, international debt crises, and a slowdown in food trade began to lead to increasing instabilities in the global food order. This has been reflected in the return of price instabilities and greater competition (and conflict) to secure markets.

The rise of the European Community (EC) as a major food exporter has highlighted the trading vulnerability of traditional export-oriented countries (Lawrence 1990). For instance, in 1985, Australia lost its place to the EC as the leading exporter of beef and is now witnessing the EC encroaching on its Pacific markets with subsidized sales. As Australian farmers have found out, adopting free trade principles under the auspices of deregulation of domestic policy can cause severe hardship if not all the competing trading blocs are prepared to follow suit (Lawrence 1990). Conflict has been most apparent in the General Agreement on Tariffs and Trade (GATT) negotiations, in which the United States has faced stiff European and Japanese opposition to its demands for a radical reduction in farm subsidies. There have been a number of "tit for tat" exchanges between the United States and Europe. In the mid-1980s, for example, the United States took before GATT the tariff advantages the EC allows on citrus fruit imports from Mediterranean countries, which placed U.S. imports at a disadvantage just when manufacturers were seeking to expand export market share. A GATT panel favored the

U.S. claims, but the GATT council failed to support the recommendations. The EC refused to discontinue the practice. The United States then decided to increase custom duties on the imports of pasta, which benefited from EC export subsidies. The EC retaliated by raising import duties on American nuts and lemons. While a truce was agreed to in 1985, no fundamental agreement was reached. This led to a new round of reprisals from the United States as it further increased import duties on pasta.

By focusing on changes at the international level, commentators have tended to understate the role of national food systems. Thus on the one hand Friedmann and McMichael (1989) have argued that the restructuring of production has undermined nation-states and their existing economic systems. One consequence is that agriculture becomes increasingly differentiated, with some parts strengthening links to other sectors such as the chemical industry. On the other hand, attention to the food crisis at the national level has largely focused on its consequences for farms and food production rather than nationally based food systems more generally. The reduced levels of financial support both through commodity markets and infrastructural grant payments has promoted downturns in farm income and upturns in debt-to-asset ratios, such that there has been some talk of a farm crisis of international proportions in the developed as well as the developing world (see Goodman and Redclift 1989).

However, both perspectives are somewhat flawed. The latter, with its preoccupation with the consequences of policy change on *farm-based production*, tends to obscure a broader assessment of the consequences for the relatively more powerful and influential food industry during more unstable times. Meanwhile, the former view ignores the fact that nationally constructed systems of regulation, food consumption, and legitimation are crucial in assessing the changes of direction and the relative sustainability of the international food system. Moreover, as we will argue, it is at the national level that the most comprehensive (and relevant) food crises (as opposed to farm crises) are realized and that, given specific political and cultural conditions, severe constraints can be placed on the tendencies toward industrialized and homogenized food production and consumption. While nation-states may be increasingly losing their sovereignty over the ways food is produced, manufactured, and consumed, the evolving and adjusting forms of nationally based regulation can combine to cross-cut transnational restructuring during a period of increased international instability. A growing emphasis on consumption by food manufacturers and retailers is by no means a synergistic process. National governments and their agencies face the combined pressure to adjust over the long term as well as to cope with more immediate crises of legitimacy associated with their traditional support for agricultural producer interests.

The National Food System in an International Context

Before focusing on the specific factors determining the nature of food crises, it is necessary to outline some of the key emerging tendencies associated with the structure of the nationally based food system, albeit within its increasingly internationalized context. In advanced capitalist societies the food system has represented a competitive arena in which different sectors and companies struggle for ascendancy. It is worthwhile to look at some of the principal emergent trends in each of these sectors.

Input Suppliers

This is the most concentrated sector within the food system, with fertilizers now in the hands of three multinational firms (Norsk Hydro, ICI, and Kemira). Together they have the potential to supply 90 percent of the British market. BOCM Silcock, Dalgety, and Pauls and J. Bibby (Barlow Randt) control 57 percent of animal feedstuffs. The interdependencies of the food system are well represented by the animal feedstuffs sectors. First, the bulk of their raw materials is derived from the farming production sector itself, representing, in large part, an industry based on waste agricultural products that are inappropriate for food manufacturing and processing in their raw form. The bulk of cereal, soya bean, and other feed crop products in Britain are sold downstream to the feed manufacturers. As a result their profitability is heavily influenced by fluctuations in farm incomes and farm-based policy. Second, related to this point, considerable increases (in absolute terms) during the last twenty-five years in the consumption of prepared feedstuffs are largely due to an expanded national herd size. This has masked the tendency for the use of more highly concentrated feed, which holds higher conversion rates.

Input suppliers have also collaborated with banks to provide their own semiautonomous leasing companies in order to offer farmers favorable credit packages. The development of such credit links and particularly the growth in leasing and sell-back arrangements on farm machinery have increasingly tied the farm sector to the progressively concentrated input sector, while also protecting input suppliers' market share.

Farmers

In contrast with the nonagricultural sectors of the food chain, the farming sector in Britain is characterized by a large number of producers. According to the Ministry of Agriculture, Fisheries and Food (MAFF) about 144,000 full-time holdings produce more than 97 percent of total output (MAFF 1988) thus giving individual farm businesses minute market shares and negligible influence over market prices. The farming sector now accounts for little more than 15 percent of the value added in the food production process (Harvey 1987). Agricultural policy in the postwar period has tended to encourage, among other things, the specialization and regional concentration of production and increased output. These trends have also led to a more intensive use of farmland and, indirectly, to fewer, larger businesses, owned and occupied by a more profit- and asset-conscious generation of farmers. Since the mid-1970s real prices for most farm products have been falling. New technologies and credit relations have tended to favor the larger farm producer, but the decline in farmers' incomes and agricultural support during the last decade brings uncertainties for the future viability of many full-time farm businesses.

Food Manufacturers

In food manufacturing, the ten largest companies hold 44 percent of the British market, most of them being large multinational corporations (i.e., Unilever, Allied Lyons, Grand Metropolitan, Dalgety, and Hillsdown Holdings). Unlike the input suppliers, most of these companies are wholly or partly British owned, with the British market representing a larger proportion of their total activities.

Food Retailers

The top four food retailing firms (Tesco, Sainsbury's, Gateway, and Argyll) are British with, on average, 95 percent of their sales occurring within the U.K. (Ward 1990). While the vertically integrated interest of food manufacturing companies remains strong, food retailers are increasingly dictating to these companies and their subsidiaries strict regulations concerning the quality of food produce and are developing their own brand labels that undercut traditional manufacturers. Retailers' influence is also increasing in the storage and distribution sectors, with the larger companies establishing their own centralized distribution systems. This growth of influence of retailers has corresponded to increasing levels of concentration in the subsector. A series of corporate mergers and acquisitions have occurred since the

1970s. While price cutting has been a conventional mechanism for maintaining retail market share, the process of product innovation and presentation and the ability to provide flexible methods of food preparation are now key features in retailers' strategies. Such strategies lead to the backward integration and control over the production and manufacture of food.

Strategies within the Food System

With their margins squeezed, the food manufacturing and processing sectors have adopted a combined set of strategies that have led to further levels of overall concentration and correspondingly to more sophisticated internal organizational behavior. Some have purchased retailing outlets, but a higher proportion holds major interests in agro-input industries. Unilever, Nestlé, and BSN are three of the largest conglomerate food-processing/manufacturing firms in Europe. They run input supply firms, such as BOCM Silcock, as well as specialist food-processing firms (e.g., Mattesons Walls Ltd., pig meat processors). Such backward integration allows firms to regulate and direct technological innovations, so as to monitor inputs into specific food-manufacturing processes. For instance, the development of particular brands of seed potatoes (by Dalgety) can allow the provision of required yields and quality control of a diverse range of potato value-added products at the manufacturing stage. Producers' margins are squeezed, and their levels of control over the actual production process are reduced (Hawkins 1991).

Technological innovation takes diverse forms, and the food manufacturers increasingly depend upon it for their survival. Currently innovation is directed toward the obstacles associated with the vulnerability and perishability of food products, such as diversifying the methods and techniques of food preparation in the home (e.g., prepared foods, deep freeze and microwave products) and developing new forms of packaging (such as Tetra Pak and resealable laminated packaging) that allow more natural food to be stored longer. The continual need for innovation fuels the acquisition strategies of food firms, such that small firms within particular research and development sectors become particularly vulnerable to takeover. Leveraged buyouts undertaken by transnational food companies serve both to *engineer growth* in unchartered and often culturally resistant food markets and to *consolidate* the research and development function. Such acquisition strategies are increasingly leading to pan-European manufacturing control and distribution, with several of the leading competitors taking over the relatively less concentrated Southern Mediterranean national food sectors where the demand for value-added products is likely to continue to grow (Glover 1989).

In the context of the British food system these tendencies have several important implications that we shall explore. First, whatever the possibilities of the increasingly internationalized food system, it is likely to continue to diminish the economic and, as we shall see, the political significance of the agricultural production sector, which is increasingly dependent on the rest of the food system. Second, a combination of technology-push and progressive concentration and integration within the food system (as well as between the food system and other manufacturing sectors) confronts and often superimposes itself upon preexisting nationally and culturally based modes of consumption, transforming some and protecting others. The accumulative tendencies of the transnational food sector can only be realized and eventually sustained if they are grounded in the consumption practices of national and culturally based groups. Hence they increasingly need to absorb and transform cultural tastes and preferences and to bring the full weight of technological food production to bear down upon them.

So far we have looked at global processes of change at work in the food system and how they apply to Britain. But in understanding any particular food crisis, this approach can take us only so far. What is crucial is the conjunction of global processes with substantive features within a national food system. It is to an explanation of these substantive issues that we now turn.

Agriculture in British Society

The 1980s witnessed a declining role for agriculture in British society in a number of ways: As part of the increasingly sophisticated food chain, its economic power diminished. In addition, and just as importantly, its political power has declined, both in terms of its representative organizations (National Farmer's Union—NFU—and Country Landowners Association—CLA) and in the legitimacy of their claims on government (and society). For instance, the contribution of agriculture to the national economy, which had been much vaunted until the end of the 1970s (MAFF 1974; 1979), was no longer seen as such a strategically important industry. Indeed, in an economy suffering from the rigors of industrial recession and associated urban-based problems, such as civil disorder and growing disquiet at the cost of agricultural support, the consensus on agricultural policy waned. Moreover, it was increasingly recognized that the real contribution of agriculture to the nation's balance of payments and export trade was relatively low (cf. France).

While Britain's agriculture minister, John Gummer, has said that agricultural support and export subsidies will have to be cut, the German farm minister has argued, "If I am offered the choice between the collapse of the GATT talks and the ruination of 70% of my farmers I will choose the former" (*Guardian*, Feb. 1990). In addition, there has come a heightened but negative visibility of farming within Britain. Most notably this has been associated with changes in farm practices and the use of new technologies to degrade the environment. More recently, farming has been identified, rightly or wrongly, as the site at which contaminated food production is initiated. It was at agriculture that fingers were pointed both by the public and increasingly by other sectors of the food system when hygiene crises emerged in the 1980s.

MAFF and the Regulation of the Food System: Managing the Emerging Contradictions

MAFF lies at the heart of the food regulatory system in Britain. Unfortunately little is known about how MAFF goes about its task or how it works with other government departments. Political scientists have not been much concerned with a critical analysis of public administration, and a department with the glamour of MAFF has attracted virtually no attention. Of the two books that deal specifically with the ministry (Foreman 1989; Winnifrith 1962), neither offers a rigorous scrutiny of the work of the department.

Much more, however, is known about the links between the farming industry and MAFF. Most attention has been devoted to the relationship between the ministry and the NFU and to whether this should be regarded as a form of corporatism. In this sense corporatism is a form of state and not a theory of the state (Marsh 1983: 2). From the very earliest studies of the links between MAFF and the NFU (see Self and Storing 1962) it was apparent that there was a sense of partnership between the two at both national and regional levels. In an explicit comparison of British and American farm groups, Wilson pointed out their differences in access to government and added that within Britain "there is a widespread feeling in academic and government circles . . . that the relationship between the NFU and the Ministry of Agriculture is far closer than is normal" (Wilson 1977: 35). Subsequent analysts have sought to portray this relationship as one in which authority for policymaking is shared and, moreover, from which other interests were actively excluded (Cox et al. 1985, 1986; Grant 1983).

Such a relationship is most likely to arise where a key (sectoral) producer interest is involved. It provides the state with support for its policies and assistance in their implementation; for the interest group it provides the opportunity to shape both the formulation and implementation of policy. Such a relationship places responsibilities on both sides: The state must deliver on a policy that has been negotiated, and the group leadership must ensure that the membership complies with the policy.

Although the debate on the links between the NFU and MAFF has undergone many twists and turns as agriculture's relationship to public policy concerns has shifted, the insights that it offers to the workings of MAFF have stood the test of time. The first is that in organizational terms MAFF is a somewhat exceptional department. Like other departments it has a Whitehall base, but where it differs is in its direct chain of command that goes from a regional level to a local level and ultimately to the individual farmer. Many departments, while retaining responsibility for a policy area, carry out most of their work through other agents. Second, because of the close links that have been fostered between MAFF and farmers and their organizations, there have been allegations of *agency capture* such that MAFF seeks to represent the views of farmers at the expense of consumers and other sectors of the food industry. Third, it is widely believed that farmers favor a system of self-regulation, that is, they wish to regulate their own activities free from external control. MAFF has actively participated in this strategy and is by no means unique in Whitehall in doing so. Self-regulation relieves government of a task and, it is thought, industry of an unnecessary burden (i.e., regulation by an external agency).

If this is the framework within which MAFF operates in its dealings with the agricultural industry, it is worthwhile trying to extend the analysis to other elements in the food system and to elucidate MAFF's position as it faces unprecedented change in its environment. In terms of personnel, MAFF is one of the larger government departments, employing about 12,000 civil servants out of a total of about 600,000. The Ministry of Food was formed in 1939 but was not merged with agriculture until 1955, much to the unease of some contemporary commentators who feared that the interests of distributors and consumers would be weakened in a department that would be primarily concerned with farmers' needs (Foreman 1989: p. 57).

Both before and since it merged, the food section of MAFF seems to have adopted an administrative and regulatory style similar to that of agriculture. Favored interests are incorporated into the decision-making structure in an attempt to ensure that government and industry move in the same direction and at the same time. Perhaps the most obvious indication of the close relations between the ministry and industry is the Food Standards Committee established in 1947, which set up two subcommittees, one on food contaminants and the other on additives, amalgamated into the Food Additives and

Contaminants Committee in 1964. In 1983 a further reform took place when both committees were replaced by the Food Advisory Committee (Foreman 1989). Throughout, the aims of the committees have been to assess the latest scientific evidence on additives, contaminants, and the composition of food and to advise the minister on the need for any updating of the regulations. Both the Food Advisory Committee and its predecessors have been increasingly criticized for their lack of independence, their unrepresentative membership, and the secrecy of their proceedings (National Consumer Council 1988: p. 18).

Despite its undoubted influence, the Food Advisory Committee is not at the center of government's food committees. That privilege belongs to the Steering Group on Food Surveillance chaired by MAFF's chief scientist. Its members are drawn primarily from MAFF and the Department of Health (National Consumer Council 1988: 24). The steering group, too, is concerned with additives and contamination of food but has a more general remit to consider the safety and nutrition of food (National Consumer Council 1988: 20). It has a series of Working Parties dealing with specific topics such as pesticides under its direction. Working Party reports are considered by the steering group before being passed on to the Food Advisory Committee, a Department of Health–run body, and the Committee on the Toxicity of Chemicals in Food, Consumer Products, and the Environment (National Consumer Council 1988: 20).

The deliberations of these committees and their recommendations are significant because they are continually modifying the boundaries of existing regulations as the food companies, retailers, and input suppliers search for new products and processes. These changes have been reflected in MAFF's attitude toward food regulations, which has "tended to move away from imposing compositional standards on food . . . to provide more effective ingredient and nutritional labelling" (Foreman 1989: 118). The extra flexibility this modified stance has given food manufacturers is reflected, for example, in low-fat products previously outlawed by restrictions on minimum fat content. Although MAFF retains responsibility for food matters, the EC is making an increasing impact. Thus the Food Acts of the 1980s have more often been a response to EC directives than to consumer or producer pressures.

Unlike the situation of farmers, where MAFF works directly through its own agency on the ground (Agricultural and Development Advisory Service—ADAS), food legislation is enforced by local authorities through their trading standards departments or environmental health officers (EHOs) (Foreman 1989: 83). Local authorities also play a key part in the regulation of slaughtering in conjunction with veterinarians, who over time have become increasingly incorporated into the core of MAFF, culminating in their integration into ADAS in 1971. The State Veterinary Service is responsible for animal welfare on the farm, in transit, and at the slaughterhouse, but only for the first of these functions does it have sole responsibility. The rest are shared with environmental health officers. This division of responsibilities makes Britain somewhat unusual compared with the rest of Europe, where veterinarians are involved more fully in the slaughtering process, from the initial certification that the animal is fit for slaughter to the testing of them afterward.

What emerges, therefore, is a set of subtle but significant differences between MAFF's regulation of farmers and other elements in the food system. While self-regulation might be favored, close consultation with producer interests is the norm. The roles played by veterinarians and local authorities add a further twist. The powers of veterinarians are quite unlike those of other ADAS officials. They can stop an animal from going to slaughter, but a local ADAS official cannot stop a farmer from applying an excess amount of pesticide. Neither is the power of intervention of an EHO or local authority Trading Standards officer to be found in an ADAS official. Indeed, the break between MAFF's responsibility for the food system and the power of executive action that resides with local officials is quite unlike anything confronting farmers in their relationship with MAFF.

For much of the postwar period MAFF has faced few problems in regulating agriculture or food. It has operated within a stable, consensual food system, from which all sectors could profit. Increasingly, though, shifts in economic and political power within the British food system and in international trading relationships have undermined a previously settled network. Like most established organizations, when confronted with unwanted change, MAFF has sought to recreate and maintain its traditional operating pattern and mode of regulation. Unfortunately, MAFF's defensive strategy has at times looked anachronistic, allowing it to be portrayed unfavorably as a friend of the producer and an enemy of the consumer. As debates on food hygiene, for example, have moved beyond MAFF's policy environment to embrace the Department of Health and EHOs, so its authority has appeared to fray further.

Yet perhaps the greatest threat to the ministry has arisen from the unprecedented conflict between the Conservative party and the NFU. Politically the dominant forces in the Conservative party under Margaret Thatcher's premiership were antipathetic toward widespread farm support and the corporatist-type relationship the NFU enjoys with MAFF. The feelings of the free marketeers within the party were summed up in Norman Tebbit's memorable phrase that "the Foreign Office is for foreigners and MAFF is for farmers." Such attitudes have been instrumental in undermining the traditionally close relations between farmers and the Conservative party, culminating in an unprecedented vote of no confidence in a Conservative minister of agriculture at the 1987 NFU annual general meeting. A privileged group with insider status, influential Conservatives began to take a different view of the NFU. As one of them put it, "We cannot regard . . . [the NFU] . . . any longer as anything more than a mere trade association" (*Independent*, 24 December 1988).

Naturally ministers of agriculture, and MAFF itself, have not been completely immune from such sentiments, as when Minister John MacGregor thought it unlikely that farmers would think that they had MAFF in their pocket (*Times*, 13 February 1989). MacGregor's period as minister has been regarded as something of a turning point in MAFF's history. He "had no pretensions about being a farmer" and proclaimed that he was a "great believer in individual responsibility, letting the market operate, reducing government" (*Independent*, 24 December 1988). According to press reports, there was a feeling in Whitehall that under his leadership MAFF was "slowly being turned around, like an oil tanker, slowly but surely, away from the farmers and round to the interests of the politically more important consumer and environmental lobbies" (*Independent*, 24 December 1988). Under John Gummer, MacGregor's successor, further shifts can be detected in MAFF's attitude toward farmers and the food industry. Gummer has explicitly sought to ally the ministry with the consumer and on one occasion referred to the ministry as the Ministry of Food, much to the consternation of farmers.

Changes in MAFF's outlook are, perhaps, currently limited but, combined with the restructuring of the food system, have severely challenged its regulatory style and legitimacy. There can be little doubt that the food crises in Britain have also presented themselves as crises for MAFF itself, with questions being raised as to its continued "single-sector" existence. However, while the existing regulatory regime as practiced by central government has helped shape the food crises, it has by no means determined them. As is already apparent, the differing responsibilities of central and local government for regulating the food system can promote different interests and variable responses.

We now turn briefly to two case studies of food crises in Britain—salmonella in eggs, and bovine spongiform encephalopathy in cows—in order to illustrate how restructuring of the food system and changing regulatory approaches have combined to provide the mutually reinforcing circumstances within which crises of legitimacy can occur.

The Salmonella in Eggs Crisis

The salmonella in eggs crisis, which began in autumn 1988, was the food-safety issue with the highest profile in the 1980s. This crisis caused the wholesale price of eggs to be halved in a matter of weeks. It attracted massive press coverage, and the media hype of television documentaries and news stories on the subject kept the issue high on the political agenda for a long period. Emergent, high-profile consumer groups, who campaigned for improved food policy and against food adulteration (London Food Commission 1988), also did their best to keep the issue alive. Government ineptitude at dealing with a crisis led to internal divisions and resulted in the resignation of the junior health minister, Edwina Currie, adding to the controversy. Criticism of the government's handling of the crisis by the House of Commons Select Committee on Agriculture also helped to maintain food safety issues in the public's awareness.

Environmental and consumer groups generally laid the blame for the salmonella crisis on contaminated animal feed. However, the findings of the House of Commons Agriculture Committee were markedly different, arguing that attempts to place blame "served no good purpose" and that much of the crisis had been exaggerated. Despite the soothing words of the committee, the role of contaminated animal feed was at the heart of the salmonella crisis. An important outcome has been to call into question the effectiveness of industrialized and intensive livestock farming techniques and the role of an industrial, restructured food system.

The Bovine Spongiform Encephalopathy Crisis

Another high profile case of the late 1980s is that of bovine spongiform encephalopathy (BSE) or "mad cow disease affecting cattle specifically." The cause of the disease is generally believed to be the feeding of ruminant-based rations originating from scrapie-infected sheep. Worries about the effects of BSE on the public (as well as cattle numbers and welfare) brought about much controversy domestically and within the EC. Domestically, there were disputes about the compensation that should be given for destroyed cattle and concern about the transmission of the disease to other animals and to humans. Media coverage—with many pictures of cows unable to stand properly—undermined confidence in the British beef industry. At the EC level, debate was particularly fierce between Britain and Germany, with the latter wanting tighter control over Britain's beef exports to protect German consumers.

Once again, it was left to the multiparty House of Commons Agriculture Committee to reassure the public of the safety of food. The government, as represented by MAFF, had again failed to quell public anxieties in order to provide market security for the beef industry. As in the case of salmonella, inadequate regulations were seen as a major factor in precipitating the outbreak of BSE.

The BSE issue combined public concern about the possible implications of the disease with an underlying mistrust of modern farming methods and of MAFF assurances that food is safe. Within the "scientific vacuum" that presented itself, largely because of the absence of support for long-term research, the schools of thought that developed represented estimates of the best and worst scenarios. At best, because humans eat infected sheep and yet do not catch scrapie, the chances of humans catching the disease from beef are negligible. However, at worst, some notable scientists stressed the delayed incubation of the disease and the lack of effort being placed on detection in cattle entering the food-processing chain (Lacey and Dealler 1991).

Conclusion: From Producer Corporatism to Market-led Private Interest Government

There are many similarities both in the detailed origins of salmonella and BSE and in the methods of political mediation developed to alleviate the problems they cause. First, it is noticeable that the very nature of the animal feed industry, and particularly its changing practices vis-à-vis the preparation of its products, has become a major focus of concern in both cases. The use of animal protein in feed concentrates, the method by which it is rendered, and the degree to which intensive farming systems have to rely on these sources are common to both issues. However, MAFF and the respective agricultural committees of inquiry have sought to broaden the debate and fact finding away from this critical nexus. In both cases, the immediate concern has been to quell public anxieties by the publication of "quickfire," limited scientific research on the probability of human health risk, leading them down the road toward a scientific vacuum in which they have largely assumed the most optimistic (and usually least costly) scenario.

Second, it is also significant that in both cases political action has been forthcoming to quell farmer protest through the payment of compensation and that, so far, no new legislation is being developed to control more clearly the animal feed industry in the public interest. The passage of the Food Safety Act (1990) has been projected as standard-bearer for consumer protection, but it fails to deal directly with the input sector and places a strong emphasis on more sophisticated labeling of foods and on public accommodation to the pace of technological change in the food sector (see Flynn and Marsden 1992).

Third, a key feature of the food hygiene issue is the extent to which the traditional techniques of MAFF to quell producer and consumer anxieties are progressively weakened, exposing its internal inadequacies in monitoring and evaluating health risks and legitimating the food system. It is also manifested in its inability to control the supply of and demand for particular food products. Indeed, the very emphasis MAFF places upon certain types of scientific evidence (for instance the Southwood and Tyrell committees investigating BSE) has tended to divert attention from the real as well as potential market changes and fragilities incurred by the food hygiene issues themselves. This is particularly noticeable in the case of the meat trade. The period 1980 to 1986 saw beef and veal consumption fall by 19 percent, mutton and lamb by 23 percent, and pork by 12 percent. In a rapidly declining market, beef producers and manufacturing groups have become increasingly critical of MAFF for what they see as inflaming rather than dampening the problem of BSE. In addition, food processors and retailers are increasingly trying to reconstitute meat products in new ways as a way of maintaining and enhancing their market share (as well as adding value). They have found it expedient to vocally support the consumer. Retailers have thus attempted to disassociate themselves from the crisis and to place even greater stress on food quality in *their* stores. Food quality itself, once an accepted, publicly held norm, has now become commoditized, and is a particularly significant factor in maintaining consumer demand and market growth.

The implicit problems MAFF has faced during this period stem partly from the inadequacy of its dual role; that is, at its center and at the local level, it has insufficient apparatus or ability to cope with consumer-related concerns over and above more narrowly based and well-entrenched production-oriented priorities. Try as they may to quell public anxieties about food quality, the minister and, more generally, the central government have been unable to reassure consumers partly because of the lack of locally based systems of regulation. The outmoded and confined roles of veterinarians on the one hand and EHOs on the other have been shown to be insufficient mechanisms for monitoring food hygiene. EHOs, in particular, have complained of a lack of resources as a result of financial pressure on local government generally. Hygiene problems have been directed straight at the center, forcing the hurried assembly of agriculture select committee inquiries to adjudicate and resolve. The lack of consideration given to implementation of new regulations concerning the banning of offal is well illustrated by the Institute of EHOs' responses to MAFF during the select committee inquiry into BSE. They argue, for instance, that "local authority environmental health departments did not receive copies of the regulations until a week after the implementation date. In addition, many slaughterhouses were not aware of the existence of the regulations at the time of implementation. As a result there was little time, if any, to make appropriate arrangements for compliance, especially with regard to disposal of the specified offal. The Institution do not consider therefore that the Regulations initially achieved their aim of protecting the public throughout the country" (House of Commons Agriculture Committee 1990b; 107). Such gaps and weaknesses in effective food hygiene monitoring at the local level have exposed MAFF at its center, making the ministry vulnerable to widespread criticism even from its traditional clients, the producers.

At a more basic level, however, perhaps the most significant feature of the food crises of the late 1980s and early 1990s in Britain has been the degree to which the food hygiene issue has raised public awareness not only of the existence of the food chain (as opposed to agriculture or retailing) but also to its *interdependencies*. MAFF is finding this issue increasingly difficult to handle, given that its natural reference point in policy initiation and discourse is farming and the well-being of the countryside. Also as a central government ministry, it is being pushed into a new set of roles that attempt to legitimate certain types of food consumption practices as well as moderate public anxieties about food production and manufacturing practices. This is raising the specter of increased interdepartmental conflict, for instance, between MAFF and the Department of Health. MAFF is having to contend with these new pressures using an increasingly outmoded set of organizational instruments and interdepartment and national-local arrangements. Moreover, as is evident from the passage of the Food Safety Act 1990, the level of market and technological sophistication of the input, processing, and retailing sectors means that central government ministries are at best behind and at worst uninformed about some of the changes and practices taking place within the food system. These problems are heightened by both successive reviews of government departments that have tended to reduce the monitoring and research and development functions, and the partial "hiving off of functions"—not least in the food research and development sector—to the private sector.

The intention here has been to initiate a scientific concern for the changing balances evident in the production and consumption of food in one national context. Nationally based policymaking and regulation through the central government ministry are increasingly influenced by the internationalization of the corporate food sector, particularly through the development of new technologies and food brands. In addition, with the onset of European market integration, a plethora of new food-regulation standards is likely to tie the ministry into supranational negotiation in addition to national-level debates concerning food standards and quality (Waters 1991). As with agricultural pollution and environmental pressures, MAFF is increasingly having to shift its locus of concern from policies concerned with enhancing a type of self-regulation based on the long established corporatist links with the farmers' lobby. Although some of the more established environmental groups are now being consulted on a range of land-based policy issues (e.g., price reviews), there is as yet very little evidence that the food-consumer interest groups have been conferred with the same degree of political legitimacy. In addition, increasingly wide-ranging consultation has not guaranteed more effective implementation of food standards policy, given the lack of clarity concerning the future financial resourcing of regulatory authorities at the local level (Howells, Bradgate, and Griffiths 1991); and, as Painter (1981) suggests, the traditional emphasis of local enforcement is on *point of sale* inspection rather than on the monitoring of the food manufacturing *process*. The rights of consumers and enforcement officers to "look into the mixing bowl" in the food-manufacturing process are still highly restricted, and one of the principle aims of the recent Food Safety Act was to protect "the need of an innovative and competitive food industry by avoiding unnecessary burdens and controls."

Under these circumstances it is far more likely that it will be the retailers who will act to police food-manufacturing processes rather than any thinly spread public food authorities. Indeed, with retailers increasingly sensitized to consumer consciousness of food quality, it is they who are more likely to promote more precise regulation (under their terms) of the food production process.

The influence of trade associations supporting the retailing, food manufacturing, and input supply sectors may now be establishing more powerful relations (Cawson 1985) with MAFF, the national government, and the EC that far outweigh traditional producer corporatism. Private-interest government is replacing producer corporatism as the mainstay of political mediation. Thus, far from the food-processing and retailing sectors representing "a shadow industry" in terms of their relatively weak political organization in comparison with farmers (see Grant 1987), the 1980s have provided more opportunities to improve their political as well as economic position. The recent Food Act, for instance, provides retailers with de facto powers to regulate the quality of their inputs by promoting the inspection of the manufacturing processes. Moreover, as their continued substantial rates of profit illuminate, even in a period of general retailing recession, the food retail multiples and the food manufacturers continuously struggle for the political and economic space in which to sustain product diversification, technology push, and consumer-oriented safety guarantees.

After a decade of considerable growth in concentration and internal reorganization, the European food-retailing sector is likely to face the need to reinforce its regulatory role over the rest of the food system, and it will require central government authorities (particularly MAFF) to legitimize its actions to a more sensitized consuming public. The food hygiene scares have reinforced this tendency and have placed input manufacturers in a potentially more politically contentious position vis-à-vis the consumer. The evidence suggests that food hygiene will remain the responsibility of the Ministry of Agriculture rather than the Department of Trade and Industry or the Department of Health. Under these circumstances the traditional agricultural "exceptionalism" that has so characterized the postwar period will be superseded by more explicit priority given to the market-led food sector. Under current arrangements, both in terms of policy direction and apparatus, MAFF shows little indication that it can achieve this transition without raising public consciousness about the legitimacy of food quality and consumer rights.

Notes

1. We would argue here that any significant changes occurring in the accumulation system can only be sustained by modifications in the modes of social regulation, whereby a certain set of regulatory functions must be created for the accumulation system to be established (e.g., in the regulation of business relations and the formation of new norms of consumption). In this sense, regulatory systems take on concrete and geographically specific forms typically articulated at the level of the nation-state (see Boyer 1990; Jessop 1990; Tickell and Peck 1992).

2. Evidence has been collected for this analysis from a wide variety of documentary sources, interviews, and attendance at parliamentary select committee inquiries.

Bibliography

Boyer, R. 1990. *The Regulation School: A Critical Introduction*. New York: Columbia University Press.

Cawson, A. 1985. *Organised Interests and the State: Studies in Meso-Corporatism*. London: Sage.

Cox, G., P. Lowe, and M. Winter. 1985. "Changing directions in agricultural policy: Corporatist arrangements in production and conservation policies." *Sociologia Ruralis* 25: 130–154.

_____. 1986. "Agriculture and conservation in Britain: A policy community under siege." Pp. 31–50 in *Agriculture: People and Policies*, G. Cox, P. Lowe, and M. Winter (eds.). London: Allen and Unwin.

Flynn, A. and T. K. Marsden. 1992. "Food regulation in a period of agricultural retreat: The British experience." *Geoforum* 23, 1: 85–93.

Food Safety Act. 1990. London: HMSO.

Foreman, S. 1989. *Loaves and Fishes*. London: HMSO.

Friedmann, H., and McMichael, P. 1989. "Agriculture and the state system: The rise and decline of national agricultures, 1870 to the present." *Sociologia Ruralis* 14: 93–118.

Glover, J. 1989. "Post-acquisition strategies in the European food industry." *Acquisitions Monthly*, December.

Goodman, D., and Redclift, M. 1989. *The International Farm Crisis*. London: Macmillan.

Grant, W. 1983. "The National Farmers' Union: The classic case of incorporation?" Pp. 129–143 in D. Marsh (ed.), *Pressure Politics*. London: Junction Books.

———. 1987. "Introduction." In W. Grant (ed.), *Business Interests, Organisational Development and Private Interest Government: An International Study of the Food Processing Industry*. Berlin: Walter de Gruyter.

Harvey, D. W. 1987. *The Future of the Agricultural and Food System*. EPARD Working Paper no. 1. University of Reading.

Hawkins, E. H. 1991. "Changing Technologies: Negotiating Autonomy on Cheshire Farms." Ph.D. thesis, CNAA South Bank Polytechnic, London.

House of Commons Agriculture Committee. 1990a. *Salmonella in Eggs: A Progress Report*. London: HMSO.

———. 1990b. *Bovine Spongiform Encephalopathy*. London: HMSO.

Howells, G., R. Bradgate and M. Griffiths. 1991. *The Food Safety Act*. London: Blackstones Press.

Jessop, B. 1990. "Regulation theories in retrospect and prospect." *Economy and Society* 19: 153–216.

Lacey, R. W., and S. F. Dealler. 1991. "The BSE time bomb?" *Ecologist* 21, 3: 117–122.

Lawrence, G. 1990. "Agricultural restructuring and rural social change in Australia." Pp. 101–128 in T. K. Marsden, P. Lowe, and S. Whatmore (eds.), *Rural Restructuring: Global Processes and Their Responses*. London: Fulton.

London Food Commission. 1988. *Food Adulteration and How to Beat It*. London: Unwin.

MAFF. 1974. *Food from Our Resources*. London: HMSO.

———. 1979. *Farming and the Nation*. London: HMSO.

———. 1988. *Annual Review of Agriculture*. London: HMSO.

Marsh, D. 1983. "Introduction: Interest groups in Britain, their access and power." Pp. 1–19 in D. Marsh (ed.), *Pressure Politics*. London: Junction Books.

National Consumer Council. 1988. *Food Policy and the Consumer*. London: National Consumer Council.

Painter, M. 1981. "Enforcement: A rethink?" *FDIC Bulletin*, 18 July.

Self, P., and H. Storing. 1962. *The State and the Farmer*, London: Allen and Unwin.

Tickell, A., and J. A. Peck. 1992. *Local Modes of Social Regulation? Regulation Theory, Thatcherism and Uneven Development*. Working Paper 14. School of Geography, University of Manchester, U.K.

Ward, N. 1990. "A preliminary analysis of the UK food chain." *Food Policy* 15: 439–441.

Waters, P. 1991. "1992 and all what?" *Guardian*, 23 February 1991.

Wilson, G. K. 1977. *Special Interests and Policy Making*. London: John Wiley and Sons.

Winnifrith, J. 1962. *The Ministry of Agriculture, Fisheries and Food*. London: George, Allen, and Unwin.

6 Global Strategies and Local Linkages: The Case of the U.S. Meatpacking Industry

Lourdes Gouveia

At its most fundamental level, globalization entails a radical change in strategies of capital accumulation aimed at resolving the world capitalist crisis that began in the late 1960s. It is premised on the capacity of fractions of capital to move into an international market of money, commodities, and labor, unconstrained by geographical borders. But globalization means much more than economic change. Most significant for social scientists is the understanding of globalization as not only an economic but also a political process with significant social implications. Sustained globalization rests largely on the disproportionate power accruing to transnational corporations by virtue of their newfound mobility and expanded field of investment. In this new context, the state often becomes either a reluctant or enthusiastic partner and promoter of globalization strategies.

Of particular importance here is the role the state plays in the articulation of what McMichael and Myhre (1991) call the "global wage relation." This refers to the recomposition of labor markets across the globe whereby different forms of wage and nonwage, skilled and unskilled labor, are integrated into a single cost-reducing, profit-enhancing strategy. Immigrants, women, and others become new entrants to wage labor markets and compete with as well as subsidize veteran wage laborers in a climate of declining political power for all. Transnationalized capital and state agents, often jointly, facilitate this process through various explicit and implicit mechanisms.

As an accumulation strategy, however, globalization of capital concentrated within specific economic sectors and industries is uneven and its successes are far from assured. Furthermore, as with the accumulation schemes identified with the post–World War II "Fordist era,"[1] globalization may contain the seeds of its own demise.

One economic contradiction resulting from global strategies is that while lowering labor costs, these strategies also result in shrinking consumer markets. In the end this only exacerbates competition for the remaining numbers of higher-wage meat consumers. But the nemesis of globalization is not simply its economic contradictions. Politically, it is a highly contested strategy at both national and local levels. European Community (EC) farmers protesting against the proposed elimination by the General Agreement on Tariffs and Trade (GATT) of agricultural subsidies, Mexican and U.S. workers and environmental groups opposing the North American Free Trade Agreement (NAFTA), impoverished Venezuelans rioting in opposition to adjustment policies dictated by the International Monetary Fund (IMF), and U.S. rural communities resisting the relocation of labor-importing meatpacking plants into their area are a few examples.

As the contradictions of the global strategy unfold, new demands, both economic and political, are made upon central and local governments. Economically, state governments are called upon to bankroll internationalization efforts through a variety of direct and indirect mechanisms. These range from tax abatements to new forms of export promotion through the creation of state trade offices and budget lines for marketing agroindustrial commodities worldwide. For example, Nebraska has created the Office of International Trade and Investment to assist "Nebraska firms in pursuing international markets" and firms "interested in joint ventures and international investment" (NDN 1992).

Politically, nation-states continue to be important protagonists in the creation of new regulatory structures, such as NAFTA, and the reorganization of old ones to conform to the demands of the global economy. Furthermore, governments (including local ones) continue to play an important role in the articulation of economic ideologies consonant with the new economic climate.

One way to empirically observe the economic and political contradictions emerging from the globalization process is to examine a particular food sector and the main economic and political agents currently charting its course. Here I examine the relatively recent process of internationalization of the livestock sector and, more specifically, of the meat-processing firms, key agents in this process.

The chapter is divided into two parts. The first briefly reviews the history of internationalization of the U.S. meatpacking industry, specifically beef-packing, and examines the opportunities afforded to this industry by the emerging global economy. I argue that such opportunities vary widely according to the characteristics and histories of these large processing firms and that they are constrained by complex and often contradictory social, economic, political, and cultural factors. The second part of the paper examines how food conglomerates, meat processors in particular, depend on central and local states to resolve accumulation crises. The underlying argument is that globalization has brought about a bifurcation between regulatory activities and policymaking. On the one hand transnational economic policymaking has shifted upward toward entities such as the EC, GATT, the International Monetary Fund, and NAFTA. On the other hand, and especially in the United States, domestic policymaking has shifted downward toward local states and communities (Johnson et al. 1989). The latter entities are partially underwriting, as well as providing political legitimacy for, the global accumulation strategies of agroindustrial firms located in their midst. It is precisely in this context of local social dynamics that a global wage relation is ultimately constituted.

Data for this second section come primarily from an ongoing research project examining the impact of IBP Inc. (arguably the world's largest processor of beef and pork) on the state of Nebraska, and on the rural community of Lexington in particular.[2] Lexington is located in Nebraska's Dawson County, and at the time of the 1990 census its population was 6,601. A recount conducted in early 1993 placed the figure at 8,556. IBP opened its newest plant in Lexington in November 1990; by the end of 1992 the plant employed more than 2,000 workers and processed 4,000 head of cattle a day. Before the plant's opening, only 4.9 percent of Lexington's residents were Hispanic. Two years after IBP's opening, more than half the plant's work force was Hispanic, primarily newly arrived Mexican and other Latino immigrants. According to some estimates Lexington's Latino population in mid-1993 was between 20 and 30 percent. For Lexington, a relatively isolated community in the Great Plains, globalization became a reality in two short years thanks to the unique labor needs of IBP.

Internationalization of U.S. Meat Processing: From Multinational to Global Firms

The Beginning of Globalization

> It is quite within the range of possibility that a steer raised on a ranch in Wyoming may not only furnish the porter-house steak for the table of a New York business man but its hide may also reappear as the . . . raw material for the luggage which he is to carry with him on his round-the-world tour, or as the saddles he sees in a wild west movie when he stops off at Hong Kong on his trip. (Swift & Company 1937: 84)

Taken from a 1937 history of meatpacking, this quotation is suggestive of a U.S. livestock sector still largely but not entirely confined to a national sphere. To be sure, the United States was a major meat exporter around the turn of the century. The "Big Four" of the time—Armour, Morris, Swift

Hammond, and Schwarschild & Sulzberger (S&S, later Wilson & Co.)—dominated the domestic market and also controlled international trade.

When Argentina emerged as a major competitor early in the century, the four big packers quickly moved a substantial portion of their operations to this South American country. By 1911, U.S. meatpackers shipped most of the chilled and a hefty share of frozen beef coming out of Argentina. Exports of meat originating in the United States plummeted (Yeager 1981). But these early multinational packers, much like the United Fruit Company, were essentially limited to extracting a commodity produced under local forms of production, trading it within a relatively confined international market. The driving force behind this sort of investment was to gain access to commodities and markets that because of physical or market conditions could not be secured within the home country. It is unclear how much the Big Four's move into Argentina continued to hurt exports. As we shall see, it is only recently that this competitive relationship between the domestic and overseas investments of U.S. meatpackers has become a concern for producers and policymakers, as well as a defining feature of meatpacking's internationalization.

Despite U.S. packers' early excursions into the world market, until recently the livestock sector in the United States and elsewhere retained a strong domestic orientation (Friedmann and McMichael 1989). In fact, transnationalization in this sector is most advanced in those stages pertaining to the transformation of feed crops into industrial inputs by the major grain companies such as Cargill and ConAgra (Friedmann 1991). Beef production and processing stages are by necessity largely confined to domestic production sites, closed to basic inputs, and thus controlled by national capital circuits. For example, in 1988, only about 9 percent of total world beef production was involved in international trade. The United States doubled its beef exports between the seventies and the eighties, but this still amounts only to 3 percent of total U.S. production.

Continued domestic competition led to a new wave of concentration and the current market dominance by three giant companies and food conglomerates, IBP, ConAgra (and its meat company, Monfort), and Cargill (and its meat company, Excel). However, as domestic meat consumption continued to decline, the competition among the "Big Three" remained fierce. It was this latter version of packer competition, coupled with opening world economies, that ultimately thrust the industry full force into various forms of global production and marketing strategies. The latter are insufficiently captured by conventional measures of internationalization such as export figures or even direct investments.

The road to new packer concentration was paved largely by IBP's pioneering production methods. Particularly important was its development of boxed beef (vacuum packed cuts of beef), which permitted greater product standardization and lowered transportation costs. IBP was a relatively small firm that took advantage of the market opening resulting from industrial decentralization and the weakening of the Big Four. The company started its operations in 1961 in a rural area near Denison, Iowa. It built the first of a new wave of packing houses that became the industry's standard. IBP located its plants close to livestock supplies and far from the urban, high-wage, union strongholds where the industry had been traditionally located. The company was also one of the first to eliminate higher-paid skilled workers such as trained butchers (IBP 1987). This was accomplished through the fractionalizing of tasks, which enabled IBP to tap pockets of unskilled labor.

By the late 1970s, decentralization reached its peak as the larger packers moved their operations to relatively isolated rural localities. Those large packers also followed IBP's lead in transforming the production process, radically altering the old balance between managers and workers (Broadway 1992). Master contracts that had earlier been won by unionized workers were effectively undermined: Wages fell some 40 percent below those attained through these contracts (*Business Week* 1983).

A new level of industrial consolidation was achieved through the wave of mergers and acquisitions that marked the 1980s. The significance of this new wave of mergers is that, through their marriage with specialized meatpackers, old grain companies like Cargill and ConAgra acquired control over the transnationalization of the entire livestock complex. ConAgra purchased an emerging giant, Monfort, in 1987 and two of the former Big Four, Swift and Armour. Cargill, the world's largest grain trader, purchased Excel (known then as MBPXL), in 1979. Only IBP did not merge with a major grain company and was bought instead by Occidental Petroleum in 1981.

The Big Three's Global Strategies:
Beyond Domestic Restructuring and Trade

> We now face an epoch in which the meat on consumers' tables will have been developed in Europe and North America, bred in Latin America, fed with export grains . . . slaughtered under international standards, and consumed in the communities most removed from their point of origin. (Sanderson 1986: 147)

Despite the impressive performance of the new packing giants, the competition among the three remained fierce: costs of production continued to climb and demand for red meats dropped. For example, in 1976 beef consumption in the United States was about 95 pounds per capita. Ten years later consumption was 20 pounds below that level and has continued to drop (Johnson et al. 1989). By the beginning of the 1990s, the core of the meat-packing industry's restructuring strategies had moved from domestic reorganization toward increased participation in the global economy. One informal measure of this new global emphasis is the increased attention paid by industry publications to this topic in the last two years. For example, in 1992 *Beef Today* and *Meat and Poultry*, two of the most important industry journals, published their first cover stories on the globalization of meatpacking in 1992 and headlined them with "global" terminology.[3]

Globalization and its outcomes exhibit different forms for each of these firms, conditioned by their different organizational and investment histories. As noted earlier, IBP is the only one of the three large packers not part of a major grain and food conglomerate. Its participation in the global economy is primarily through trade; IBP is the largest exporter of U.S. meat and meat by-products, primarily for the Japanese market. IBP has no direct investments outside the United States, and its international physical presence is confined to service centers in Tokyo and London (IBP 1991). Indirectly, of course, this corporation is responsible for many of the organizational and technological changes in production relations and global diets that are now internalized by both peripheral and advanced capitalist countries (Sanderson 1986).

Globalization, as suggested by Sanderson's quote, implies out-sourcing of inputs and transnational integration of subsectors across geographical boundaries. But as a definitive characterization of today's entire industry, Sanderson's assessment is premature. IBP's participation in the global economy, for example, is rather limited. The company slaughters cattle that have crisscrossed such borders. But global sourcing for IBP is only applicable to its recruitment of labor from places such as Mexico and Central America. In contrast, ConAgra and Cargill have long histories of world market participation including direct investments in the various subsectors of the livestock complex. In 1992, ConAgra, also headquartered in Nebraska, was the world's largest meat company and the third largest food conglomerate. It has processing facilities all over Western Europe and recently entered into agreements with the Russian Commonwealth for distribution of its frozen food lines. It holds majority ownership rights in several Australian meat enterprises, including its largest cattle feeding and processing operation. The major portion of the beef processed in Australia is aimed at the Japanese market. But honing in on IBP's domestic market, ConAgra has begun to ship "lean trimmings" back to the United States (Effertz 1992). Cargill's Excel, the world's third largest meat company, also has invested in Australia with similar intentions. It has meat-processing facilities in fifty-five countries, including a new facility in Japan.[4]

This divergent picture of globalizing firms indicates that there are a multiplicity of strategies that firms can adopt to become global actors. IBP's participation in the global economy seems closest to the old mercantilist trading companies and the Swift-type ventures discussed earlier—minus the direct overseas investments of these old multinationals. A first-place ranking in exports no longer adequately measures a corporation's performance in the global economy or its overall strength in the industry for that matter, since beef trade is rather small relative to output. World exports of beef, although larger than those of poultry and pork, still account for only about 9 percent of total beef production (Sparks and Arnade 1992).

In contrast to IBP, ConAgra and Cargill are active integrators of feed and livestock subsectors across national boundaries. They are highly vertically integrated companies that, especially in the case of ConAgra, participate in each of the global production and circulation circuits suggested by Sanderson: ConAgra produces feed, fertilizers, and animal antibiotics; feeds some of its own cattle; processes cattle; and markets beef and beef products all over the world. Additionally, both are involved in the production of all forms of animal protein, while IBP focuses solely on red meats.[5]

Finally, as the world's second—or third—largest food conglomerate, ConAgra has the power, and openly expressed will, to accelerate the conversion of bulk agricultural commodities such as meat into mere inputs for the value-added processed foods market. Consonant with these aims is ConAgra's significant involvement in biotechnological research in-house and through funding of such research at the University of Nebraska. The latter is a potentially critical shift and an advanced global strategy because it involves nonagricultural processes that can be easily reproduced and transported worldwide, bypassing local agricultural producers. Thus, while ConAgra is looking to get out of the less profitable commodity business, IBP remains committed to this declining world market (Kay 1992a; ConAgra 1991). It is difficult not to conclude that both Cargill and ConAgra seem better situated than IBP to successfully follow a global strategy of accumulation. In its July 1992 issue, *Meat and Poultry* released its fourteenth annual ranking of the top one hundred meatpacking companies in the United States and Canada as measured by annual sales, and IBP had begun trailing ConAgra as the latter's meat products and markets rapidly diversify (*Meat and Poultry* 1992). The question that remains is whether IBP's limited global strategy necessarily translates into an endangered future.

A look at three major markets—the EC, Japan, and NAFTA/Mexico—in which these three companies hope to increase future participation reveals the limits these markets currently pose to a globalization strategy and each firm's capacity to confront them.

The European Community. In 1989 Europe banned U.S. beef produced with hormones, a step that cost the United States $100 million in exports. This dashed the hopes—at least until now—of corporations like IBP that had modernized some of their facilities to meet the EC's "Third Country Directives" for meat exporters. The Lexington plant in Nebraska was built with such specifications in mind. On the other hand, ConAgra and Cargill bypassed the ban by investing in facilities and joint ventures within the EC itself.

Japan. Japan is the golden global market of beefpackers and is the principal, though currently shrinking, market for U.S. meat exports (Ginzel 1992). It offers a large number of high-wage consumers, and beef consumption, which tripled in the 1980s, is far from reaching its peak. This was a relatively closed market until the 1988 signing of a two-step liberalization agreement. Japan had maintained a protectionist policy toward its national livestock sector made up of small family farmers. But increasing demand for beef beyond national production capacity, and unrelenting pressure from the U.S. government and industry groups, led to an incremental opening of this sector. The United States recently surpassed Australia as the major exporter of beef to Japan. But this is not a guaranteed long-term ranking given the volatility of the global economy (Ufke 1993).

IBP remains a major U.S. exporter of beef to Japan. Recently, for example, IBP signed a contract to export chilled beef with Ito-Yokado, a large retail food chain based in Tokyo. Additionally, operations in the Lexington plant were expanded to produce a cooked intestine product IBP regularly produces for the Japanese market. But the other two large packers export to Japan from their Australian base and are beginning to process beef within Japan itself. Japan also has just opened its market to France, and, probably not coincidentally, ConAgra recently purchased 20 percent of IDEA, a meat processor headquartered in Caen, France (*Meat and Poultry* 1991).

Japan's preference for high-quality cuts destined for the high end of the Japanese market has opened a niche not only for smaller livestock producers and processors in the United States, but also for Japanese investment in U.S. packing plants. A United States Department of Agriculture (USDA) report shows that Japanese investment in U.S. agribusiness, particularly in the meat sector, has increased dramatically since the late 1980s: "The beef industry has become an example of vertical integration, with cattle being raised on Japanese-owned ranches or feedlots and slaughtered in Japanese-owned packing plants. When transported by sea, 50% of the US beef is shipped on Japanese lines" (Bolling 1992: 4). Japanese companies own twenty-one meatpacking plants in nine U.S. states. Several of these plants had been closed before the Japanese purchase, unable to survive in the face of declining U.S. demand and competition from the Big Three (Bolling 1992). The differences between these small Japanese-owned plants and those of IBP are striking. The work force in the Japanese plants tends to peak at about two-hundred, work space is generous, and the pace is slower given the emphasis on quality rather than quantity (Bjerklie 1992). In contrast, the Big Three have opted for a modernization pattern based on plants of staggering proportions that employ hundreds or thousands of workers and process massive volumes of meat. This pattern has allowed the "new breed" of large packers to achieve domestic market dominance, but, contradictorily, it tends to reduce the flexibility that is required in the new global market.

Japan appears, then, as a highly contested market, and IBP's exports to that country face some clear limitations. Such limitations are exacerbated by the fact that processing beef for export to Japan is no longer confined to advanced capitalist countries. Small Mexican-based meatpacking plants are beginning to compete effectively. As a Mexican-based investor put it, "Japanese companies were buying raw materials from the U.S., shipping them to Southeast Asia for further processing and then bringing them back to Japan." He explains that now, by operating from Mexico, he can do the processing in Mexico and ship to Japan from there. The key is that Mexican wages are lower than those in Southeast Asia—and, of course, wages in the United States (Nunes 1992). It is to this Mexican market, and NAFTA, that I now turn.

NAFTA and the Mexican Market. It is not without reservations that meat industry groups have supported the North American Free Trade Agreement and the decision to grant former President Bush fast-track authority in free-trade negotiations with Mexico (Kelly and Nunes 1991). This regional agreement illustrates some of the limits and contradictions embedded in a global accumulation strategy. NAFTA represents, at least partially, a defensive response by a U.S. government hoping to arrest the erosion of its economic hegemony—most evident in the emergence of more powerful regional blocks such as the EC. Latin America continues to be viewed by some Americans as within the U.S. sphere of influence. Moreover, the devastating economic crises of recent years have made this part of the world particularly receptive to U.S. economic policies for the region.

It is clear, however, that gains from the NAFTA treaty are not assured to accrue primarily, or even significantly, to the United States as a whole, though individual sectors, localities, and corporations may benefit. Livestock is one of the North American agricultural sectors that industry analysts expect to benefit from the agreement (Elliot 1992). But others such as the International Trade Commission (ITC) predict only a short-term gain for U.S. feeders as export fees for Mexican feeder cattle are removed. In the long run, the ITC, as well as U.S. industry watchers, expect that Mexico's cheap labor (the United States–Mexico wage ratio in the food-processing sector is 14.7 to 1) will hasten the move of meatpacking plants south of the border (CRA 1992a).

The Mexican state, partly out of a lack of alternatives, is actively pursuing Mexico's integration into the global economy and the abandonment of the nationalistic goals of the past. The costs and benefits of this integration to Mexico's agricultural and food sector and, most importantly, to the masses of urban and rural poor are also less than clear. The government has moved quickly to remove the regulatory structure that, theoretically at least, sheltered many peasants from international competition. Most significant has been the recent changes made to Article 27 of the 1917 agrarian reform law, which prohibited the sale and lease of *ejido* lands. These properties can now be sold, and foreign investors can own up to 49 percent of an operation's farmland and 100 percent of all other assets associated with such operations (Elliot 1992). Some students of agrarian change in Mexico believe that the new law is especially designed to help cattle raisers expand their operations into previously protected agricultural lands (Renard 1992).

These changes, along with access to cheap labor, may provide the welcome mat to U.S. meatpackers. Labor and livestock represent the highest costs of production in the meatpacking industry; both can be potentially sourced more cheaply south of the border. Yet, the move south has so far been slow. The Big Three's presence in Mexico is still tenuous. Cargill's Excel recently purchased an old poultry and meat–processing facility in Saltillo, but processes only chicken (see note 4). IBP and Monfort export boxed and carcass beef and by-products, but only Monfort processes carcass beef within Mexico and for the domestic market (Gouveia, interview with United States Meat Export Federation [USMEF] official, Mexico City, January 1993).

In the meantime, the smaller Japanese and Mexican plants seem best suited to deal with such limitations. The contradictions embedded in NAFTA expose the limits to the globalization strategy pursued by the U.S. meat-processing industry and its allies within the state. Such limits are in part biophysical. In a recent meeting with Mexican USMEF representatives, U.S. meatpacking company managers unanimously agreed that they do not see any place in Mexico right now with the appropriate "mix of large numbers of cattle in a concentrated area, and sources of grain and water" that would hasten their move south of the border (Gouveia, interview with Horacio Recio of USMEF, Mexico City, January 1993). Similarly, Cargill's general manager is convinced that "it is ridiculous to believe it is economical to import grain [and feed the cattle in Mexico]. It is better to import the meat" (Gouveia, interview with Carlos Silva, Monterrey, Mexico, January 1993).

It is often said that globalization implies a level of technological change and homogenization in production processes, diets, and inputs that allows firms to produce almost anything anywhere—or as Friedmann (1991) puts it, to be "spatially indifferent." However, as the above discussion suggests, intrasectoral integration across national boundaries within the beef sector appears to be more constrained by such physical barriers than, say, electronics manufacturing. In addition to production, transportation of commodities like meat, unless frozen, is still problematic. The Japanese market, for example, is primarily for chilled, not frozen, meats. On the other hand, physical barriers are only relative to other economic and political considerations. Economic agents and market forces can often diminish the insurmountability of such barriers. In fact, it is a combination of recent technological changes in the areas of production and transportation, together with the need to secure low costs of production, that allows peripheral countries like Mexico to effectively compete within the United States's favored export markets. Finally, pressures exerted by environmental and political movements, coupled with the continuity of hidden barriers to free trade[6] are likely to place new limits on global strategies.

With regard to the Big Three specifically, the future is uncertain. IBP appears as the weakest and ConAgra the strongest in their capacity to remain globally competitive. But in a global economy characterized by rapid technological changes and flexible production processes that permit the recomposition of foods to suit changing tastes and pockets, the present helps little in predicting the future. As this chapter goes to print, IBP has increased its market share in both cattle and hogs and, after twelve years, has regained a spot (forty-second) in *Fortune* magazine's rankings of the largest corporations in the United States (*Clipper Herald* 1993; Kay 1992b). Much of this growth seems to be related to IBP's current aggressive gamble to regain a competitive edge by continuing to expand processing facilities and capture increasing numbers of cattle despite the serious overcapacity problem confronting the whole industry.

What is clear, so far, is that despite its integration into the global economy, the U.S. meatpacking industry continues to suffer from rather slim and, at times, declining profit margins, rising costs of production, and related shrinkages in beef supplies. In the United States and elsewhere, this has kept the price of beef above that of other meats and has transformed it into an upscale commodity for many of those moving downward and out of the middle class. In addition, the industry continues to battle strong pressure from environmentalist groups such as Beyond Beef whose aim is to reduce beef consumption by 50 percent by the year 2002 (Rasmussen 1992).

IBP registered its first quarterly earnings loss ever in 1991, largely as a result of Occidental's exodus from the company. ConAgra's more diversified structure and global presence make it more resistant to business cycles, but earnings were down for the same quarter of 1991 (Rasmussen 1992; Kay 1992c). NAFTA enthusiasts point to the 360 million consumers (25 percent more than in the EC) living in North America as the greatest opportunity opened to the meat and poultry industry in recent years. But privately industry representatives admit this is an exaggerated figure, especially if one takes into account the high quality and costs of U.S. beef exports. According to one USMEF official, "the 86 million that NAFTA supporters say will be the Mexican market for beef is not what the market research shows us. We are talking 14–20 million maximum [who eat high-quality meat] right now. A person making a minimum wage of $4.25 a day [or half of the city] is not going to be our market. We are not going after them, but after the upper and middle classes; per capita consumption right now is 45–49 lb of meat per year; that may increase by 15%" (Gouveia interview with USMEF official, Mexico City, January 1993). A USMEF publication also shows that while close to 50 percent of Mexicans eat lower-quality meat on a fairly regular basis, less than 10 percent eat high-quality beef within similar time intervals (USMEF 1991). These figures, and the realization that NAFTA's success is premised largely on Mexico's comparative advantage in cheap labor, make it hard to be terribly optimistic about an exponential growth of U.S. meat exports to this country. Industry watchers, like the USMEF representative, insist that U.S. producers are going after a selective clientele of upper-income Mexicans and international tourists (Elliot 1992). But unfortunately for these U.S. producers, so are the Australians and the Europeans.

Globalization for all of these corporations involves serious and conscious attempts to achieve the greatest possible degree of flexibility and synchronization of profit-maximizing activities such as sourcing of cheap livestock and labor. Until NAFTA and related developments change the playing field, the packers are making use of their unique capacity to out-source cheap labor from Mexico on a "just-in-time" basis (Gouveia 1992b). At the same time, national governments, but especially states and local communities are losing control over their own economic development strategies while being called upon to support economic globalization in the name of uncertain medium- and long-term benefits.

Local States, Imported Labor, and Nebraska Rural Meatpacking Communities

Nebraska provides a useful example of the rural and debt crisis of the 1980s and of the forces that precipitated this crisis. An agricultural state par excellence, by the 1960s Nebraska was highly specialized in grain production, particularly corn and soybeans. Both commodities enjoyed an expanding international market. By the 1970s, Nebraska surpassed other states in exports of corn to the Japanese, and local farmers and speculators invested heavily in land and expensive irrigation equipment (Strange et al. 1990). As a result, between 1972 and 1982 corn production increased by 44 percent. However, by 1985 when the international markets for grain collapsed because of a widespread economic crisis and the arrival of new global producers, Nebraska corn prices dropped to 25 percent of their peak in the 1970s.

By 1983, Nebraska crop cash receipts were the lowest since 1979, and a drop in livestock receipts followed closely behind (NDA 1983). Between 1982 and 1987, land values fell by 50 percent, and Nebraska was the top state in farm bankruptcies (SRI 1988; Nebraska Department of Economic Development (DED) 1990–1991; Thompson 1992). Manufacturing employment, an increasingly significant source of revenue, also declined sharply, and 632,000 people abandoned rural counties between 1985 and 1986, a considerable reversal from the 1970s, when the state experienced a net gain of 350,000 people (CAUR 1987).

The impact of the crisis was deeply felt by the state treasury as the gross domestic product declined continuously between 1982 and 1985 (Nebraska Department of Economic Development 1990–1991). Politically, the crisis precipitated a wave of activism among Nebraska-based business leaders, particularly within the very important agroindustrial sector. Mike Harper, then ConAgra's chief executive officer, soon emerged as the spokesperson and powerful ideologue of this "entrepreneurial movement." He was joined by labor leaders, prominent media organizations, and local and state representatives. This loosely articulated coalition began then to develop its own vision of the state's economic development strategy. One of the main thrusts of that strategy was, not surprisingly, the strengthening of Nebraska's livestock sector, and particularly its upstream side—all the way to biotechnological research. The other thrust was in the expansion of communication services, which, among other things, has turned Omaha into a major telemarketing center for the country. The entire strategy was also premised on a rechanneling of state and local revenues for economic development directly through those businesses that fit the new strategies, among which are the expanding meatpacking plants.

These events forged a new capital-state relationship, consonant with the reduced power of this economically battered state and the newfound mobility of private capital in a globalizing economy. ConAgra's Mike Harper offers us a perfect illustration. In a controversial and astute move, Harper drafted a tax exemption bill and threatened to abandon plans to build Con-

Agra's global corporate headquarters and state-of-the-art food preparation lab in Omaha unless the bill was approved by the legislature (Limprecht 1990).[7] The bill, LB775 or the Nebraska Development and Investment Growth Act, was passed in 1990, meeting virtually all of Harper's requests. Today, a plethora of international flags, signaling the company's global conquests, fly smartly in front of its impressive Omaha headquarters (except during the Gulf War when all the flags displayed were U.S. flags).

Multiple plants of all three of the major packers have benefited substantially from LB775 as revealed by a report by the Nebraska Department of Revenue in 1991. IBP-Lexington alone obtained a property tax exemption of $47 million (Loughry 1991).

Efforts to redirect economic development policies at the state level were accompanied by a sophisticated political campaign paid for by ConAgra and other members of this ad hoc coalition. The new economic discourse was reflected in a batch of publications produced by California-based SRI International. SRI, through a locally established organization called Nebraska Futures, produced an influential 300–page report, "New Seeds for Nebraska. Strategies for Building the New Economy." The report was widely distributed and presented in public forums all over the state, including those communities most affected by the farm crisis. Its recommendations were often reproduced verbatim in several state government publications outlining the state's economic development policies and priorities (see, for example, the 1987 publication "Targeted Industries for Nebraska" from the DED).

The report and its follow-ups emphasized the need to compete in a global economy via, in part, support for large agroindustries such as meat-processing firms and for the expansion of the most efficient (meaning the largest and most capitalized) farm and livestock units of production. Conversely, the report lambasted Initiative-300, a 1982 act commonly known as the Nebraska Family Farm Amendment, which restricted the ownership of farmland by corporations. The act was a manifestation of the political will of rural communities most affected by the farm crisis and their alternative view of economic development (Roberts et al. 1990).

In the several years since the report was written, ConAgra's Harper set a new tone for state-capital relations in Nebraska; many other types of state economic development funds have been almost exclusively channeled toward corporate interests, particularly to food-processing industries. This has been done in a variety of ways and at various state levels. For example, federally allocated community development block grants (CDBGs) are ostensibly used to complement operational needs of meatpacking plants locating or expanding in rural communities. In less than two years IBP's Lexington plant has benefited from more than $2 million in CDBG funds (Broadway 1992; Gouveia 1992a).

Demands for tax abatements and training funds are not confined to IBP or Nebraska. Recent studies in Iowa and Kansas reveal a similar pattern (see, for example, McNaughton 1991; Stull and Broadway 1990). State training funds specifically aimed at the creation of skilled, high-wage jobs have been utilized by ConAgra, Cargill, and IBP in their Midwest locations. Claims made by representatives of these multimillion dollar operations that subsidies intended for small rural community development are crucial to their survival are somewhat baffling—though not entirely unreasonable in the context of global competition. Additionally, it is highly debatable whether meatpacking jobs can honestly qualify for the "skilled jobs" state planners promised when garnering support for the transfer of such generous subsidies to the business community. In fact, I would argue, based on numerous conversations with workers, that on the contrary, most of the jobs performed within a meatpacking plant require little training and provide almost no skills transferable beyond meatpacking work (Gouveia 1992b).

But as the founders of IBP indicated a decade ago, meatpacking, an industry of typically small margins per unit of output, relies heavily on fractional savings at every stage of the production process (Tintsman and Peterson 1981). As global competition reaches new heights, these savings become even more important. Sourcing cheap factors of production, particularly livestock and labor, appears to be the true central strategy of the meatpackers and to a large extent of state planners—even if reluctantly. The natural or externally shaped biophysical and social milieu of particular localities are inevitably critical to industrial relocation decisions. Nebraska constantly trades first place with Texas as the nation's largest cattle feeding state. Feed grain is relatively cheap and water is abundant as Nebraska sits atop the Ogallala aquifer. Water is important not only for feed grain irrigation, but for meatpacking plants like Lexington's IBP facility, which uses more than 2 million gallons a day.

The meatpacking industry itself has become a major force in creating or enhancing the "comparative advantage" of selective cattle-growing areas like Dawson County, Nebraska. The popular media often cite the abundance of cattle as the main reason for meat-processing concentration in the High Plains. However, a reverse cause-and-effect relationship may be just as true. There is evidence that the increasing concentration of cattle and processing plants in the Central Plains is the result, at least partly, of an appreciating difference in the relative prices of grain between states such as Texas versus Nebraska or Iowa (Stalculp 1989). Others add such factors as lower workers' compensation, water, and transportation costs in the midwestern states (Kenyon 1990). The packers' move to these states provides an automatic incentive for local cattle feeders to expand and for others to move in (Gouveia and Stull 1992; Kenyon 1990). Feeders understand that, on average, more than 70 percent of their livestock will be bought by one of the Big Three and that packers are actively searching for ways to minimize the number of cattle suppliers.[8]

Expansion of feed production and processes, and thus the cheapening of both feed and livestock input, follows the trend of this geographic restructuring of packers and feedlots. Nebraska's cattle prices are consistently reported in the press as being $.50 per hundredweight below the national average, and the Nebraska-Texas competition to retain cattle in their area has become fierce in recent years (Stalcup 1989).

Labor costs continue to be an important portion (though not the most important) of production costs given the stubbornly labor-intensive character of this industry. Reducing the price of labor can, in any industry, be achieved through a variety of mechanisms beyond lowering wages. Accessing state funds for training the packers' labor force is one such mechanism. Increasingly important as a cost-saving mechanism is the mobilizing of pools of the poorest and politically weakest workers. And, finally, labor costs can be reduced through deregulation in the areas of health and safety, as well as weakening legislation in areas such as workers' compensation. As a right-to-work state, antiunion sentiments run deep in Nebraska, especially in smaller communities. A brochure promoting Lexington, Nebraska, as a good place to locate a business (used at the time IBP was recruited), emphasizes the fact that Nebraska has the lowest number of days lost because of work stoppages and of workers' compensation payments of any state (NPPD, 1990).

The most important cost-reduction strategy currently used by meatpackers is the incorporation of new immigrant workers, primarily Mexican and Central American, and including women (Grey 1992; Griffith 1990; Stanley 1991).[9] Many of these workers have been recruited from agricultural labor markets both outside and inside the United States, and many have become permanent U.S. residents through the 1986 agricultural amnesty program. These workers encounter in meatpacking a degree of seasonality not unlike that of agricultural work. When cattle prices are high and demand low, work weeks in meatpacking are often reduced by ten hours or more, and, occasionally plants shut down completely for days, as occurred during the winters of 1992 and 1993. Unemployment insurance seldom applies or immigrant workers fail to use it during these downtimes, which do not quite fall under the legal definition of a "layoff."

High labor turnover is normal in today's meatpacking industry (7–10 percent a month is not unusual). And while not exactly cost-free, this can para-doxically become a form of savings for the industry. For example, workers engage in a cycle of "injury and therapy," to borrow a term from Griffith (1992). Interviews with Latino workers in Lexington who are suffering from injuries and repetitive motion afflictions show that they often quit their job without ever filing for workers' compensation insurance. In the meantime, they may travel to Mexico or look for less-physically demanding jobs within or outside the community. In time, some return and begin work at the plant all over again. Additionally, during times of unemployment, workers' sub-sistence is partly subsidized by a combination of local communities' social agencies (often staffed by volunteers) and informal social networks that ex-tend back to the workers' native countries (Gouveia and Stull 1992). All of this provides year-round survival for this meatpacking labor force at the same time that it reinforces the industry's low wage structure.

Meatpacking wages in the 1960s could go as high as $15 an hour; today they generally remain below $10. In Nebraska, meatpacking wages were above the national average during the 1970s. Since then wages have slipped below the national average and below the average manufacturing wage in the state (Lamphear 1992). Wages at the IBP-Lexington plant start at $7.15 an hour, which is actually higher than wages at IBP's unionized plants. But they cap around $9.50 an hour, regardless of years of work or job skills. The legal status of most workers in Lexington, whether working for IBP or else-where, is both fragile and cost-saving. Many are either undocumented or hold "bad" papers. Those legalized under the general amnesty program along with political refugees from Guatemala and El Salvador, face numer-ous restrictions in social service benefits. Under these circumstances, work-ers are reluctant to quit or demand better working conditions and the bene-fits to which they are entitled.[10] Local communities and municipalities pick up much of the tab for a development strategy built on the hopes of their "city fathers" for the long-term success of their newly arrived meatpacking plants. Since IBP's arrival, Lexington has experienced a severe housing crunch, built its first homeless shelter, passed several school bond issues, hired increasing numbers of regular and bilingual teachers for federally mandated English as a second language programs, and built a new and big-ger jail.

School enrollments and turnover rate reflect IBP's employment patterns. In March 1991, 9.56 percent of Lexington's students (all grades) were minor-ities (up from about 6 percent the year before), and less than 10 percent were Hispanic. By November of that year, the percentages were 16 percent and 14 percent respectively. Minority percentages have continued to climb sharply as housing has become available and by 25 September 1992 the percentages were 23 percent minority, including 21 percent Hispanic (Lexington Superintendent of Schools 1993). More problematic than suddenly becoming the fastest growing school district in Nebraska (Loughry 1991) is high student turnover, which hampers budget and academic planning. Only five months into the 1991–1992 school year, 7.75 percent of the student population had changed, or the equivalent of about 20 percent a year (Loughry 1992).

The disproportionate growth of the poor and uninsured population has also strained health facilities and staff. Most significant has been the rapid increase in the number of births and in the proportion of such births not covered by medical insurance. In 1992, 51 percent of the bills for births at the local hospital were either not paid or covered by Medicaid, compared with 44 percent the year before. This also contrasts with earlier years, during the 1970s and much of the 1980s, when Medicaid payments seldom accounted for more than 17 percent of total payments, and unpaid bills were rare (Gouveia, interview with hospital administrator 5 June 1993).

Crime also has increased, and for the first time in its history Lexington in early 1993 had the highest crime rate in the state. Local law enforcement officials complain that a majority of their hours are now spent in "reactive" as opposed to preventive police functions (Gouveia, interview with police chief, 5 July 1993).

The mere presence of IBP also alters the local livestock production and market structure. Large production units are better equipped to handle the growing demands for standard quality beef; small packers find it hard to withstand the pressures exerted by large packers on wages and cattle. Lexington's oldest meatpacker, Cornland Beef, closed less than a year after IBP's plant opened. A few months before they closed the plant, Cornland officials remarked bitterly that IBP's presence in the area made it very difficult to remain competitive (Gouveia and Stull 1992).

The impact of global forces on local communities goes beyond easily quantifiable observations and is often paradoxical. Cultural diversity, for example, is touted as a positive development in today's globalizing society. But when people are thrust into radical life changes not entirely of their choosing, and in a context of fierce competition for meager resources, diversity can also mean community fragmentation and conflict. In Lexington, diversity's positive and not-so-positive elements coexist in tension with each other; and the outcome of such tension remains unclear. Though overt ethnic clashes have so far been rare, resentment about poor Hispanics' seemingly endless needs grows day by day. This is expressed in a variety of ways—from an increasing number of sarcastic jokes, to previously sympathetic service providers becoming increasingly impatient with their Hispanic clients' demands. Emerging local Hispanic leaders, in return, grow critical of the Anglo community and often accuse Anglos of cultural insensitivity (Gouveia, fieldnotes May 1993).

Some of these personally felt frustrations, as well as the more positive attitudes toward cultural diversity, are turned into criticism of and demands on city officials regarding resource redistribution and quality-of-life improvements for various social groups. Those include requests for additional police officers as well as special services for the Latino population.

Within the IBP plant itself, the fragmentation of the work force along ethnic lines is also evident—albeit in subtle ways. In personal interviews, Latino respondents often contended that the worst jobs are reserved for them. A woman I interviewed put it this way: "The artistic jobs are for the Asians, the supervisory jobs are for the Anglos, and the dirty jobs are for the Mexicans" (Gouveia, interview 10 May 1992).

Community fragmentation can indirectly contribute to corporate strategies for demobilizing labor and ultimately reducing production costs. Today, a growing number of meatpacking community members do not share a common language, history, or cultural strategies for survival. They also misdirect their anger and blame each other for their misfortunes, rather than demand a higher degree of social responsibility from the corporate sector.

Summary and Conclusions

Global strategies of accumulation are intricately interwoven with the histories of local crises, the strategies to overcome them, and the resulting balance of power between communities, workers, and capital agents. States like Nebraska, or for that matter countries like Mexico, transfer funds to globalizing firms in the hope of resolving their own fiscal crises. But in today's global economy local and central polities are poorly equipped to secure a return on their investments. Firms like meatpacking's Big Three have the capacity—albeit uneven—to shift or threaten to shift investments quickly and thus to dictate the economic development agenda. Costs to states and communities can be high. Nebraska recently experienced a severe tax crisis as the ambiguous and unevenly applied policy of property tax exemptions provoked an onslaught of claims from all corners of the state for similar treatment. The state's Supreme Court declared the tax laws unconstitutional. ConAgra's former chief executive officer, Mike Harper, was said to have been once again actively involved in drafting a constitutional amendment that would protect LB775 contracts and other tax exemptions (Gouveia 1992a). Whether he drafted the amendment or not is inconsequential. According to a study by the Center for Rural Affairs (CRA 1992b), ConAgra will in fact pay even less tax today than it did before the passage of the amendment.

Capital's hypermobility engenders a similar, though much slower, rate of labor mobility (Gouveia 1992b). The largest percentage gain in nonmetro employment in recent years has been among Hispanics and women (USDA 1990). It is reasonable to assume that this gain has been largely due to meatpackers' recent concentration in this area and their active mobilization of these labor pools. Recently released USDA data support this last conclusion by showing that meatpacking employment is the only type of employment expanding within the food-processing sector and that Nebraska, where meatpacking jobs are highly concentrated, is one among a small number of midwestern states that has experienced a parallel increase in its nonmetro Hispanic population (USDA 1992).

Both central and local polities have found themselves deeply involved in the globalization process. Nation-states are clearly important for the negotiation of trade agreements like NAFTA and the unending battles to protect and open economic sectors to international competition. National governments can also facilitate the mobilization of labor pools across nations and labor markets. Immigration laws, including the latest amnesty law, while seemingly closing doors open new ones as well (Gouveia 1992a).

Whether to locate in Lexington or in Mexico is in itself an almost irrelevant question for globalizing firms looking to overcome their profit squeeze. Instead, it is the creation of similar, that is, devalued, global-wage relations that has been at the core of corporate strategies in recent years.

Yet, capital mobility and similar global strategies do not occur and do not produce desirable outcomes entirely at the will of individual firms. Serious economic and political contradictions and limitations emerge in the process. Economically, these firms confront a crowded world market coupled with declining income and employment levels. Politically, these firms and especially the local governments in locations where they operate must still respond to pressures from domestic constituencies—however weakened these constituencies may be.

Notes

Research for this chapter was funded by the ASA/NSF Small Grant Program for the Advancement of the Discipline, the University of Nebraska at Omaha (UNO) Committee on Research, and an Aspen–Ford Foundation grant. The trip to study the impact of NAFTA on the rural sector was financed by UNO's International Studies and the Center for Rural Affairs in Walthill, Nebraska. I am grateful to Bob Antonio,

Bill Friedland, Philip McMichael, Marty Strange, and Donald D. Stull for their generous comments on various drafts of this chapter.

1. Much has been written about the crisis of Fordism. See, for example, Liepietz (1987) for an analysis of the crisis of Fordism and globalization in general. See the seminal paper by Harriet Friedman (1982), and Kennedy et al. (1989), for analyses dealing specifically with the agricultural and food sector.

2. Donald D. Stull from the University of Kansas and Michael Broadway from the State University of New York–Geneseo have participated in different phases of this research project.

3. *Beef Today*'s "U.S. Meat Companies Go International" was published in February 1992; and *Meat & Poultry*'s double issue on "Global Meat Companies" was published in March/April 1992. In addition, early in 1992, *Issues*, a publication of the National Cattlemen's Association, changed its format to include a section on international trade.

4. Much has been made of Cargill's alleged opening of a beef-and-poultry-processing plant in Saltillo, Mexico, in anticipation of NAFTA (for example, Kay 1992a). Some industry watchers contend that this is but the first of "runaway meat-packing plants" that will take advantage of Mexico's cheap labor and unregulated business environment (Ritchie 1991). In reality, this is based on misinformation put out by Cargill (whether intentionally or not no one can be sure) and hasty extrapolations made by these industry watchers. Cargill did purchase an old meat- and chicken-processing plant from Mexican owner Carlos Silva (now the general manager). But it had been processing only chicken before Cargill's purchase. According to Silva, there are no plans to convert it to beef processing anytime in the foreseeable future (Gouveia, interview with Carlos Silva, Monterrey, Mexico, January 1993).

5. See Heffernan and Constance, Chapter 1 in this volume, for a more detailed view of these food conglomerates' global investments.

6. As a case in point, as Mexico advanced in its free-trade negotiations with the United States and Canada, it simultaneously imposed a new form of nontariff trade barrier for boxed beef through new sanitary regulations. It required that a sample box from each load be inspected at the Center of Parasitology in Cuernavaca, at the importers' expense. U.S. industry writers attribute this move directly to pressure from Mexican beef producers and their fears NAFTA will mean more meat imports (NCA 1992).

7. See Broadway (1992) and Strange et al. (1990) for a detailed analysis of this bill and its impact on Nebraska's economic development. Broadway's essay gives the reader further insight into ConAgra's power at the state level. He mentions a newspaper story, for example, in which the chairperson of the Nebraska legislature's Revenue Committee, upon hearing about Harper's "conditions," is reported as having asked ConAgra to provide him with a list of specific items the company wanted from the state.

8. Both Monfort and IBP have been reported by industry journals to be searching for ways to standardize the quality of their beef by forcing the "bad apples" to shape up or get out. *Beef Today*, the trade journal, recently reported that IBP was looking to reduce its total number of cattle suppliers to the amazing number of fifteen.

9. The 1992 conference on "New Factory Workers in Old Farming Communities: Costs and Consequences of Relocating Meat Industries" examined the entire gamut of meat, poultry, and fish processing. This meeting revealed that hiring of Hispanics is a generalized trend in the industry. Even in the case of poultry, where black women have been the dominant labor force, new immigrants from Mexico and Central America are beginning to take such jobs, particularly in the state of Georgia.

10. Partly because of her deficient English and not-so-amicable relationship with her floor supervisor, one woman worker I interviewed, for example, "waited until my nails got purple from the vibration of the air-gun to ask for permission to see the nurse. . . . I finally did" (Gouveia, interview no. 8, 10 October 1992).

Bibliography

Bjerklie, Steve. 1992. "Built-in quality." *Meat and Poultry* 38, 2 (February): 38–39.
Bolling, Christine H. 1992. "The Japanese presence in U.S. agriculture." *Foreign Agricultural Economic Report* (USDA) 244.
Broadway, Michael. 1992. "Economic development programs in the Great Plains: The example of Nebraska." *Great Plains Research* 1, 2: 324–344.
Business Week. 1983. "The slaughter of meatpacking wages." June 27: 70–71.
CAUR (Community Affairs and Urban Research). 1987. "Recent Trends in Rural Community Development Policy." Briefing Report no. 4.
Clipper Herald. 1993. "IBP sales are up during 1st. quarter." 28 (April): 4.
ConAgra Inc. 1991. *Fiscal 1990 Annual Report*. Omaha, Nebr.: ConAgra.
CRA (Center for Rural Affairs). 1992a. "North American free trade—what price exports?" *Center for Rural Affairs Newsletter*, July: 1.
_____. 1992b. "Amendment 1—the aftermath." *Center for Rural Affairs Newsletter*, June: 2.
Dawson County Herald. 1991. "IBP is biggest taxpayer in Dawson County." August 3, 1–3.
Effertz, Nita. 1992. "A frustrated giant." *Beef Today*, February: 48–53.
Elliott, Ian. 1992. "Canada tries to find agricultural niche in Mexico." *Feedstuffs*, April: 19, 31.
Freidmann, Harriet. 1991. "Changes in the international division of labor: Agrifood complexes and export agriculture." Pp. 65–94 in William H. Friedland, Lawrence Busch, Frederick Buttel, and Alan P. Rudy (eds.), *Towards a New Political Economy of Agriculture*. Boulder, Colo.: Westview Press.
_____. 1982. "The political economy of food: The rise and fall of the postwar international food order." *American Journal of Sociology* 88s: 248–286.
Friedmann, Harriet, and Philip McMichael. 1989. "Agriculture and the state system: The rise and decline of national agricultures, 1870 to the present." *Sociologia Ruralis* 29, 2: 93–117.
Ginzel, John. 1992. "Livestock outlook." *Agricultural Outlook* January/February: 5–9.
Gouveia, Lourdes. 1992a. "El estado, municipalidades, e immigrantes lations en la internacionalizacion del circuito de la carne: Un caso de Nebraska, Estados Unidos." *International Journal of Sociology of Agriculture and Food* 2, 2: 93–110.
_____. 1992b. "Immigrant labor in the internationalization of meat-processing." Pp. 93–110 in A. Bonanno (ed.), *The Agricultural and Food Sector in the New Global Era*. London and New Delhi: Concept Publishing Company.
Gouveia, Lourdes, and Donald D. Stull. 1992. "Dances with Cows: Beefpacking's Impact on Garden City, Kansas, and Lexington, Nebraska." Paper presented at a national conference on New Factory Workers in Old Farming Communities: Costs and Consequences of Relocating Meat Industries, Queenstown, Md., 12–14 April.
Grey, Mark A. 1992. "Lao Porkpackers in Storm Lake, Iowa: Implications for Education and Health Provisions." Paper presented at the national conference on New

Factory Workers in Old Farming Communities: Costs and Consequences of Relocating Meat Industries, Queenstown, Md., 12–14 April.

Griffith, David. 1990. "The Impact of the Immigration Reform and Control Act's (IRCA) Employer Sanctions on the U.S. Meat and Poultry Processing Industries." Final report submitted to the Institute for Multiculturalism and International Labor. Binghamton: State University of New York.

Griffith, David., M. Valdes Pizzini, and J. C. Johnson. 1992. "Injury, therapy, and trajectories of proletarianization in Puerto Rico's artisanal fisheries." *American Ethnologist* 19: 53–74.

IBP, Inc. 1987. *Annual Report*. Dakota City, Neb.: IBP.

_____. 1991. *Annual Report*. Dakota City, Neb.: IBP.

Johnson, Gale D., John M. O'Connor, Timothy Josling, Andrew Schmitz, and G. Edward Schuh. 1989. "Competitive Issues in the Beef Sector: Can Beef Compete in the 1990s?" Humphrey Institute Report no. 1. Minneapolis: University of Minnesota.

Kay, Steve. 1992a. "A global business." *Meat and Poultry* 38, 3 (March): 30–38.

_____. 1992b. "Carving a niche." *Meat and Poultry* 38, 10 (October): 20–23, 52.

_____. 1992c. "Light at the end of the tunnel?" *Meat and Poultry* 38, 1 (January): 29–40.

Kelly, Jane, and Keith Nunes. 1991. "Mexico. Boom or bust." *Meat and Poultry* 37, 10 (October): 26–41.

Kenney, Martin, Luida M. Lobao, James Curry, and Richard Coe. 1989. "Midwest agriculture and U.S. Fordism." *Sociologia Ruralis* 29, 2: 131–148.

Kenyon, Sevie. 1990. "IBP shifts its weight." *Cattle*. Supplement to *Nebraska Farmer* C-5.

Lamphear, Charles. 1992. "The meatpacking industry in Nebraska and surrounding states." *Business in Nebraska* 47, 570: 1–3.

Lexington Superintendent of Schools. 1993/Various years. School enrollment data.

Liepietz, Alain. 1987. *Mirages and Miracles: The global crises of Fordism*. London: Verso.

Limprecht, Jane E. 1990. *ConAgra Who? The Story of ConAgra's First 70 Years*. Omaha, Nebr.: ConAgra.

_____. 1991 "Enrollment milestone." *Dawson County Herald*, 23 October.

_____. 1992. "Turnover teaches flexibility." *Clipper Herald*, 18 January, 1, 3.

McMichael, Philip, and David Myhre. 1991. "Global regulation vs. the nation state: Agro-food systems and the new politics of capital." *Capital and Class* 43, 2: 83–106.

McNaughton, Marie Thomas. 1991. "On the dark and bloody ground." *Meat and Poultry* 37, 9 (September): 18–26.

Meat and Poultry. 1991. "Companies." 37, 7 (July): 5.

_____. 1992. "The 14th annual TOP 100." 38, 7 (July): 33–48.

NCA (National Cattlemen's Association). 1992. "Boxed beef restrictions in Mexico." *Issues . . . Affecting the Beef Industry* June/July: 16.

NDA (Nebraska Department of Agriculture). 1983. *Nebraska Agricultural Statistics*. Lincoln: Nebraska Agricultural Statistical Service.

Nebraska Department of Economic Development (DED). 1991. *Nebraska Statistical Handbook*. Lincoln, Nebr.: DED.

_____. 1987. "Targeted Industries for Nebraska: Report of the Nebraska Industry Targeting Committee." Lincoln, Nebr.: DED.

Nebraska Development News (NDN). 1992 "International trade office established at DED." *NDN* April: 13.

NPPD (Nebraska Public Power District). 1990. "Industrial Facts. Lexington, Nebraska." Columbus, Nebr.: NPPD Area Development Department.

Nunes, Keith. 1991. "What can be done about workers comp?" *Meat and Poultry* 37, 10 (October): 42–44.

_____. 1992. "Doing business in Mexico." *Meat and Poultry* 38, 6 (June): 52–54.

Rasmussen, Jim. 1992. "Beef packers find profits elusive." *Omaha World Herald*, 19 April.

Renard, Marie-Christine. 1992. "Mexico: El Fin de la Reforma Agraria." Paper presented at the eighth World Congress of Rural Sociology, Pennsylvania State University, 11–16 August.

Ritchie, Mark. 1991. "Unlimited meat imports bad for U.S." *PrairieFire Journal* 2, 3: 10.

Roberts, Rebecca S., Frances M. Ufkes, and Fred M. Shelby. 1990. "Populism and agrarian ideology: The 1982 Nebraska corporate farming referendum." Pp. 153–175 in R. F. Johnston, F. M. Shelby, and P. J. Taylor (eds.), *Developments in Electoral Geography*. London and New York: Routledge.

Sanderson, Steven E. 1986. "The emergence of the 'world steer': International and foreign domination in Latin American cattle production." Pp. 123–148 in F. Lamond Tullis and W. Ladd Hollist (eds.), *Food, the State and International Political Economy*. Lincoln: University of Nebraska Press.

Sparks, Amy, and Carlos Arnade. 1992. "World agriculture and trade." *Agricultural Outlook*, April: 19–21.

SRI International. 1988. *Seeds for Nebraska*. Omaha, Nebr.: Nebraska Futures.

Stalcup, Larry. 1989. "The battle for cattle." *Beef Today*, August: 16–17.

Stanley, Kathleen. 1991. "The Role of Immigrant and Refugee Labor in the Restructuring of the Midwestern Meatpacking Industry." Paper presented at the Midwest Sociological Society meeting, April.

Strange, Marty, Patricia E. Funk, Gerald Hansen, Jennifer Tully, and Donald Macke. 1990. *Half a Glass of Water*. Walthill, Nebr.: Center for Rural Affairs.

Stull, D. D., and M. J. Broadway. 1990. "The effects of restructuring on beefpacking in Kansas." *Kansas Business Review* 14, 1: 10–16.

Swift & Company. 1937. *The Meat Packing Industry in America*. Chicago: Swift & Company.

Thompson, David. 1992. "Chapter 12 and the family farm." *Omaha World Herald*, 23 January: 21–23.

Tintsman, Dale C., and Robert L. Peterson. 1981. *Iowa Beef Processors, Inc.: An Entire Industry Revolutionized!* New York: Newcomen Society in North America.

Ufke, Frances M. 1993. "Trade liberalization, agro-food politics, and rural restructuring." *Political Geography* 12, 3 (May): 215–231.

USDA (United States Department of Agriculture). 1990. "Nonmetro employment growth exceeds metro." *Rural Conditions and Trends* 1, 1 (Spring): 6–7.

_____. 1991. *Trade Highlights*. Foreign Agricultural Service. Washington, D.C.: Government Printing Office.

_____. 1992. "Rural employment edges up in first quarter of 1992." *Rural Conditions and Trends*, Summer: 6–7.

USMEF (U.S. Meat Export Federation). 1991. "Consumer Attitudes toward U.S. High Quality Beef in Mexico." Executive Summary, September. Denver: U.S. Meat Export Federation.

Yeager, Mary. 1981. *Competition and Regulation: The Development of Oligopoly in the Meat Packing Industry*. Greenwich, Conn.: JAI Press.

7 The Behavior of U.S. Food Firms in International Markets

Michael R. Reed and Mary A. Marchant

The level of processing involved in agricultural exports is currently a popular topic. Increased exports of processed food products will not only stimulate farm income, but also provide manufacturing jobs. The General Accounting Office (GAO) recently charged that the U.S. Department of Agriculture (USDA) must rethink its priorities if it is to help increase the exports of processed foods. In particular, the GAO insists that the USDA must engage in more strategic marketing in cooperation with the private sector.

The Foreign Agricultural Service (FAS) of the USDA classifies agricultural exports in three categories based on how close they are to their final consumer form: bulk (which are free from processing), intermediate (which are principally semiprocessed), and consumer-oriented (which require little additional processing). In 1990 the United States exported 53.8 percent of its agricultural products in bulk form, 22.7 percent in intermediate form, and 23.5 percent in consumer-oriented form (FAS 1990). These percentages are the reverse of those in world trade in agricultural products, where in 1988 consumer-oriented trade totaled $141.3 billion, intermediate product trade $52.9 billion, and bulk food trade $56.9 billion (FAS 1990).

The problem with concentrating on bulk commodities is exacerbated by the fact that world trade in consumer-oriented food products grew at a 4 percent annual rate, compared with 1 percent for bulk and intermediate products (FAS 1990). Hence, as incomes across the world increase, there are likely to be increased export opportunities for consumer-oriented food products. A vital question is, How can the U.S. agricultural industry best take advantage of these growing markets?

This paper deals with globalization of one part of the U.S. agricultural industry—the food manufacturing sector.[1] The food-processing industry is extremely important for the United States. In 1987, it accounted for $330 billion in sales (or 13.3 percent of the $2.476 trillion manufacturing segment of the U.S. economy), $18 billion in exports, and 1.45 million jobs (Bureau of Census 1987).[2] Obviously, small changes in this huge industry can have significant ramifications for the entire U.S. economy. However, foreign sales from affiliates of U.S. food-manufacturing firms in 1987 totaled $41 billion—more than double their direct and indirect exports. An analysis of why firms invest in food-processing facilities overseas is certainly needed to guide policymakers and government agencies.

Why Direct Investments? Existing Arguments

The classical theory of comparative advantage is goods-oriented in that it assumes free, unrestricted trade and that countries export goods in which they have comparatively low production costs and import goods in which they have comparatively high production costs. Each country gains from trade as long as markets are perfectly competitive and there are differences in production possibilities between countries. The only reason for trade in goods is that some factors of production (such as land and labor) cannot be moved across national boundaries.

When technology and capital are mobile, or trade barriers on goods are introduced, some scarce factors of production may move instead of the goods. Direct investments or productive capital are examples of factor flows that can substitute for goods flows. Foreign investment allows the country receiving capital to capture some of the gains from the other country's superiority in production of goods without having to import the goods themselves. However, the capital investment flow will not totally compensate for the potential gains from free trade (Ethier 1986). Yet the investment-receiving country has increased employment while increasing the variety or reducing the price of the goods it imports.

The decision on foreign direct investment occurs at the firm level. There are generally five reasons for firms to operate in a foreign country:

1. ownership advantages of the firm (e.g., patent, technological, or managerial capabilities). The firm can capitalize on special advantages that it has in more markets.
2. locational considerations (e.g., high transportation costs, trade barriers, or lower production costs). These barriers can be overcome through direct investment as long as foreign-owned firms receive national treatment.
3. establishment of processing facilities in anticipation of future trade restrictions (Bhagwati et al. 1987). Some argue this is why the Japanese automakers have invested in the United States.
4. reduction of exchange rate risks for larger markets (Cushman 1987). Foreign exchange risk is lowered because much of the processing costs are denominated in the currency of the country where the facility is lo-

cated. Thus, only potential repatriated earnings will fluctuate in value (in the investing firm's currency).

5. tailoring of the product to local tastes when consumer needs for the product differ significantly or product specifications vary. A local processing facility will allow this to occur.

All of these advantages must be balanced against the major disadvantage with respect to foreign investment—the loss of scale economies. Scale economies exist for most manufacturing enterprises. In fact, from a conceptual basis, the existence of scale economies and imperfect competition are the major reason for intraindustry trade (Helpman 1981; Krugman 1980).[3]

There are generally two types of foreign direct investment: vertical and horizontal. Vertical investment involves a firm investing in foreign facilities to produce successive stages of the production process. An example would be a confectionery firm having its chocolate made in Europe and exporting the chocolate to the United States for final processing into a candy bar. Horizontal investment involves a firm investing in the same type of processing in more than one country. Vertical investment is usually undertaken because of cost differences, whereas horizontal investment is usually aimed at overcoming locational disadvantages.

Michael Porter (1990) takes a more comprehensive view of international trade (and the theory of comparative advantage), which he labels as the theory of competitive advantage. His theory focuses on explaining the large increase in intraindustry trade in recent years and the fact that most developed countries trade with each other. His theory also helps explain why there tend to be within a country clusters of closely related industries that are globally competitive. In Porter's framework, a particular country's industry is competitive if it exports a high proportion of its output and if its firms have a significant amount of outbound foreign investment. His framework works best in explaining vertical investment, where firms spin off lower-order processing activities to countries with lower wages and other costs. In this sense, foreign investment and international trade are complementary because much trade takes place between a parent firm and its foreign subsidiaries (affiliates).[4] The parent will focus on sophisticated, high-technology enterprises in order to keep pace with its constantly upgrading labor force and will rely on its affiliates to provide components.

Raymond Vernon's (1966) product life cycle is an alternative view of foreign direct investment that is similar to Porter's. During this life cycle, changes in production and marketing characteristics occur as the product matures. A key element in the model is the slow diffusion of technology or product characteristics. This dynamic model specifies four stages within a

Table 7.1. Size of the Industries Analyzed, 1987

Industry	Sales ($billions)	Employment (1,000 jobs)
Food and kindred products	330	1,449
Tobacco products	21	45
Textile mill products/apparel and other textile products	127	1,753
Lumber and wood products	108	1,209
Paper and allied products	109	611
Printing and publishing	136	1,494
Chemicals and allied products	230	814
Petroleum and coal products	130	126
Rubber and miscellaneous plastic products	87	831
Stone, clay,and glass products	61	524
Primary metal industries/fabricated metal products	267	2,159
Industrial machinery and equipment	218	1,844
Electronic and other electric equipment	171	1,565
Transportation equipment	333	1,817
Instruments and related products	107	982

Source: Bureau of Census, *Census of Manufacturing*, 1987.

product's life cycle. The first stage is when the product or process is invented and the country (or firm) is a monopolist. As information and technology diffuse, foreign production develops and increases, restricting the markets for the initial innovator (stage two). Soon, foreign-produced goods are competitive not only in their home markets, but also in third-country markets (stage three). As the life cycle reaches maturation, foreign-produced goods are actually imported by the innovating country (stage four). Within the life cycle, firms in the innovating country can decide to invest in foreign facilities during stage two of the cycle. However, the foreign markets must be large enough to overcome scale economies.

U.S. Food Manufacturing in an International Comparative Perspective

For the purpose of this study, manufacturing is divided into fifteen industries—all are at the two-digit Standard Industrial Classification (SIC) code level (Table 7.1). The Bureau of Economic Analysis classifies twenty different two-digit SIC industries, but the data on U.S. direct investment overseas is combined for some industries (textiles and apparel, SIC 22 and 23, are combined; lumber and furniture, SIC 24 and 25, are combined; and primary metals and fabricated metals, SIC 33 and 34, are combined). Leather goods

Table 7.2. Measures of the Importance of the Foreign Sector by Industry, 1987

Industry	Export Percentage	Foreign Sales/Exports	Output per Worker ($1000)	International Ratio
Food	5.4	2.33	227.6	17.8
Tobacco	13.8	1.73	464.4	37.7
Textiles	6.3	0.46	72.5	14.5
Lumber	7.6	0.19	88.7	9.0
Paper	14.7	0.68	178.3	24.6
Printing	4.9	0.38	91.1	6.8
Chemicals	19.1	1.73	281.9	52.1
Petroleum	10.2	12.63	1,125.2	139.1
Rubber/plastic	14.9	1.10	104.2	30.7
Stone/glass	7.9	1.08	117.5	16.6
Metals	20.8	0.33	123.9	27.7
Machinery	28.3	1.14	118.0	60.7
Electronics	32.0	0.55	109.5	49.6
Transport equipment	15.2	1.75	183.2	41.9
Instruments	16.0	1.01	109.2	32.1

Source: Bureau of Census, *Census of Manufacturing*, 1987, and Bureau of Economic Analysis, *U.S. Direct Investment Abroad*, 1988.

are included in the "other" category for U.S. direct investment data, and this category was excluded from the analysis.

In 1987, the $330 billion in food manufacturing sales was the second largest in terms of sales (only $3 billion behind transportation equipment), and its 1.45 million jobs ranked seventh largest in terms of employment (Table 7.1). The food manufacturing industry is a relatively capital-intensive industry. Its output per worker was $228,000, which was the fourth highest industry (Table 7.2)—behind petroleum, tobacco, and chemicals.

More precise measures of the food industry's capital-intensity is available at the four-digit SIC level.[5] A random assessment of capital-intensity for some segments of food and nonfood industries was made using the following ratios: book value per dollar spent on wages, average hourly earnings of production workers, and value added per production worker hour. A higher value for each of these ratios would imply higher capital intensity. Soybean mills were consistently ranked as one of the most capital intensive segments, along with cereal/breakfast food manufacturing. Other capital-intensive industries were pharmaceutical, fertilizers, and steel mills. Automobile manufacturing and most machinery manufacturing sectors had low book values per dollar spent on wages, despite having high wages in some cases. Their value added per worker hour was in the $30–50 range, whereas it was above $60 for flour, breakfast food, baked goods, candy, and soybean mills. The

Table 7.3. Food Manufacturing Affiliate Sales by Country, 1987

Country	Sales (billion dollars)
European Community	25.13
Other Europe	0.77
Canada	5.43
Japan/Australia/New Zealand/South Africa[a]	3.44
Developing Countries	6.46

Source: Bureau of Economic Analysis, U.S. Direct Investment Abroad, 1988.

[a]Aggregated to avoid disclosure of individual firm performance.

meat processing segment, though, had relatively low wages, book values per dollar of wages, and value added per worker hour.

The food-manufacturing industry exports a very low percentage of its output from the United States (Table 7.2). In 1987, it exported only 5.4 percent of its output, which placed it second to the last among the fifteen industries—only the printing industry was lower. The industry with the highest proportion of exports was electrical machinery, where 32 percent of U.S. shipments were exported.

Instead of exporting, many food-processing firms have chosen to invest in foreign processing facilities. In 1988, U.S. food-manufacturing parents held at least 10 percent equity in 661 foreign affiliates with total sales of $60.26 billion (Bureau of Economic Analysis 1988). If only those affiliates that are majority-owned by U.S. parents are included, sales of affiliates totaled $49.15 billion in 1988.

The food-manufacturing industry had the second-highest ratio of foreign affiliate sales to U.S. exports (the investment/export ratio) with a value of 2.33—the highest ratio was for the petroleum industry where foreign affiliate sales were more than twelve times U.S. petroleum exports. Data from the Economic Research Service indicate that the largest food-processing companies tend to have an even higher investment/export ratio of foreign affiliate sales to exports. For the sixty-four largest food-processing firms, sales of their foreign affiliates were $40.43 billion, while their exports equaled $3.82 billion in 1988—a ratio of 10.58. Only one of the top twenty food-processing firms had no foreign affiliate sales, and these top twenty firms accounted for $36.28 billion in foreign affiliate sales, but only $2.47 billion in exports from U.S. operations—a ratio of 14.69.

A measure of the importance of the foreign market can be obtained by adding exports from the United States to sales of foreign affiliates and dividing by U.S. shipments (this is called the international ratio). This ratio gives an indication of how important the international market is for the U.S. parent and is used to operationalize the Porter paradigm.[6] Food-processing companies rank eleventh out of the fifteen industries for the international ratio, with a value of 17.8 (Table 7.2). The industries ranking below food processing are printing, lumber, textiles, and stone/glass. The highest ratios were for petroleum (139.1), industrial machinery (60.7), and chemicals (52.1).

The international market is less important for most food-manufacturing firms than for other manufacturing firms, and exports from food-manufacturing firms are also relatively minor. Examining the pattern of U.S. investment in foreign food manufacturing will give an indication why this is so and provide other clues regarding foreign investment decisions.

U.S. Food Manufacturing and Foreign Affiliates

The information on the operation of foreign affiliates of U.S. food-manufacturing parents is aggregated to the two-digit SIC level, in part to preserve the identity of individual firms when some of the cross-tabulations are reported. Of particular interest will be analyzing foreign operations to investigate whether they indicate potential reasons for their existence.

If U.S. foreign investments in food processing are vertically integrated, then the facilities should be in areas of the world with lower wages than in the United States. This would be consistent with Porter's idea of upgrading skills within a country and pushing lower-grade skills to foreign countries. However, most foreign affiliate sales are in Europe and Canada. In 1987, foreign affiliate sales in the European Community (EC) totaled $25.13 billion, or more than 60 percent of foreign affiliate sales (Table 7.3). Canada accounted for another 13 percent of affiliate sales, or $5.43 billion, and other developed countries had sales of $4.21 billion. Affiliates in developing countries sold $6.46 billion in processed foods; most of that was in Brazil, Mexico, and Argentina.

Significant vertical linkages in foreign investment would also imply that a large percentage of the sales of affiliates would flow to the U.S. parent or other foreign affiliates. This is not borne out in the data for food processing (Table 7.4). Eighty percent of foreign affiliate sales are in the local country ($33.02 billion of the $41.23 billion in sales). Most of those local sales are to unaffiliated locals. Shipments to the United States were small ($707 million), though most (71 percent) of the U.S. shipments were to the U.S. parent. The remaining $7.45 billion in sales were to other foreign countries, with 51 percent going to affiliates.

EC countries receive most of the shipments from foreign affiliates (Bureau of Economic Analysis 1987). In 1987, affiliate exports to the EC to-

Table 7.4. Sales of Food Manufacturing Affiliates by Destination, 1987

Destination	Sales (billion dollars)
Sales to local affiliates	1.05
Sales to unaffiliated locals	31.97
Total local sales	33.02
Sales to U.S. parent	0.54
Sales to unaffiliated U.S. companies	0.22
Total U.S. sales	0.76
Sales to other foreign affiliates	3.81
Sales to nonaffiliated foreigners	3.64
Total sales to other countries	7.45
Total sales to affiliates/parents	5.40
Total sales to unaffiliated firms	35.83
Total sales	41.23

Source: Bureau of Economic Analysis, U.S. Direct Investment Abroad, 1988.

taled $6.34 billion, or 77 percent of the foreign affiliate exports to "other countries." Developing countries were more prominent in receiving food products from foreign affiliates than as a location for processing—receiving $804 million in 1987. Foreign affiliates export a much higher percentage of their output (19.9 percent versus 5.4 percent for U.S. parents), but much of that trade seems to be within the EC, where trade barriers are lower.

Finally, foreign affiliate trade of processed food with their U.S. parents is very small—only $707 million was shipped from foreign affiliates to the United States, and only $1.27 billion was shipped from U.S. parents to their foreign affiliates. If vertical strategies were prominent, one would expect more fluid trade between affiliates and parents. Furthermore, vertical investment would imply that more shipments to the United States would come from Latin America or other developing areas. However, most of the affiliate shipments to the United States come from Europe (45 percent) and Canada (22 percent). Developing countries accounted for $232 million in affiliate shipments to the United States.

Conclusion

One obvious conclusion emerging from this analysis is that most foreign investment by U.S. food processors is horizontal—the same type of processing is performed in the foreign affiliate as in the U.S. parent. This is due to the fact that trade between U.S. parents and their affiliates is small and most affiliate production occurs in developed countries. Horizontal investment is feasible in developed countries where plants can reach a large enough scale to operate efficiently. Lower wages are not a significant concern because of the need for significant capital outlays per worker. Further, trade barriers on more highly processed products could be prohibitive.

Three possible explanations for the pattern of U.S. food-processing investment overseas are to escape high trade barriers on processed food products, to overcome high transportation costs, and to allow food products to be tailored for local conditions. Little can be said about transportation costs given the aggregate level at which relevant cost data is collected (however, exporting bulk products is commonly thought to be more costly than exporting processed products). There is no question that tariff escalation is prevalent for processed foods, but it is difficult to quantify the effect of these tariffs with such aggregated statistics. However, the predominant position of the EC in receipt of foreign affiliate exports indicates that intra-EC shipments may account for a large percentage of these exports. There is still a great deal of cultural diversity among EC countries, so product tailoring might not be an important reason.

The ease of establishing a processed food sector may be a reason for these high trade barriers and other government incentives unique to food. Most countries want to capture this added value associated with the food industry, and they are probably suffering little welfare loss from the inefficiencies of these firms because technology is not complex and is easily transferred. In addition, a viable food-processing sector improves markets for raw agricultural commodities, which is an important concern for most countries.

The U.S. food-processing industry does not seem to be very competitive in the Porter sense, that is, its international ratio is not particularly high. There could be institutional factors that determine this noncompetitive position—for example, trade barriers in foreign countries coupled with small and thus unprofitable markets. Yet little is known about the true causes of the U.S. food-processing industry's lower level of competitiveness vis-à-vis its foreign counterparts. This suggests a need for research constructed around more narrow case studies.

It seems that if the United States is going to promote exportation of high-value processed food products, it must concentrate on the small to medium-sized firms. These are the firms that are too small to establish processing facilities overseas, but they still have food products that have receptive foreign markets. Most of the largest firms already have processing facilities overseas and are increasingly less interested in exporting products. The USDA, or any other agency working to assist exporters, should be willing to work with small-scale companies that must export if their product is to reach international markets. These small U.S. food companies may have to compete with

U.S. multinational firms in foreign markets, but the uniqueness of their food products may give the small processors a niche market. However, as the introduction and several chapters in this book contend, nation-states are currently withdrawing from domestic capital circuits, and thus support for small, nonglobalized firms is less than certain in today's economy.

Given the growing tendency toward "global sourcing," U.S. food affiliates do not obtain a significant amount of their inputs from the United States. In this sense, it may be more beneficial for U.S. agricultural commodities markets to have foreign firms building plants in the United States than to have U.S. firms building plants in non-U.S. sites. Several studies in this volume illustrate some of the consequences resulting from each of these investment patterns.

The interaction between U.S. foreign investment and trade is a question crucial to the North American Free Trade Agreement (NAFTA). The results of this study provide some insights into these interactions. To the extent that Mexico provides a market for U.S. food processors, the possibility exists that U.S. multinational food companies will locate plants in Mexico to reach those consumers (which U.S. food processors have done in other areas of the world). Conversely, a free-trade agreement could actually decrease the possibilities of that occurring because barriers to U.S. processed food exports should be lower, thereby reducing the economic incentives for direct investment.

The main questions, which cannot be completely answered from this analysis, are, Does NAFTA increase the possibilities of downstream food processing locating in Mexico (the focus of Porter's paradigm where lower-level processing is performed in Mexico to support higher-level processing in the United States), or will U.S. food processors locate in Mexico and export to the U.S. market? These questions cannot be answered by looking at the historical pattern and existing institutional framework for U.S. investments in this area. Because of U.S. trade barriers and a lack of incentives for foreign direct investment in Mexico, few U.S. food processors have located across the border. NAFTA will certainly change this institutional framework, but it is unclear whether this new framework will be enough to move U.S. food-processing plants to Mexico.

Notes

1. For this paper, the food manufacturing industry is Standard Industry Class 20, which is food and kindred products. It does not include tobacco products, textiles, or wood products.

2. The base year for this study is 1987 for most information because it is the last year when foreign investment data and U.S. manufacturing data were available.

3. Intraindustry trade is defined as exporting and importing the same SIC classification of goods at the three-digit level.

4. The parent is the home base of the firm that is investing in foreign processing facilities. Those foreign processing facilities are affiliates of the parent.

5. Unfortunately two–digit and three–digit measures are not yet available from the 1987 Census of Manufacturers.

6. This will overstate the importance a bit because of shipments from foreign affiliates to the U.S. parent, covered in the next section.

Bibliography

Bhagwati, Jagdish N., Richard A. Brecher, and Elias Dinopoulos. 1987. "Quid pro quo foreign investment and welfare: A political-economy-theoretic model." *Journal of Development Economics* 27: 127–138.

Bureau of Census. 1987. *Census of Manufacturing.* Washington, D.C.: Department of Commerce.

Bureau of Economic Analysis. 1987. *U.S. Direct Investment Abroad.* Washington, D.C.: Department of Commerce.

_____. 1988. *U.S. Direct Investment Abroad.* Washington, D.C.: Department of Commerce.

Cushman, David O. 1987. "The effects of real wages and labor productivity on foreign direct investment." *Southern Economic Journal* 54: 174–185.

Ethier, Wilfred. 1986. "The multinational firm." *Quarterly Journal of Economics* 101, 4: 805–833.

Foreign Agricultural Service, U.S. Department of Agriculture. 1990. *Desk Reference Guide to U.S. Agricultural Trade.* Agriculture Handbook no. 683, March.

General Accounting Office. 1991–1992. *U.S. Department of Agriculture: Strategic Marketing Needed to Lead Agribusiness in International Trade.* GAO/RCED, January.

Helpman, Elhanan. 1981. "International trade in the presence of product differentiation, economies of scale and monopolistic competition: A Chamberlin-Heckscher-Ohlin approach." *Journal of International Economics* 11: 305–340.

Krugman, Paul. 1980. "Scale economies, product differentiation and the pattern of trade." *American Economic Review* 70: 950–959.

Porter, Michael. 1990. *The Competitive Advantage of Nations.* New York: Free Press.

Vernon, Raymond. 1966. "International investment and international trade in the product cycle." *Quarterly Journal of Economics* 80: 190–207.

8 An Introduction to the Japanese Juice Industry: Trading Firms, the State, and New Liberalization Policies

Raymond A. Jussaume, Jr.

In academic and policymaking circles, interest has been increasing during the past decade in the process of globalization. This has been especially true in the United States, where recent economic developments have underscored U.S. interdependence with the rest of the global economy. One expression of this trend in agricultural studies has been analyses of international commodity trade, particularly grain crops, and its impact on national development strategies. Some scholars have developed a political economy of agricultural commodities trade with an emphasis on the role of the state in promoting and controlling food trade regimes (Friedmann 1982; Friedmann and McMichael 1989). Others have examined the roles multinational corporations play in controlling the terms of international trade in basic commodities such as wheat, corn, and soybeans (Bertrand, Leclercq, and Laurent 1983; Hamilton 1972; Morgan 1980).

While these and related efforts have helped stimulate intellectual curiosity about the developing patterns of international agricultural commodities trade, little work has been done on the globalization of other aspects of the food marketing system and its linkages with farm families, rural residents, food industry employees, and consumers. For example, wholesaling is a critical aspect of any modern food delivery system, and in the United States at least, wholesale food companies have begun expanding vertically into food warehousing as well as retailing (Gallo 1986). Very little work has been done in the United States or elsewhere on the increasing concentration of the food wholesaling industry and the potential consequences of this trend for the international food marketing system. As Chapter 7 by Reed and Marchant in this volume makes clear, much remains to be learned about the implications of international trade of bulk versus processed and semiprocessed foods. Processing commodities not only adds to their value, but in many cases makes those foods easier to handle and distribute. Consequently, world trade in high-value farm products in the 1970s increased at a rate of 17 percent per annum (Economic Research Service 1983).

Finally, while we have learned much from empirical examinations of U.S. and European-based food processing and trading firms, such as Cargill and ConAgra, analyses of the globalization process are handicapped by a dearth of research on the growing and intricate role of Japanese firms in that process. This seems quite astonishing when one considers that during the mid-1980s, Japanese agricultural imports accounted for 10 percent of the total world trade in agricultural and food products (Ministry of Agriculture, Forestry, and Fisheries 1989). In addition, Japanese general trading companies are very active in international food and commodity markets, while Japanese food processing companies have established food processing facilities around the world, particularly in Pacific Rim countries. In other words, Japan is a major paying importer and a principal market for trade in food and agriculture. Japanese companies are playing an increasing role in controlling that trade, especially within that other cluster of paying East Asian customers: Korea, Taiwan, Singapore, and Hong Kong. Finally, although Japanese trading firms share many similarities with U.S. and European trading firms, there are some important differences as well. As we shall see, they are larger and organized differently, and they have traditionally had a unique relationship with the Japanese state.

My goal here is to expand the empirical foci of studies on the world food marketing system by examining the production, distribution, and importation of fruit juice in Japan. A major reason for selecting the juice products industry for a case study is that at the time the research was being conducted, in early 1991, the Japanese juice market was in the process of adapting to liberalization. Grapefruit juice imports had been liberalized in 1986, apple and grape juice in 1990, and orange juice on 1 April 1992. The latter was a particularly sensitive political issue, as oranges are a major fruit crop in Japan, and the unrestricted importation of orange juice was strongly opposed by agricultural interests on the grounds that the subsequent decline in the price for domestic orange juice would adversely affect orange growers, who are generally able to sell only 40 to 60 percent of their crop on the fresh market because of stringent quality standards. However, over the long run, the Japanese government has been unable to resist external political pressures to liberalize agricultural commodity imports. These pressures began mounting in the 1960s, with one of the better-known cases being the liberalization of lemon imports in 1966 (Kada 1989), and continue on to the present. Thus, the juice industry provides an example of how Japanese food processing and trading companies are adapting their marketing strategies to cope with the liberalization process that is being vigorously promoted within the context of the General Agreement on Tariffs and Trade negotiations.

The evidence presented here was collected during a study of the Japanese soft drink industry during January and February of 1991. The primary methods of data collection were interviews with informants from private firms and industry associations, and collection of available public and private secondary information on the structure of the industry. During the interviews, a series of open-ended questions were asked. Each informant was asked to describe the role of his firm or organization in the Japanese juice industry as well as respond to questions about the structure of that industry. In addition, informants occasionally provided privately held information on the soft drink industry in Japan, including information on market shares of major firms in various soft drink sub-markets.

The Japanese Juice Market

While the consumption of fruit juice products is a comparatively new phenomenon in Japan, it has grown rapidly in recent years. There has been a substantial increase in the consumption of most types of fruit juice drinks in Japan during the 1980s (Table 8.1). Since the rate of population increase is very slow in that country, this means that the per capita consumption of fruit juice products in Japan has approximately doubled. Growth in fruit juice consumption has been centered around a boom in 100 percent juice beverage sales. Per capita consumption of pure fruit juice products more than doubled between 1985 and 1989 alone (Table 8.2)!

This tremendous growth in juice consumption, as well as that in other types of soft drinks, like canned coffee and tea, is one reason why many Japanese food processing companies have developed soft drink divisions or subsidiaries. Another reason is the relatively high rate of return on investment. Food manufacturing industries in general have a lower added value ratio, but a higher investment ratio, than non–food manufacturing industries (Table 8.3). However, the index for beverages is higher than the average for food manufacturing industries. In other words, food processors can expect a relatively high rate of return on their investments in soft drink production. Since juice processing and bottling technologies are comparatively easy to obtain and use, it is hardly surprising that so many major Japanese food processing firms have become involved in either producing or distributing juice products.

Seven of the top fifteen Japanese food processing companies (see Table 8.4) have soft drink divisions. These include Kirin and Asahi breweries,

Table 8.1. Japanese Juice Consumption by Fruit Type (in tons of natural juice base)

	1980	1981	1982	1983	1984	1985	1986	1987	1988	1989
Orange	59,387	63,049	58,731	59,581	61,706	56,072	57,348	62,741	71,457	85,921
Apple	13,950	14,289	13,963	17,830	22,005	24,893	25,747	31,148	37,338	49,757
Grape	2,117	22,884	3,387	4,577	4,632	4,993	5,388	6,352	8,693	9,046
Pineapple	*	*	*	1,653	1,831	1,906	1,610	1,635	1,738	1,659
Peach	2,650	2,446	2,326	2,176	2,160	2,383	2,724	3,096	3,090	3,272
Grapefruit				4,484	5,249	5,298	5,885	7,720	9,342	9,717
Others				2,584	2,983	4,020	4,526	6,126	6,637	6,857
Total	78,104	82,668	78,407	92,849	100,566	99,565	103,228	118,818	138,295	166,229

Source: Ministry of Agriculture, Forestry, and Fisheries, internal document.

*Not reported.

Table 8.2. Average per Capita Consumption of Soft Drinks in Japan (in milliliters)

	1985	1986	1987	1988	1989
Carbonated Beverages					
Carbonated cola	7,476	7,232	7,650	7,249	7,706
Clear carbonated	6,609	5,802	5,841	5,229	5,256
Fruit-based carbonated	1,404	1,488	1,407	1,409	1,444
Fruit-colored carbonated	3,800	3,123	3,232	3,152	3,245
Milk-based carbonated	1,090	945	753	741	713
Carbonated water	554	403	360	326	309
Other carbonated beverages	1,900	1,561	1,808	1,482	1,387
"Small bottle drink" carbonated	1,487	1,438	1,620	1,751	1,963
Subtotal	24,320	21,992	22,671	21,339	22,023
Fruit Drinks					
Natural juice (100%)	1,652	1,816	2,209	3,038	4,299
Juice (50-100%)	1,314	1,036	1,091	1,059	1,030
Juice nectar (20-60%)	467	436	462	424	424
Juice-based (10-50%) soft drinks	8,451	9,287	10,370	10,095	9,239
Juice pulp (10% +) beverages	609	460	425	342	308
Other "direct" fruit drinks	1,817	1,561	1,636	2,036	3,488
Diluted drinks	1,941	1,849	1,964	1,853	1,825
Fruit syrups	165	148	155	143	150
Subtotal	16,416	16,593	18,312	18,990	20,763
Total	40,736	38,585	40,983	40,329	42,786

Source: National Soft Drink Association and Japan Carbonated Beverage Testing Association 1990.

which are the two largest food processing firms in Japan and which outsource the bulk of the production of their brand name juice products. Kirin and Asahi, like other juice distributors, have juice products bottled for them under their own labels by contracting firms or agricultural cooperatives and merely control the distribution and marketing of those products. Other top companies active in the juice drink industry are Snow brand milk products, Sapporo Breweries, Ajinomoto, Meiji milk products, and Morinaga milk industry. In other words, Japanese milk and alcohol producers dominate the list of leading food processing firms, and all are active in the fruit juice market.

Although sales figures for the Japanese companies may be slightly misrepresented by the translation from yen into dollars, most leading Japanese food processors have not achieved the same size as their American counterparts (see Table 8.4). However, when one considers that the size of the Japanese consumer market is roughly half that of the United States and that these firms typically control dozens of subsidiaries, it becomes evident that the role of Japanese food processing firms within the Japanese economy is

Table 8.3. Profitability of Capital Equipment Investment in Food Manufacturing in Japan, 1987

Food Industry Type	Capital[a] Equipment Ratio (Yen,000)	Capital Equipment Ratio Index	Added[b] Value Ratio (%)	Added Value Ratio Index	Investment[c] Ratio (%)	Investment Ratio Index
All manufacturing industries	7,358	100.0	35.0	100.0	1.40	100.0
Food manufacturing industries	6,344	94.0	30.8	84.8	1.53	101.5
Livestock and dairy products	5,961	53.4	26.1	85.8	1.55	109.7
Fish products	3,386	50.8	26.4	116.3	1.68	106.7
Vegetable products	3,224	138.5	35.8	160.2	1.63	137.5
Seasonings	8,788	274.6	49.3	86.6	2.10	68.6
Sugar	17,423	252.1	26.7	64.6	1.05	75.9
Modified cereals and flour	15,996	68.6	19.9	161.7	1.16	118.5
Bread and cakes	4,353	365.3	49.8	90.8	1.81	69.8
Fats and oils	23,178	58.3	28.0	126.0	1.07	102.2
Other food products	3,696	198.4	38.8	112.1	1.56	114.1
Beverages	12,587	274.8	34.5	85.4	1.74	95.1
"Sake" brewing	17,432	183.3	26.3	60.8	1.45	51.6
Tea, coffee	11,632	280.1	18.7	64.9	0.79	69.1
Feedstuffs, organic fertilizer	17,768	296.3	20.0	42.2	1.05	60.1
Tobacco	18,796		13.0		0.92	

Source: Ministry of International Trade and Industry, as cited by Nakajima 1991.

[a]Capital Equipment Ratio = Fixed Material Assets divided by Number of Employees
[b]Added Value Ratio = Amount of Value Added divided by Production Costs
[c]Investment Ratio = Amount of Value Added divided by Fixed Material Assets

Table 8.4. Top Fifteen Food Processors in the United States and Japan Based on Sales ($million)[a]

American Company	1989	Rank	Japanese Company	1988
Philip Morris Companies, N.Y.	25,802	1	Kirin Brewery[b]	9,068
RJR Nabisco, Atlanta, Ga.	9,888	2	Suntory Brewery[c]	4,855
Anheuser-Busch Company, St. Louis, Mo.	9,363	3	Asahi Breweries	4,191
ConAgra, Omaha, Nebr.	8,591	4	Sapporo Breweries	3,767
IBP, Dakota City, Nebr.	8,502	5	Snow Brand Milk Products	3,663
Pepsico, Purchase, N.Y.	8,153	6	Toyo Seikan (cans)	3,584
Coca-Cola, Atlanta, Ga.	8,000	7	Nippon Suisan (fish, canned & frozen foods)	3,569
Archer Daniels Midland, Decatur, Ill.	7,200	8	Ajinomoto (seasonings, food processing)	3,538
Nestle Holdings, Purchase, N.Y.	5,961	9	Nippon Ham (meats)	3,414
Campbell Soup Company, Camden, N.J.	5,700	10	Yamazaki Baking	2,954
H. J. Heinz Company, Pittsburgh, Penn.	5,492	11	Meiji Milk Products	2,881
Borden, New York, N.Y.	5,386	12	Nichirei (frozen foods)	2,622
Sara Lee Corporation, Chicago, Ill.	5,255	13	Nissin Flour Milling	2,467
Quaker Oats Company, Chicago, Ill.	4,879	14	Morinaga Milk Industry	2,462
CPC International, Englewood Cliffs, N.J.	4,701	15	Taiyo Gyogyo (fish, canned & frozen foods)	2,231

Source: Economic Research Service 1990 and Shokuhin Sangyo Center 1990.

[a]Japanese figures calculated at 130 Yen/$1
[b]Soft drink division turned into subsidiary as of 1 January 1991
[c]Privately owned corporation

Table 8.5. Interfirm Structure of Top Fifteen Japanese Publicly Owned Food Processors

Rank	Firm	No. of Known Subsidiaries	No. of Overseas Subsidiaries	Known International Relationships
1	Kirin Brewery	33	5	Seagrams/Molson/Tropicana
2	Asahi Breweries	62	0	Coors
3	Nippon Meat Packers	178	7	Swift & Co.
4	Snow Brand Milk Products	77	1	Dole/Quaker Oats/Hershey
5	Sapporo Breweries	20	1	Miller[a]
6	Itoham Foods	23	2	Carnation
7	Ajinomoto[b]	62	7	Kraft–General Foods
8	Yamazaki	14	3	Nabisco
9	Nichirei	86	8	—
10	Nissin Flour Mills	16	4	—
11	Meiji Milk Products	51	0	Borden/Bulgarian government
12	Prima Meat Packers	43	0	Broke with Oscar Mayer
13	Morinaga Milk Industry	23	1	Kraft-General Foods/Sunkist
14	Q.P.	9	1	—
15	Toyo Suisan	10	1	—

Source: Toyo Keizai Inc. 1990, *Nihon Keizai Shimbun* 1988, and personal interviews.

[a]Sapporo licensed its draft beer brewing techonology to Miller.
[b]Merged soft drink division with Calpis, which has ties to Welch, in April 1991.

at least equivalent to that of American firms. Also, the Japanese firms are certainly large enough to enable them to develop significant overseas contacts, both in terms of setting up their own overseas subsidiaries as well as setting up joint ventures with non-Japanese firms. Gouveia's analysis of conglomerates like ConAgra versus domestically constrained firms like IBP also reveals this important connection between size and overseas contacts (see Chapter 6, by Lourdes Gouveia, in this volume).

An important reason for investigating the Japanese juice industry is that many Japanese food processing firms marketing juice are becoming increasingly active internationally. Six of the seven top food processors who market juice have overseas subsidiaries, and all seven have known links with Seagrams, Molson, Tropicana, Coors, Dole, Miller, Borden, Kraft-General Foods, and Sunkist (see Table 8.5). Other firms that have important overseas ties affecting the juice market are Pokka Corporation (Ocean Spray and Tree Top) and Suntory Whiskey (Strauss World, which recently terminated a two-year relationship with Ueshima coffee). This information suggests the economic strength of Japanese food processing firms and their global position. It also indicates that an analysis of changes in the Japanese juice market and the ongoing process of juice import liberalization can be useful for developing an understanding of the role of the Japanese food industry within the international food order.

Organizational Environment of the Japanese Juice Industry

The organizational climate of industrial groupings in Japan has been fairly well studied by both Japanese and foreign scholars. Of particular interest has been the relationship between the national government and private firms and whether the comparatively direct role the Japanese government plays in economic planning is one of the secrets to the success of the Japanese economy and companies (Dore 1986; Okimoto 1989; Vogel 1980). While the pervasiveness and effectiveness of Japanese industrial policy can be debated, one clearly cannot understand the structure of the Japanese economy without analyzing the ability of the government to direct most industrial sectors.

The powerful role of the government is also a common theme in studies of Japanese agriculture, particularly among American writers whose underlying intent is to promote the expansion of American agricultural sales to Japan by demonstrating the economic inefficiencies of government policies that protect small-scale agriculture in that country (Bale and Greenshiels 1978; Coyle 1983, 1987; Tallent 1983). The Japanese government is very active in promoting both rural and agricultural development, not only because of the historical tradition of Japanese governmental involvement in promoting capitalist development in that country, but also because of the political power farmers have had in post–World War II Japan. Many elected politicians within the powerful Liberal Democratic party have been dependent on the farm vote (George and Hayami 1986; Stockwin 1982). In addition, the political influence of farmers is supported by the organizational and economic power of the national association of agricultural cooperatives (George 1981), to which virtually every Japanese farmer, as well as most nonfarming rural residents, belongs.

Given the pivotal role of the Japanese government, particularly the Ministry of International Trade and Industry, in setting industrial policy, as well as the history of government interventions in agriculture, it is surprising that the food industry, including food processing, is one of the least controlled of all industrial sectors in Japan. In effect, the Japanese food industry has fallen through the cracks. Although food processing is indeed a form of manufacturing, because agricultural commodities are used as an input, supervision of food processing is not under the jurisdiction of the Ministry of

International Trade and Industry, but under the Ministry of Agriculture, Forestry, and Fisheries (MAFF). MAFF, however, like its counterpart in the United States, has been much more concerned with regulating and supporting petty commodity producers than it has been with guiding firms that use what farmers grow in their production processes.

This does not mean that food processors, including those who produce and distribute juice, are not subject to any government supervision. The Japanese government does introduce policies relating to food manufacturing, but these initiatives originate in various ministries and are thus frequently uncoordinated. For example, food safety issues come under the jurisdiction of the Ministry of Health. The Treasury Ministry's role is to collect tariffs and duties on imported agricultural commodities and food products, which has a major impact on food processors because of Japan's high degree of dependence on imported agricultural commodities. The Ministry of International Trade and Industry affects food processors through its control of the retail sector and in particular its enforcement of the Big Store Law, which limits the flexibility of large supermarket and department store chains in opening new stores in urban districts. Even the Ministry of Foreign Affairs enacts policies affecting agricultural commodity trade and, subsequently, Japan's food industry. "The stated aim of Japan's foreign aid to agriculture is to obtain imports of feed grains and oil seeds from developing countries" (Goldberg and McGinity 1979: 95) in order to decrease its dependence on the traditional suppliers of these commodities. In spite of all this, the Japanese MAFF has no detailed industrial policy for food processing, which makes this industry fairly unique in that country.

Technically, supervision of food processing falls under the jurisdiction of MAFF, but MAFF has been more interested in farming and rural issues than in keeping a supervisory eye on the Japanese food industry. This does not mean that the ministry has no influence at all over food processors. In the case of fruit juice, four industry-wide associations represent institutions active in that industry and thus serve as a link between fruit juice producers and distributors and the Japanese government. These organizations are *Zennoh*, the trading arm of the agricultural cooperatives—the Japan Fruit Juice Agricultural Cooperatives, which is the national office for those specialty cooperatives dealing in juice production, the National Soft Drink Association, and the National Fruit Juice Association. The latter two organizations represent private industry and are governed by executive committees whose members include executives from private firms as well as retired MAFF bureaucrats. These individuals help facilitate communication between MAFF and the firms represented in these associations, but they have no governmental authority to back up any recommendations they may make to the industry.

This relative lack of governmental leadership in food processing, in comparison to industries like semiconductors, may be one reason, along with the large profit potential, for the great number of firms currently active in the Japanese juice market. Juice consumption in Japan is a relatively new phenomenon, beginning in the post–World War II era, which means it was possible for a number of both new and old food processing firms to get involved in that industry. It is possible that the Japanese government would have attempted to limit the number of firms entering that market if it had played a more direct role in supervising the food industry in the 1950s and 1960s, although it should be remembered that even the Ministry of International Trade and Industry has not always been successful in getting private firms to follow its recommendations. Concern with, and attempts to limit, "excessive competition" (*Kato Kyoso*) has been a major element of overall Japanese industrial policy (Okimoto 1989). Regardless, the Japanese government has not played an active role in regulating its domestic juice market, which is now characterized by a comparatively high degree of competition, at least in terms of the number of firms involved in either producing or distributing juice products. It is important to keep this in mind when one discusses the nature of that competition and the current trends in the Japanese juice market.

Juice Production and Distribution in Japan

To understand the evolutionary trends in the marketplace for juice products in Japan, a number of the key elements that characterize this industry must be appreciated. The first, and one that has already been reviewed, is the large number of firms active in that market. Second, it is vital to recognize that in Japan juice drinks are considered to be part of the larger product family of soft drinks. This explains the role of the National Soft Drink Association in the fruit juice market as well as why firms that produce other types of soft drinks, such as carbonated beverages and dairy drinks, have expanded horizontally into juice drink production and/or distribution. A third consideration is that nearly 60 percent of all juice products sold in Japan are not bottled by the company whose name appears on the label. This bottling, or canning or packaging as the case may be, is done through subcontracting arrangements. The final consideration, and one that is related to all of the others, is that a diverse number of market channels are used to distribute juice drinks.

The Japanese soft drink market is complex (see Table 8.6). There are six major classifications of fruit juice drinks, according to the guidelines established in accordance with the Japan Agricultural Standards. The numbers reveal that not only are there a variety of container sizes and market channels used to sell soft drinks to consumers, but that a correlation exists between the popular sizes of a product and which channel has the dominant share for each item. This in turn is linked to the firms that have dominant market shares. For example, more than 43 percent of pure juice products are sold in containers of one liter or greater in size, and more than 50 percent of pure juice products are sold in either convenience stores or other major retail outlets. This is because 100-percent juice is frequently consumed at meal times. Thus, the Ehime Cooperative,[1] which distributes its brand name juices primarily through retail food stores, has a slight lead over the Coca-Cola Bottling Group as the top marketer of 100-percent juice products. Meanwhile, carbonated juice beverages are sold primarily in the 300–500 millileter size and nearly half of these beverages are sold through either vending machines or package stores, which in turn frequently sell products in their own vending machines outside their front door. Kirin Brewery, which retails more than half of all beer sold in Japan and which has an extensive distribution network, sells 35 percent of all 50–100 percent juice-based beverages in Japan. Coca-Cola, on the other hand, which has more vending machines than any other company in Japan, is the market leader in colas, canned coffee, and carbonated fruit colored beverages.

This information outlines one of the major trends taking place in juice production and distribution in Japan. It was noted that in 100-percent juice products, the consumption of which is growing faster than any other category of juice beverages, there were two primary market leaders: the Ehime Producers Cooperative and the Coca-Cola Bottling Group. Generally speaking, the Ehime Cooperative specializes in selling large-size juice containers through supermarkets, department stores, and convenience stores. Coca-Cola, meanwhile, takes advantage of its vast system of vending machines to sell small—less than 200 millileter—bottles of 100-percent juice directly to consumers. The difficulty for the Coca-Cola group is that as the consumption of 100-percent juice becomes more commonplace in Japan, it is also becoming a meal rather than a snack item. For many consumers on the run buying soft drinks from vending machines, small containers of 100-percent fruit juice do not satisfy their thirst as well as 350 millileter containers of carbonated beverages or juice drinks with a 10–30 percent juice base, particularly during Japan's hot, sticky summers.

However, this trend should not be taken as an indication that the agricultural cooperatives will strengthen their position in Japan's juice market. In-

Table 8.6. Evolution of Japanese Beverage Production and Sales Distribution, 1990

Product Type	Percentage Sales by Size of Container (liters)						Percentage Sales by Channel						Top Producers and Share (%)
	.20	.20–.30	.30–.50	.50–1.0	1.0–1.25	1.25	Stores	Convenience Stores	Vending Machines	Package Store	Restaurant	Other	
Natural (100%) juice	25.5	18.3	0	12.9	41.3	2.0	36.4	15.8	20.3	19.8	3.2	4.5	Ehime 12/Coke 11
Juice (50–100%) beverages	5.6	28.5	1.0	56.0	8.9	0	35.1	7.4	4.2	44.5	3.5	5.3	Kirin 35
Juice-based (10–50%) soft drinks	0.9	28.8	18.4	5.5	14.3	32.1	30.1	6.5	14.1	15.7	19.4	14.2	Asahi 11/Suntory 9
Carbonated juice beverages	0	27.2	55.9	0	0	16.9	23.3	10.2	36.4	12.6	4.4	13.1	Kirin 32/Fujiya 22
Juice pulp (10% +) beverages	93	—	—	—	—	—	21.9	2.2	38.6	11.0	0	26.3	Nagoromo 24
Juice nectar (20–60%) beverages	—	—	—	—	—	—	44.4	11.7	12.8	10.0	16.7	4.4	Fujiya 52
Tomato juice	72.0	8.0	14.5	2.0	3.5	—	24.2	4.9	6.3	10.3	31.4	22.9	Kagome 44/Kikkoman 38
Vegetable juice	66.9	30.0	3.1	0	0	0	27.3	8.5	0.6	33.3	9.1	21.2	Kagome 59/Yakult 18
Colas	9.7	26.0	33.4	1.2	0.6	29.1	18.3	8.7	44.1	13.8	11.8	3.3	Coca-Cola 88
Transparent carbonated beverages	0	31.3	42.7	1.1	0.6	24.3	34.5	8.6	16.3	10.9	10.4	19.3	Coke 30/Asahi 23
"Ramune" beverages	27.8	66.4	5.8	0	0	0	32.7	9.1	5.8	—	—	52.4	Soft Drink Japan 57
Carbonated fruit colored beverages	0	28.0	40.8	2.6	6.4	22.1	21.3	5.4	33.1	11.7	3.0	25.5	Coke 73
Wine-type carbonated fruit beverages	44.6	16.1	39.3	0	0	0	10.7	0	0	7.2	70.7	11.4	Otsuka Seiyaku 59
Ginger ale	1.0	22.8	52.7	0	0	23.5	13.2	14.6	31.8	21.9	15.2	3.3	Cadbury 42/Coke 40
Milk-based soft drinks	82.2	17.8	0	0	0	0	6.6	23.3	58.9	5.6	0	5.6	Calpis 78
Milk	9.5	19.6	1.5	8.8	60.4	0.2	35.9	17.0	0.0	9.5[a]	22.0	15.6	Yuki 15/Meiji 14
High-fat milk	21.1	9.1	7.7	15.0	47.1	0	31.9	31.7	0.0	23.4[a]	—	13.0	Morinaga 26/Yuki 26
Low-fat milk	0	3.0	0	2.4	94.6	0	43.1	31.7	0	10.1[a]	—	15.1	Yuki 43/Morinaga 24
Canned coffee	34.6	63.7	1.7	—	—	—	12.0	14.0	64.6	—	—	9.4	Coke 37/Ueshima 18

Source: Personal interview.

[a]Milk stores

Table 8.7. Purveyors of Top Ten Brands of 100 Percent Bottled Juice in Japan

1983				1988		
Brand Name	Cases[a]	Market Share	Rank	Brand Name	Cases[a]	Market Share
Pon[b]	3,300	33.5	1	Pon[b]	6,800	28.0
Coop[c]	800	8.1	2	Dydo	6,300	25.9
Join[b]	650	6.6	3	Kirin	2,100	8.6
Sun-Ray[b]	600	6.1	4	Join[b]	1,600	6.6
Morinaga-Sunkist	500	5.1	5	Calpis	1,300	5.3
My	400	4.1	6	Sunkist	900	3.7
Juicy[b]	400	4.1	7	Welch's	800	3.3
Shizuoka-Ren[b]	300	3.0	8	Coop[c]	700	2.9
Welch's	220	2.2	9	HI-C	600	2.5
Fuku-Ren[b]	200	2.0	10	Byerley's	500	2.1
Total	7,370	74.8			21,600	88.9

Source: Nikkan Keizai Ryutsu Sha 1989.

[a]One case equals six liter bottles.
[b]agricultural cooperative.
[c]brand of consumer cooperatives.

deed, the opposite is taking place. While the Ehime Cooperative's "Pon" brand is still the market leader in this subsector of the 100-percent juice market, between 1983 and 1988 four out of six producer cooperatives dropped out of the top ten brands (see Table 8.7). It is true that the decline of the agricultural cooperatives is due in part to their inability to maintain market share in a rapidly growing market, and most of the cooperatives remain active in producing brand name juice for private firms, like the alcoholic beverage companies (Kirin, Asahi, Suntory, and Sapporo). Nevertheless, as the 100-percent juice market quiets down and market leaders solidify their sales positions, major producers may increase the percentage of the juice products they bottle in-house, thus further undermining the cooperatives' role in the juice market. Such a change could have a major impact on the economic viability of many Japanese fruit farmers, not only because the economic position of their cooperatives will be weakened, but also because the major producers may go increasingly to foreign sources of fruit concentrate for their raw material. Some cooperatives have recently begun to respond to this challenge by privatizing their juice processing operations, giving them more freedom to import raw material.

A related trend that is just beginning to develop in the Japanese juice industry is the movement toward straight and chilled juice. As Japanese consumers increase their consumption of 100-percent juice products, it is expected that their ability to distinguish between different levels of juice quality will also mature. One of the keys to the delivery of higher-quality juice products to consumers is to keep these products chilled throughout the distribution system. This practice is not commonly followed by the alcohol beverage firms or members of the Coca-Cola Bottling Group but is sometimes followed by the milk producers. There has been a great deal of talk in juice industry circles about the possibility of establishing ties between milk and nonmilk companies in order for the latter to gain access to chilled distribution systems without having to incur the expense of developing them on their own. Another advantage would be the possibility of moving into distribution of larger-sized products. Should these ties materialize, it could lead to a quick increase in market concentration, further weaken the position of agricultural cooperatives, and result in an interesting set of organizational relationships between firms that already hold dominant positions in the Japanese juice market. Some of the largest food processing firms in Japan are alcoholic beverage makers and milk producers (Tables 8.3 and 8.4). Should ties be established between pairs of firms from these two industries, it could alter the organizational environment of the entire Japanese food processing industry.

Although Japanese juice firms may be looking to the future for links with other Japanese firms, they have already been very active in establishing relationships with overseas firms to strengthen their domestic market position (see Table 8.5 for examples of known international relationships). The objectives and advantages of these relationships differ by case. For example, Morinaga's relationship with Sunkist is primarily for publicity purposes. According to a company officer, Morinaga does not purchase any fruit juice either directly or indirectly from Sunkist. It has simply purchased the Sunkist label for use on its products in Japan. The Dole relationship with Snow Milk Products, on the other hand, has led to the creation of a jointly owned subsidiary that is using imported Dole juice concentrate, whenever possible, to produce juice that is bottled in Snow plants and distributed by a wholly owned Snow subsidiary. Another interesting relationship is between Kirin Beer and Tropicana of Florida. Few details of this recently announced relationship are available, but it is assumed that one of the major reasons for Kirin's courting Tropicana was to assure itself of supplies of high-quality orange juice.

In spite of these affiliations, however, it is interesting to note that companies like Snow and Kirin are still purchasing imported juice concentrate through large trading companies and not directly on their own, although under the terms of liberalization they are allowed to do so. Whether Japanese food processors will eventually bypass the large trading companies and purchase concentrate directly from overseas suppliers is a key question for the

Japanese juice industry whose resolution will have impacts not only on Japanese consumers but also on overseas suppliers of juice products. The origin of the trading companies' involvement in juice imports is linked to the manner in which juice import restrictions were enforced by the Japanese government. If the general trading companies are successful at maintaining their current role in handling juice imports, it will be a manifest indication of their economic and political power, as well as of their ability to provide functional services for their business clients.

Juice Import Liberalization and Japanese Trading Companies

One of the most intriguing of all Japanese organizations is the general trading company, or *sogo shosha*. The six largest of these are the linchpins of industrial groupings known as *kigyo shudan*, which are the latter-day descendants of the prewar *zaibatsu* (Kojima and Ozawa 1984). The history of the *zaibatsu* and how they evolved into *kigyo shudan* is a fascinating topic, but it would require a lengthy discussion not of central concern to the arguments covered here. What is vital to the current discussion is that the *kigyo shudan* exist, that the *sogo shosha* play an important role within them, and that these trading companies have become some of the most important companies in the world. As Yoshino and Lifson recount:

> A *sogo shosha* is like no other type of company. It is not defined by the products it handles or even by the particular services it performs, for it offers a broad and changing array of goods and functions. Its business goals are equally elusive, for maximization of profits from each transaction is clearly not the major goal, at either the operating or philosophical level. There are really no other comparable firms, although important business and government leaders in the United States and elsewhere have become convinced that there should be. . . .
>
> These six companies (the largest *sogo shosha*) affect the lives of most participants in the world economy. From the oil used to cook french fries at a local fast food restaurant to subway cars running beneath our streets, products passing through their hands are all around us. *Collectively, they are the largest purchaser of U.S. exports in the world, accounting for 10 percent of our overseas sales, 4 percent of world trade,* and influencing the jobs and fortunes of tens of millions of people all over the world (Yoshino and Lifson 1986: 2, emphasis added).

One of the major functions of the *sogo shosha* for the Japanese economy has been to locate and import raw materials (Tsurumi 1976), a vital task in a resource-dependent country like Japan. This function includes the importation of agricultural commodities and semiprocessed foods, which the trading companies sell to domestic food manufacturers. It was thus inevitable that the Japanese government would use these trading companies to implement juice concentrate import quotas. The Japanese government, as it continues to do with many other commodities, assigned import quotas to general trading companies and a handful of other importers, such as *Zen-noh*. While this practice has been terminated for apple and grape juice, the Japanese government has never publicized the size of past import quotas in either absolute or relative quantities. However, an appreciation for the role of the *sogo shosha* in juice trade can be had by listing their trading relationships.

The six major *sogo shosha* are predominant among the buyers of apple and grape juice concentrate imported into Japan during 1989, the last full year of preliberalization imports (see Tables 8.8 and 8.9). In the vast majority of cases, an overseas supplier sold product to a single Japanese buyer. This type of exclusivity in purchasing arrangements is a noteworthy practice, for it is not followed by the *sogo shosha's* domestic customers. Japanese food processors who buy juice concentrate from trading companies commonly make purchases from at least two different trading companies and renew contracts yearly. Although there is a tendency to return to the same source, in large part because of the necessity of maintaining trust and communication between buyer and seller, Japanese domestic firms are understandably wary about placing all of their business in the hands of one supplier.

One problem trading companies now face is that in an era of liberalization, domestic buyers and overseas sellers are no longer obligated to trade through companies that hold an import quota. This became especially problematic in 1992, when orange juice trade was liberalized. It would be in the obvious economic interest of a trading company to preserve its position in the juice trade. Although it is impossible to determine precisely what the possible strategies for doing so are and which one(s) the trading companies will use, the current situation in apple juice trade may offer some insights.

As mentioned previously, apple and grape juice imports into Japan were liberalized on 1 April 1990. One of the most amazing subsequent events has been the colossal increase in the volume of apple juice concentrate imports into Japan. In 1989, 14,867,969 liters of apple juice were imported into Japan. In the following year the number expanded to 42,723,691 liters, or an increase of almost 300 percent (Table 8.10). This increase is all the more amazing when one remembers that liberalization did not commence until

Table 8.8. Interfirm Relationships in International Apple Juice Trade (Preliberalization—1989)

Country	Overseas Maker	Japanese Trading Company
New Zealand	Apple and Pear Marketing Board	Mitsui Bussan[a]
Poland	Agros	Mitsui Bussan[a]
Chile	Prodassa	Mitsui Bussan[a]
	Agrona	Nissho Iwai[a]
	S.B.A.	Toushoku
	Iansa	Marubeni[a]
West Germany	Elunde Bando	Mitsui Bussan[a]
	Big Apple	Nissho Iwai[a]
	Jyawky	Nissho Iwai[a]
	Mein Fruits	Nisshin Tsusho
	Dein Ta	Nisshin Tsusho
United States	Shonan	Mitsubishi Shoji[a]
	Seneka	Itochu Shoji, Nissho Iwai[a], Marubeini[a]
	Barley	Nissho Iwai[a], Toushoku
	Hanson	Toushoku
	High Country	Nissho Iwai[a]
	A.D. Lance	Nisshin Tsusho
	The Brother	Nisshin Tsusho
	Tree Top	Takasago Kouryou
	Continental	Ogawa Kouryou
China	Santosho	Mitsubishi Shoji[a]
	Nyuzan	Toushoku
Austria	Staiyaobusto	Itochu Shoji
	Raohi	Nissho Iwai[a], Kumiai Boeki, Ogawa Kouryou
	Sugan	Nissho Iwai[a]
	Yo	J. B. Honda
Hungary	Bekestchaba	Itochu Shoji
	Elgihaza	Itochu Shoji
	Peco	Marubeini[a]
	Osuheigt	Marubeini[a]
Australia	Maryland	Itochu Shoji
	Reitona	Itochu Shoji, Kumiai Boeki
Argentina	Zumosu	Nissho Iwai[a], Toushoku
France	Bernier	Nissho Iwai[a]
Italy	Trent Walter	Marubeini[a]
South Africa	Apple Tyser	Nisshin Tsusho
Brazil	Subaran	Takasago Kouryou
Spain	Nufuri	Ogawa Kouryou

Note: Spellings may not be standard because of difficulties translating from Japanese phonetics.

[a]Indicates one of the six largest *sogo shosha*.

Table 8.9. Interfirm Relationships in International Grape Juice Trade
(Preliberalization—1989)

Country	Overseas Maker	Japanese Trading Company
United States	Seneca	Mitsui Bussan[a], Nissho Iwai[a]
	Mirune	Mitsui Bussan[a], Nissho Iwai[a], Itochu Shoji, Toushoku, Ogawa Kouryou
	Yakima Valley	Mitsui Bussan[a], Mitsubishi Shoji[a], Kumiai Boeki, Itochu Shoji, Nissho Iwai[a], Toushoku
	Bydel	Itochu Shoji
	Cliff Star	Nissho Iwai[a], Toushoku
	Brague	Nissho Iwai[a], Toushoku
	Welch	Nisshin Tsusho
	WAF	Meikyo Shoji
	Angel Lance	Meikyo Shoji
	Tree Top	Takasago Kouryou
Austria	Raohi	Itochu Shoji, Kumiai Boeki
	Eebu Star	Itochu Shoji, Kumiai Boeki
Australia	Maryland	Itochu Shoji, Kumiai Boeki
	Benford	Meikyo Shoji
Brazil	Subaran	Takasago Kouryou

Note: Spellings may not be standard because of difficulties translating from Japanese phonetics.

[a]Indicates one of the six largest *sogo shosha*.

April 1 of 1990, which means that this phenomenal growth took place during a nine month period.

A number of considerations make this increase even more amazing. To begin with, while grape juice imports have increased during the same time frame, the increase has not been nearly as large as in the case of apple juice. Another point of interest is that data obtained from MAFF indicate that domestic consumption of apple juice in 1990 was down slightly from 1989, from 49,757 concentrate ton equivalents (1:5 ratio) to 48,397 tons. Thus, the tremendous increase in apple juice purchases cannot be attributed to a release of pent-up demand. Nor could it have been caused by a severe shortfall in domestic supplies of apple juice, for a typhoon in Aomori prefecture, by far the dominant apple producing region in Japan, in the fall of 1990 led to a surge in the volume of apples going to processing facilities.

Another possible explanation could be that prices were so low that buyers purchased juice to stock up in anticipation of higher prices in the near future. While information on apple juice prices from around the world is difficult to obtain, prices for "juicers" in Washington state, the major apple producing region in the United States, went from $50 a ton during the spring and summer of 1990 to $100 a ton by December because of a very good pro-

Table 8.10. Apple Juice Import Volume into Japan, 1989–1990 (in liters)

Country	1989 December	1989 Calendar Year	1990 December	1990 Calendar Year
China	11,240	216,913	—	1,301,608
Israel	—	—	—	222,643
Belgium	—	18,410	—	—
Holland	—	—	—	3,000
Italy	—	—	—	378,086
France	—	67,081	—	25,530
West Germany	508,409	5,890,824	94,980	4,049,129
Spain	—	13,200	37,504	238,299
Austria	280,162	1,560,291	211,266	4,969,946
Hungary	—	20,900	—	2,251,516
Turkey	243	6,383	—	334,961
Canada	—	3,825	—	5,865
United States	119,325	2,680,410	1,074,857	14,110,904
Chile	—	224,479	674,934	4,274,962
Argentina	—	367,041	47,644	2,838,569
Mozambique	64,922	26,481	—	—
South Africa	—	412,592	125,120	2,704,489
Australia	13,310	1,210,383	—	1,525,567
New Zealand	—	2,037,106	9,236	3,480,617
Western Samoa	—	111,650	—	—
Total	997,611	14,867,969	2,275,541	42,723,691

Source: Ministry of Finance.

Note: Apple juice imports liberalized on 1 April 1991.

duction year in terms of quality and a healthy increase in overseas shipment of fresh apples. Yet the frenzied importation of apple juice into Japan continued into December 1990 (see Table 8.10). Shipments of apple juice to Japan in December of 1989 had been 997,611 liters, but increased to 2,275,541 liters in December of 1990, with almost half, 1,074,857 liters, coming from the United States. It is possible that importers had already made commitments to purchase this product, but that would be curious behavior given that Japanese trading companies have traditionally not made commitments to purchase overseas goods without lining up potential customers first and that by December of 1990, 40,000,000 liters of apple juice had already been imported into Japan during that year.

One possible explanation for this curious phenomenon, suggested by a high-ranking member of an agricultural cooperative, is that Japanese trading companies are attempting to sign exclusive marketing contracts with potential overseas suppliers of apple juice. One of the unique properties of apples, when compared with grapes and citrus fruits, is that they are grown in diverse climates throughout the Northern and Southern hemispheres. Given that juice processing technology is well developed and comparatively easy to purchase, it is conceivable that the dramatic surge in apple juice imports is the consequence of a business strategy on the part of the Japanese general trading companies to assure themselves a continuing role in juice imports.

Of course, there can be no conclusive evidence to prove this hypothesis, short of access to privileged company documents. However, it would be an understandable development and one that needs to be investigated in more depth, not only for the insights it could provide into the nature of the international trade regime in food products, but also for the direct consequences this development could have on events in the United States and Japan. For example, in Japan there was a large stock of frozen apple juice concentrate for which there was no immediate demand. Who was holding it? How and when did they release it into the marketplace? What was the effect on juice concentrate prices in Japan? What impact did this have on domestic apple juice production and the profitability of Japanese apple farms? What about overseas apple juice makers who had rather high expectations about trade with Japan? What were the economic consequences for them and what were the political repercussions on Japanese foreign trade relations?

Conclusions

The Japanese juice market is volatile and competitive, and it is likely to remain that way for the immediate future. The ongoing process of liberalization is creating a great deal of uncertainty for the managers of the food processing and trading firms that have a stake in the juice market. For this reason it is difficult to predict the future of the Japanese juice industry.

Certainly, liberalization affords an opportunity for non-Japanese firms to establish a foothold in the Japanese market, and some are attempting to do so. Perhaps the most celebrated case is Cargill. This well-known multinational firm has already established feed and fertilizer plants in Japan, and through a subsidiary known as Cargill Foods Japan has announced plans to construct a major warehouse for handling beef it will import directly into Japan (*Nihon Keizai Shinbun* 1991). Much of the frozen orange juice concentrate imported into Japan is currently purchased from Cargill, and it would be reasonable to hypothesize that after liberalization Cargill will make an attempt to handle imports of frozen orange juice concentrate into Japan on its own.

However, Cargill may be an exceptional case, in part because of its size and in part because its specialty lies in supplying inputs to commodity pro-

ducers and food processors. The strategy most non-Japanese food processors are currently using is to establish relationships with Japanese partners. The time and capital required to set up production and distribution
facilities in Japan, which has an old, saturated, and competitive marketplace, is too prohibitive for most foreign firms. Working together, Japanese
and overseas firms can take advantage of each others' strengths to ensure
that the resulting joint venture will survive the era of instability in Japanese
food markets. The partnerships that survive the current turmoil will be in a
strong position to secure solid market shares not only in the U.S. and Japanese markets but also in other markets around the world. This scenario is
not farfetched. It is exactly the pattern that has been unfolding in a number
of other industries, including automobiles and steel.

What is more difficult to predict is what effect these relationships will
have on these firms' employees, as well as on farms and other businesses that
engage in commerce with them. Small, locally based firms may be put into
an increasingly difficult bargaining position because of their comparative
inability to act globally. Even in cases where Japanese and American partners remain legally independent of one another, it is possible that the more
successful relationships will result in greater coordination of activities and
information, which in turn should give these firms a more powerful bargaining position vis-à-vis suppliers and clients.

One final question is what will become of the *sogo shosha's* role in the international juice trade and, eventually, in international food products trade
in general. Certainly, the economic viability of these firms in the long run is
not in question. What is debatable is whether they will decide that it is important for their overall profitability to do what is necessary to maintain
their position as agricultural commodity and food brokers between Japanese and American firms. It is telling that none of the Japanese businessmen
interviewed for this study reported that their firms had plans to begin directly importing juice concentrate from abroad. The services the trading
companies can provide, in particular information gathering, are too valuable for domestically based firms to forgo at the moment. In addition, the
sogo shosha may also be flexing their economic muscle in the international
juice-trade arena. If the trading companies make a concerted effort to preserve their position in international agricultural trade and succeed, which is
a distinct possibility, the emerging world food order and the relationship of
consumers, workers, and small producers to it will be very different than if
they do not. Put another way, the future structure of the global food order
will most definitely depend, in part, on the Japanese trading companies'
role in organizing trade in agricultural commodities and food products specifically.

Notes

The research carried out for this article was supported by the U.S. Department of Agriculture under agreement number 88–33574–4054, by a fellowship from the Japanese Science and Technology Agency administered by the National Research Institute of Agricultural Economics, and by the Japan International Agricultural Council. Any opinions, findings, conclusions, or recommendations expressed in this publication are those of the author and do not necessarily reflect the views of any of these institutions.

1. Like all prefectural cooperatives, the Ehime Cooperative belongs to the national association of cooperatives known as *Nokyo* in Japan. Virtually all Japanese farm households belong to this organization, which in postwar Japan has played a central role in providing capital, inputs, marketing services, and other forms of assistance to farmers.

Bibliography

Bale, Malcolm D., and Bruce L. Greenshiels. 1978. "Japanese agricultural distortions and their welfare value." *American Journal of Agricultural Economics* 60, 1: 59–64.

Bertrand, Jean-Pierre, Vincent Leclercq, and Catherine Laurent. 1983. *Le monde du soja*. Paris: Editions la Découverte.

Coyle, William. 1983. *Japan's Feed-Livestock Economy*. Foreign Agriculture Report. Department of Agriculture.

——. 1987. "Information sources and research completed—Pacific Rim beef export opportunities." Pp. 120–128 in William D. Gorman and Gail A. Welsh (eds.), *Research Opportunities in Beef Export Markets: U.S. and Pacific Rim Opportunities*. Tucson: University of Arizona.

Dore, Ronald. 1986. *Flexible Rigidities*. Stanford, Calif.: Stanford University Press.

Economic Research Service. 1983. "High value agricultural exports: U.S. opportunities in the 1980s." Foreign Agriculture Economic Report no. 188. Washington, D.C.: Department of Agriculture.

——. 1990. *Food Marketing Review, 1989–90*. Agricultural Economic Report no. 639. Washington, D.C.: Department of Agriculture.

Friedmann, Harriet. 1982. "The political economy of food: The rise and fall of the international food order." *American Journal of Sociology* 88: S248–S286.

Friedmann, Harriet, and Philip McMichael. 1989. "Agriculture and the state system." *Sociologia Ruralis* 29, 2: 93–117.

Gallo, Anthony E. 1986. "Food marketing—from farm to table." *National Food Review* (United States Department of Agriculture/Economic Research Service) 35 (Fall): 1–7.

George, Aurelia. 1981. "The Japanese farm lobby and agricultural decision making." Australia-Japan Research Center Research Paper no. 80.

George, Aurelia, and Yujiro Hayami. 1986. "The politics of agricultural protection in Japan." Pp. 91–110 in Kym Anderson and Yujiro Hayami (eds.), *The Political Economy of Agricultural Protection*. Sydney, Australia: Allen and Unwin.

Goldberg, Raymond A., and Richard C. McGinity (eds.). 1979. *Agribusiness Management for Developing Countries—Southeast Asian Corn System and American and Japanese Trends Affecting It*. Cambridge, Mass.: Ballinger Publishing Co.

Hamilton, Martha. 1972. *The Great American Grain Robbery and Other Stories*. Washington, D.C.: Agribusiness Accountability Project.

Ishiboda, Seiro. 1989. *Sakerui shokuhin sangyo no seisan, hanbai shea (Production and Market Shares in the Food and Liquor Industry)*. Tokyo: Nikkan Keizai Tsushin Sha.

Kada, Ryohei. 1989. "Boeki to nougyou (Trade and agriculture)." Pp. 32–41 in *Tsu de miru showa nougyoshi (A View of the History of Showa Agriculture in Charts)*. Osaka: Fumin Kyoukai.

Kojima, Kiyoshi, and Terutomo Ozawa. 1984. *Japan's General Trading Companies: Merchants of Economic Development*. Paris: OECD.

Ministry of Agriculture, Forestry, and Fisheries—Japan. 1989. "Japan's agricultural trade." *Japan's Agricultural Review* 17.

Morgan, Dan. 1980. *Merchants of Grain*. New York: Penguin Books.

Nakajima, Masamichi. 1991. "Seiryouinryougyou no kozo (Structure of the soft drink industry)." Pp. 131–216 in *Shokuhin sangyo no kozo bunseki (Structural Analysis of the Food Industry)*. Chouki Kinyuu Series no. 72. Tokyo: Nourinsuisan Chouki Kinyuu Kyoukai.

Nihon Keizai Shinbun. 1988. *Japanese Companies*. Tokyo: Nihon Keizai Shinbun.

———. 1991. "Shokuhin Gyoukai." *Foods Business World* 28 March: 11.

Okimoto, Daniel I. 1989. *Between MITI and the Market*. Stanford, Calif.: Stanford University Press.

Stockwin, J. A. A. 1982. *Japan: Divided Politics in a Growth Economy*. London: Weidenfield and Nicolson.

Tallent, David R. 1983. "Japan's trade barriers see problems for U.S. citrus exporters." *Foreign Agriculture* 21, 10: 21.

Toyo Keizai. 1990. *Japan Company Handbook—Winter 1990*. Tokyo: Toyo Keizai.

Tsurumi, Yoshi. 1976. *The Japanese Are Coming*. Cambridge, Mass.: Ballinger Publishing Co.

Vogel, Ezra F. 1980. *Japan as Number 1*. New York: Harper Colophon Books.

Yoshino, M. Y., and Thomas B. Lifson. 1986. *The Invisible Link*. Cambridge, Mass.: MIT Press.

9 Opening Economies and Closing Markets: Latin American Agriculture's Difficult Search for a Place in the Emerging Global Order

Luis Llambi

Latin America is experiencing a profound agricultural restructuring in the transition from an inward-oriented import-substitution industrialization to an outward-oriented free-market growth strategy. Two forces are inducing this process. The first is the emerging world order, itself a result of opposing trends leading to increased market globalization and trading bloc formation. The second is the adjustment and restructuring policies resulting from the debt crisis imposed by the International Monetary Fund and the World Bank.

Here I address three main issues. First, how are the whole globalization and bloc formation processes affecting Latin American agricultural systems? Second, can the outward-oriented growth strategy (as it stands today· in most Latin American countries) produce economic development while achieving other national goals, such as long-term self-reliance in the capital accumulation process, political sustainability, and social equity? Third, in the current world order are there other options still open to Latin America?

To tackle these issues, I depart from the standard international trade theories, which focus on comparative advantage and surplus productive capacity to explain exchange flows across national borders. Instead, I develop a political economy perspective, which highlights the strategies adopted by national governments, multilateral agencies, and transnational corporations trying to shape the conditions in which these flows take place, within the constraints imposed by natural, political, and economic structures.

Furthermore, a critical review of Latin American agricultural trade relationships will assess the external constraints affecting both the internationally traded commodities and the domestically oriented agricultural sectors. "Opening up" economies in a context of shrinking, although increasingly global, markets is an option full of hazards. The current global transition is an uncertain environment for the kind of "structural adjustment" imposed on Latin America, to say the least. Current trends in bloc formation also suggest risks characterized by increasing "closing market" protectionist measures, fears of a Fortress Europe, Japan's insurmountable culturally embedded trade barriers, and the U.S. Super 301 provision of the 1988 Omnibus Trade and Competition Act. Thus, I call for an alternative mode of insertion of Latin America into the emerging global economy.

The Outward-oriented Growth Strategy

The Transition

From 1945 to 1971, the Bretton Woods and GATT agreements set the rules for the post–World War II economic order. Fixed exchange rates and reductions in tariffs were to complete the efforts of the industrialized countries to attain high growth rates through the Keynesian policies of the welfare state in tandem with increasing industrial productivity. In other words, state intervention in domestic markets supported a free-trade ideology in world affairs (Lipietz 1987; Kenney, Kloppenburg, and Cowan 1989; Gereffi 1989). In 1971, the U.S. abandonment of the Bretton Woods agreement impelled the search for a new world order and provoked a transition characterized by volatile exchange rates and increased uncertainty.

Underpinning these developments, profound changes took place in production techniques. Sayle characterized this process as "a transition from 'energy-intensive' to 'knowledge-intensive' industries" (quoted in Gilpin 1987: 383). In the meantime, Latin America experienced the decline of the inward-oriented import-substitution industrialization strategy. This strategy has frequently been accused of leading to the stagnation of most Latin American agricultural sectors while creating food dependency.

As Gomes and Perez (1979) asserted for the first time, import substitution did not necessarily mean in Latin America that the whole agricultural sector became depressed or stagnated. In fact, during the last decades of its full application, while a considerable restructuring took place within traditional export sectors, some nontraditional agroexports flourished. Yet from the mid-1960s onward, an industrially biased policy of exchange rates combined with spiraling inflation led to severely overvalued currencies. These policies hampered the agricultural export thrust, encouraged food imports, and aggravated the balance-of-payments deficit. Furthermore, during the 1960s some Latin American countries promoted policies to stimulate nontraditional exports, such as manufactured and value-added mineral and agricultural products (Colaiacovo 1990). However, the catalyst for this full-blown policy shift was the debt crisis in 1982. Consequently, within the context of the "structural" crisis brought about by the impairment of previous growth strategy, and swelling debt burdens, each country had to find new forms of insertion within an emerging world order.

The New Growth Strategy and Its Rationale

The policy recipe for outward-oriented growth consists of the elements of fiscal discipline, an open economy, and the neoliberal state. The first is a concern that budget constraints are respected *ex ante*, implying fiscal discipline and government austerity measures (Williamson 1990). The second is based on three main policy prescriptions: (1) a competitive exchange rate through currency devaluations; (2) a commercial liberalization policy, with unilateral tariff reductions and elimination of all qualitative trade restrictions; and (3) financial liberalization to guarantee free entry of foreign direct investment in more profitable areas. Three basic assumptions underlie this unilateral trade and capital liberalization component: that each country should specialize in the production of those export items that have evident advantages of location, natural resources, or low labor costs in order to increase foreign exchange earnings and enhance import and debt payment capabilities; that foreign direct investment is necessary to finance the new technologies that will lead to efficient competition in world markets; and that "if 'barriers' are removed then the 'correct' pattern of trade will ensue" (Kuttner 1990: 39).

The state is viewed as a market developer and as a guardian of the principle of "free" market mechanisms. This doctrinal component does not necessarily rule out *all* state intervention to curb disturbances in free market operations. Neither is it the nineteenth-century laissez-faire liberal state, nor the Keynesian state of the post–World War II era, but a "neoliberal" state whose basic assumption is that more free trade is invariably better than less.

Another assumption underlies the whole open-market cum free-trade doctrine, as applied to debtor countries in the currently emerging world order. If debtors are to take advantage of opening up their economies to international trade it is assumed that the global economy must already be based on unhindered, "perfectly" competitive markets and, if not, creditor nations should lower trade barriers to open up their markets for debtor nations in return (Gilpin 1987). Consequently, to assess the prospects of an outward-oriented growth strategy, particularly in Latin America, it is necessary to analyze how these markets really work as well as what are their trends.

A Comparative Commodity Circuit Analysis

In this section, Latin American agricultural trade relationships, both importing and exporting, are analyzed in a commodity-circuit perspective (Gereffi 1989; cf. Hopkins and Wallerstein 1986). The objective here is to discern some common market structures and trends that underlie these commodity groups. Particular emphasis is given to the strategic interactions by which nation-states, transnational corporations (TNCs), and multilateral agencies (each one acting on behalf of its own interests) try to shape international trade flows. Additionally, some historical case-study materials are presented to provide illustrations of the processes by which international competitiveness in particular commodities were achieved by some Latin American countries vis-à-vis First World economies.

A preliminary distinction must be made between the patterns of agricultural trade and specialization that characterize Third World countries, especially in Latin America, and those that have characterized First World exporters. To this end, three different commodity groups and their respective trade relationships can be identified: "tropical" agricultural commodities; "temperate" food staples and agricultural raw materials; and, so-called nontraditional agricultural exports.

Most Latin American countries had specialized as producers of tropical agricultural commodities by the end of World War II as a result of the colonial division of labor. From 1945 to 1971, i.e., the period in which the Bretton Woods and General Agreement on Tariffs and Trade (GATT) set up the basic rules of international trade, some First World countries had achieved undisputed international competitiveness as producers of temperate food staples. Most Latin American countries have been trying to develop international competitiveness in such products as off-season fresh fruits, vegetables and flowers, "exotic" plants, and live tropical fishes since the post–Bretton Woods flexible exchange-rate system.

Tropical Agricultural Commodities: The Comparative
Disadvantages of a Colonial Division of Labor

Tropical commodity plantation economies, predominant in some regions of lowland Latin America, emerged in response to an increasing international demand for tropical foods and agricultural raw materials. In contrast to other productive forms, plantation lands were frequently owned by large foreign enterprises.

Coffee, tea, cocoa, rubber, jute, sisal, and bananas are the typical plantation products from the tropical Third World. In spite of their historical prominence in the development of long-distance trade, currently these commodities account for only 3 percent of international trade (GATT 1989). However, they provide an important source of foreign currency as well as jobs and income for rural populations.

After the Great Depression of the 1930s, the large export plantations experienced radical restructuring of their productive organization. Stirred by increased domestic and international demand for tropical commodities and fearing social upheaval brought about by agrarian reforms during the import-substitution period, the TNCs developed a new strategy aimed at concentrating capital in the final links of the agro-industrial chain. Furthermore, this strategy aimed at increasing vertical integration through various forms of contract arrangements with "independent" growers and central processing and distributing units.

The provision of credit to planters, the introduction of productive technical packages, and an oligopolistic control of both the domestic and international markets provided these corporations with great leverage to control both the productive and exchange conditions within exporting countries. TNCs control market outlets within importing countries through global sourcing, product differentiation, and the development of market "niches" (Gargiulo 1989; Kuwayama 1988). The main concern for governments of importing countries has been to protect their markets from tropical imports that are not, or cannot, be produced domestically. Therefore, in contrast to most First World temperate agricultural exports (in which tariffs are no longer the main concern at GATT negotiations), high tariffs are still in force for tropical agricultural exports. Overall, the markets of tropical agricultural products have been characterized by unstable boom-and-bust behavior. Furthermore, since 1945 tropical Third World governments have seen their terms of trade deteriorate vis-à-vis manufacturing imports from the advanced capitalist countries (UN ECLA 1989).

The main reason for this deterioration is the steady growth of production due to the adoption of improved technical packages. Also, the incorporation of new producing areas and new exporting countries in search of badly needed international currency has added to this situation. Hence, while high tariffs are a disincentive for demand on the "affluent" markets of the advanced capitalist world, supply has been growing steadily, giving rise to what is usually referred to in economic jargon as a "low income elasticity of demand."

Import-substitution industrialization, as a means to diversify production, was the main strategy designed by Third World countries to try to break the curse of excessive tropical product specialization. Other strategies were the creation of state trading companies to try to diminish transnational control of main currency-generating exports and exporter "cartels" and "international commodity agreements" between producer and consumer countries to give markets some long-term stability.

Yet, with the advent of the "neoliberal" open-economy strategy, state trading companies were identified as one of the main targets of privatization. Furthermore, most producer cartels and international commodity agreements are no longer active or are disappearing in the conditions created by the post–Bretton Woods era of market globalization and trade bloc formation. Coffee and bananas provide two historical illustrations of how these forces have been in operation in the tropical commodity circuits.

Transnational Forces and Multinational
Agreements in the Coffee Market

As with many other tropical agricultural commodities, coffee is an example of a division of labor in which the tropical countries produce the raw material while First World–based transnational corporations control the processing and marketing operations in their home countries. Although Brazil, Colombia, Indonesia, and Mexico are by far the major producers, coffee is an important source of hard currency and national income for fifty tropical countries throughout the world. In contrast, the European Community (EC) and the United States, which together account for 45 percent of world coffee consumption, control between 55 and 60 percent of world sales mainly through six transnational processing and trading corporations.

Introduced in the New World during the eighteenth century, coffee experienced a swift but steady expansion. From the mid-nineteenth century onward, U.S. consumers fueled an extraordinary surge in international coffee prices. Since then, Brazil has become the world's major coffee producer, despite European incentives for coffee plantations in their former colonies to break Brazil's control of the market (Renard 1989).

The export boom, with the exception of occasional dips, lasted until the Great Depression of the 1930s. Chronic oversupply and climatic instability have since become central features of the international coffee market. In 1962, the first International Coffee Agreement was signed by twenty-six exporting and thirteen importing countries. Since then, four agreements have been signed (in 1962, 1968, 1976, and 1983) achieving control of 90 to 95 percent of the world market through a system of national quotas.

Yet, during the 1970s and 1980s rapidly increasing world supply in tandem with a slowly rising or stagnant demand led to ever-growing surpluses, thus pushing prices downward. In 1975 Brazilian production was affected by a severe frost. Brazil lost control of the stock levels, which led to increased disagreements between new exporters (mainly African) and old exporters (mainly Latin American) over the quota allocation mechanism (Gilbert 1987). This lack of agreement caused Brazil to lose interest in the producer/consumer International Coffee Agreement (ICA) and to create a producers' cartel with some of its Latin American counterparts.

In 1977 Brazil, Colombia, Mexico, Venezuela, Panama, and Jamaica reached an agreement in Bogota to coordinate their sales and to set up a fund to support prices. The Bogota Group, as it was called, operated in the London and New York futures markets by establishing large long positions. There reached a point, however, when financial resources were insufficient to both maintain stocks and service their debt. So in 1980 the group attempted to absorb the losses and to support new stocks through the creation of a multinational trading corporation: PANCAFE. However, in September 1980 the United States made as a condition to its participation in a new ICA the dissolution of PANCAFE (Renard 1989).

From 1974 to 1984 a strong dollar provided coffee producers with higher real prices; however, the United States felt that the 1983 ICA was a price-raising rather than a price-stabilizing device. In 1988 the United States announced that it would quit the agreement if nonmember states did not join and decided not to support any market intervention mechanism that made them pay double the spot market price paid by other consumer countries. No agreement was reached, and the quota provisions under the ICA were suspended in 1989. The large stocks held by both the exporting and consumer countries were released, causing a sharp drop in coffee prices.

Now, the market is basically controlled by the hedging and speculative strategies of transnational trading corporations on the futures and spot markets. At the consumer-outlet level, global sourcing, that is "diversifying supplies and playing off one region against another" (Friedmann and McMichael 1989: 28), product differentiation based on the promotion of brand names, and product innovation (e.g., soluble coffee, freeze-dried coffee, etc.) are the main strategies of control (Girvan 1987; cf. Maizels 1984, 1987).

The Comparative Disadvantages of Being a "Banana" Republic

Bananas have been grown for export since the 1870s by large corporate plantations in the humid tropics on the Caribbean coast of Central America and Mexico (Grigg 1974). Until the 1940s, the United Fruit Company, mainly based in its Central American possessions, held an almost undisputed world monopoly on both production and marketing. After World War II, the monopoly market structure receded and was replaced by a cartel formed by three large and three medium transnational enterprises (Clairmonte and Cavanagh 1984; Ruhl 1983).

Within the context of social upheaval and agrarian reform brought on by the later stages of import substitution, the large transnational corporations designed a new strategy encompassing a radical restructuring of their productive operations. The agricultural stage, being the riskier and less profitable part of the agro-industrial chain, was relinquished by selling or leasing the land to domestic planters and signing long-term contracts for the sale of produce and the purchase of inputs. Meanwhile, capital was injected into the packing, transportation, and distribution operations to enhance productivity and reach wider markets (Carles 1987). Global sourcing and brand differentiation were to complement this strategy by transforming the original commodity into a less-valued, and therefore easily substituted, product (Girvan 1987).

In 1974, some Central American countries, together with Colombia and Ecuador, the two major South American exporters, took advantage of the relative tightness of the market by forming a cartel: the Union of Banana Exporting Countries (UBEC). As a result, the Central American countries were in the position to raise export levies on the TNCs; and in Colombia and Ecuador, where local ownership is more prevalent, an increase in export prices was made possible.

The 1982 world recession stagnated demand and led to oversupply, deteriorating the UBEC bargaining power vis-à-vis transnational corporations (Girvan 1987). More recently, the banana-producing countries lost their other main buffer mechanism through the dissolution of most state marketing companies. The current ideological shift in favor of the beneficial effects of the "invisible hand" market mechanism was seen as a source of this dissolution.

Temperate Agricultural Commodities: Bargaining Power
and International Competitiveness in the First World

The "temperate" agricultural commodities can be divided into three subgroups: feed and food grains (essentially wheat among the cereals, and soybeans among the oilseeds); livestock products (mainly bovine meat and dairy products); and easily substituted agro-industrial products (mainly sugar and cotton fibers). These agricultural commodities have few things in common, except that they are all oriented toward the mass-consumption markets in which the advanced capitalist countries (in particular the United States and the EC) have achieved undisputed international competitiveness.

The 1930s New Deal national price support and supply management programs to save the family farm (Friedmann 1989, 1990) and the 1954 P.L. 480 Agricultural Trade Development and Assistance Act to reduce domestic agricultural surplus mark the start of an astonishing increase in productivity. This increase led the United States to become, in less than three decades, the world's largest exporter of wheat and soybeans, as well as an important producer of livestock products and agricultural raw materials. The EC's Common Agricultural Policy, founded on the principles of food security and preferential trade with its former colonies, was also the basis of spectacular agricultural growth, which in the 1970s converted the EC into a major exporter of wheat and dairy products. In the 1980s the EC became a net exporter of sugar and a significant producer of beef and poultry products.

As a result of this three-pronged strategy during the last five decades of domestic farm support, import substitution, and export agricultural promotion, some of the markets of the tropical exporting countries of Latin America closed. But more significantly, some of the markets of the Southern Cone temperate exporters, Argentina and Uruguay in particular, were eroded.

First-World Grain Oversupply versus
Third World Food Dependence

Once self-sufficient in grain staples (maize, rice, and even wheat), most Third World countries are currently importing significant quantities of food and feed grains (mostly wheat, maize, and sorghum) to provide for their rapidly expanding urban populations. In the 1930s wheat, in particular, was produced by most, and exported by some, countries. Today wheat represents 45 percent of all Latin American agricultural imports, Argentina remaining as the only net wheat exporter in the region (UN ECLA 1989; Vidali 1989).

The extraordinary productivity increases of U.S. and EC farms in the last fifty years, which other countries have been unable to duplicate, only partly explain this turnaround. U.S. and EC success is also linked to their long-standing and deliberate policies of protecting their domestic producers while dumping heavily subsidized grain surpluses on world markets. The origins of this export promotion policy can be traced back to the Marshall Plan and the P.L. 480 Agricultural Trade Development and Assistance Act of 1954. In particular, P.L. 480 allowed the Europeans to pay the United States in devalued currencies for their purchases of U.S. grain (Friedmann 1989). Nevertheless, in the 1950s the Europeans began to perceive food as a security problem and erect barriers to protect their own farmers.

In the 1950s and 1960s P.L. 480 was reformulated to provide food aid to Third World countries. These countries, in turn, welcomed U.S. food aid, because their attention was focused mainly on developing a domestic industrial base. Import substitution of manufactured imports and a cheap food policy targeted for the increasing working- and middle-class urban populations were two primary agendas for developing this base (Gouveia 1990).

From 1947 onward, the GATT became the privileged scenario of a United States versus EC confrontation over world food and agricultural markets. In 1964–1967, at the Kennedy Round negotiations, a truce was signed clearing the way for EC wheat expansionism and U.S. control of the soybean market. Moreover, in 1969, following a contraction of demand, the U.S.-EC wheat agreement became unworkable and the trade war broke out again between the two superpowers (Tubiana 1989).

Yet, by 1971 the United States chalked up the first commercial account deficit in this century. Two devaluations lowered currency expenses for wheat-importing countries while a new grain policy, setting aside areas for wheat production, was aimed at raising domestic prices. Parallel with this policy, an aggressive export promotion program was built by expanding the activities of the Commodity Credit Corporation (CCC) to provide favorable conditions for foreign importers of U.S. commodities and to establish U.S. agricultural trade offices abroad (Byerlee 1987; Robinson 1985). Furthermore, several institutions were created to defend this market penetration policy: the U.S. Feed Grain Council, the U.S. Wheat Associates, and U.S. Agency for International Development (AID) (Stander and Becker 1990; Tubiana 1989).

The Soviet-U.S. grain deals of 1972–1973 inflated international wheat prices, which resulted in even greater food import expenses in the Third World (Gouveia 1990). Luckily, the Green Revolution rescued formerly huge Third World importers, such as Mexico, India, and China, from some of the specters of chronic hunger. Yet, these increased yields resulted in expanded First World stocks and reinforced food grain dependency for countries that did not benefit from the Green Revolution.

In 1980, the grain embargo on Soviet wheat purchases reinforced Third World fears of the United States as an unreliable supplier. Thus, after the embargo, a number of countries took immediate steps to encourage domestic production. Mexico's short-lived staple self-sufficiency policy (so-called SAM), which raised domestic prices and provided credit under favorable conditions to wheat and bean producers, is a good example. As dollar exchange rates rose again, particularly after 1983, the United States set up a new "payment in kind" export promotion program, which further subsidized wheat and flour sales (Paarlberg and Abbot 1986).

As wheat surpluses increased in the world markets, Argentina, unable to match U.S. and EC domestic support programs and export subsidies, saw its market share diminish considerably. Although temporarily relieving food shortages, wheat imports for other Latin American countries depressed domestic production and created a long-term dependence on First World exports (Morrison 1984). Potential large exporters of rice, such as Colombia, Venezuela, and Costa Rica, have seen their domestic staple production shrink as cheap food policies and wheat export subsidies have favored a change in diets toward increased wheat-bread consumption (Byerlee 1987; Gouveia 1990).

The U.S.–Latin American Nondeclared Trade War in the Soy Oil and Animal Feed Markets

Before World War II, the United States imported 40 percent of its fat and vegetable oils from Indonesia, China, and the Philippines. In 1941, the United States established a guaranteed price-support program for soybeans. However, not only were former markets for imported tropical oils closed temporarily for temperate oilseeds (mainly soybeans, but also sunflower and rapeseed), but a guaranteed price support for soybeans was introduced to help replace oilseed imports. From 1945 to 1964, during the Marshall Plan years, the United States shipped soybean products to Europe and introduced the soybean-feedgrain-livestock complex all over the world (De Albuquerque 1989; Friedmann and McMichael 1989). Soy displaced other vegetable oils in margarine manufacture and cooking oil during the 1950s (Bredahl, Schmitz, and Hillman 1987).

In the 1964–1967 Kennedy Round of multilateral negotiations at GATT, the United States achieved an international division of labor in temperate agricultural products, becoming the EC's main soybean supplier in exchange for accepting the EC's domestic protection and export subsidies of wheat (Goodman and Redclift 1989). Even so, as early as 1958 Brazil started a national research program, with U.S. AID financing, as a component of a program to eradicate coffee trees in the Southeast (Bertrand, Laurent, and Leclerq 1984). The U.S. embargo on exports of oilseeds and oilseed products in 1973—imposed to protect its domestic market and to assure the supply for its livestock producers—forced its traditional customers to turn to other oilseeds (Bertrand, Laurent, and Leclerq 1984; Faminov and Hillman 1987).

In the early 1970s Brazil reduced the impact of its former overvalued exchange rate through repeated minidevaluations and offset subsidies, thus creating new incentives for nontraditional exports. Therefore, after the 1973 embargo Brazil was in the position to become a serious competitor to U.S. exporters of soybeans in the European markets.

Meanwhile, the development of new strains, adapted to various ecological conditions, permitted the expansion of the soybean frontier into the Brazilian hinterland (Gargiulo 1989). In the 1970s the crawling peg exchange rate favored Brazilian exports (Bertrand, Laurent, and Leclerq 1984). By 1985 Brazilian exports occupied 40 percent of a world export market that had almost tripled in size (Faminov and Hillman 1987). Argentina also multiplied by sevenfold its soybean production after the 1976 military coup. As a result of the new outward-oriented policy, farm gate prices were raised, export taxes reduced, and marketing privatized. The Soviet Union became Argentina's main trade partner (Bertrand, Laurent, and Leclerq 1984).

Today, the United States, Argentina, and Brazil account for 95 percent of total soybean and soybean product exports, while Japan and the EC are the biggest world customers. About ten processing firms concentrate the processing capacity of soybeans in the United States, Brazil, and Europe (Bertrand, Laurent, and Leclerq 1984). Meanwhile, these firms obtain supplies at lower prices through strategies of global sourcing and trading in vegetable-oil substitutes (Delpeuch 1989).

Since 1947, the primary futures market for trading soybeans has been the Chicago Board of Trade. Five large transnational traders and soybean processors control the market, through their attempts to "lock in" as much soybean crush as possible when processing margins are favorable, and as little as possible when margins are unfavorable. Even so, U.S. agricultural policy (through its level of loan rates), Europe's demand and stocks, the size of the Brazilian and Argentinean crops, and the prices attained by alternative oils (such as palm kernel oil and rapeseed oil) also influence the international prices of the bean (Garramon and De Obschatko 1990). Although the Kennedy Round negotiations dealt a severe blow to Brazil and Argentina, there is an ongoing market competition in soy products.

The Export-Subsidy War in the Meat and Dairy Markets

The intensive production of livestock is a by-product of the U.S. soybean export promotion policies starting from the 1950s (Friedmann 1989). Parallel to the market penetration of soybean oil in the European and Third World markets, the soybean-feedgrain-livestock complex was established. This complex is based on a technical package of feedlot ratios, which significantly reduced fattening time, and on lowered production costs due to low prices in oilseeds and feedgrain production, cheap transport and marketing developments, and advances in veterinary science (Rama and Rello 1979).

For a long time Argentina and Uruguay were Latin America's largest meat exporters. Between 1924 and 1928, Argentina alone contributed 61 percent of world supplies. However, in 1978 Argentina supplied only about 10 percent of the world total, and Uruguay just 3 percent. In the 1930s, England imported 90 percent of Argentinean beef exports and more than half of Uruguay's (Ojala 1985). Today, according to Pineiro, "the developed countries represent three fourths of the world exports in fresh meat" (1988: 9).

Prior to the 1950s, England had an almost undisputed control of the world market by financing production and packing houses in Australia, New Zealand, Argentina, and Uruguay (Rama and Rello 1979). During the 1980s, due to the EC's heavily subsidized meat and dairy production, Uruguay's exports to the EC were reduced from a 70 to 80 percent high during the 1950s to only 10 to 20 percent. Meanwhile, England imported virtually nothing from Latin America, and U.S. exports occupy only 25 percent of the world market (Rama and Rello 1979; Sanderson 1986).

In the 1970s, however, a binational beef production system began in the Mexico-U.S. borderlands: a sort of *maquila* beef industry, in which cattle are raised in Mexico, fed in the United States, and returned to Mexico for slaughter (Sanderson 1989a). Yet, while Mexico's frontier cattle industry is mainly oriented toward the U.S. low-quality beef fast-food market, U.S. domestic production is reserved for the high-quality beef markets in the United States. Following this U.S. strategy, the EC has also created a high-quality beef market for the European producers, while importing low-quality meats destined for intermediate use or for the low-price mass-consumption markets (Green 1990).

In dairy products, only Uruguay in Latin America is still a net exporter, although Argentina also exports small amounts of cheese and Costa Rica exports some butter (UN ECLA 1989). As a result of the many decades of strong EC domestic support programs for its dairy producers, large stocks of dairy products have grown, causing an increasing burden on European taxpayers. Nevertheless, by the end of 1989 export subsidies had virtually wiped out these stocks (GATT 1989).

At the current Uruguay Round of multilateral negotiations, export subsidies are one of the major areas of contention, particularly meat and dairy products. Whereas the EC position recommends a gradualist approach to their reduction, the Cairns group of "temperate" agricultural exporters (a group of nonsubsidized exporters including Argentina, Uruguay, Brazil, Colombia and the United States) seeks a commitment to the elimination of all trade-distorting measures on an agreed-upon schedule (Goodman and Redclift 1989; Huekman 1989; IMF 1990). Behind these seemingly antagonistic positions lie the U.S. need to get rid of its agricultural surplus and the EC's attempt to maintain its preferential trade agreement with its former colonies. For Latin America, whose imports of grains (including oil seeds) amount to 46 percent of all its agricultural imports (adding livestock products this reaches 66 percent), the current export subsidy war is contrary to its long-term interests (Vidali 1989).

The First World's Import-Substitution Strategies in Agro-Industrial Products

Sugarcane and cotton, unlike raw materials produced exclusively in the tropics (e.g., coffee, cocoa, tea, natural rubber, jute, and sisal), are grown in a large number of countries in temperate, subtropical, and tropical climates. For centuries, both commodities were important sources of hard currency for Third World countries and provided cash income and jobs for rural populations. However, in the postwar era, they ceased to fuel growth for these countries: The development of alternative raw materials and the import substitution-cum-export promotion policies of the advanced capitalist countries have undercut Third World export prospects. Sugar and textiles also provide good illustrations of managed trade and market-sharing arrangements favoring the interests of large transnational corporations and selected interest groups in their home-based economies.

"Free" and Managed Trade in the Fiber Markets. In Latin America, Brazil, Mexico, and Argentina are the largest cotton producers. Yet even for Paraguay cotton provides 38 percent of all foreign exchange earnings as well as cash incomes to 140,000 families. In Nicaragua, Guatemala, and El Salvador cotton ranks third after coffee and bananas both in terms of production and exports. In Peru, raw cotton exports account for only 6 to 10 percent of all agricultural exports, mainly because of the price premium commanded by the high value of its long-staple cotton.

Since the end of World War II, global cotton consumption has grown by an annual average of 3.3 percent. However, during the 1930s synthetic fiber substitutes began to compete with natural fibers. Thus, while cotton consumption has continued to increase, its share in the global textile market had fallen to less than 50 percent in the 1980s (Morris 1988). According to Girvan, "Fifteen large companies control between 80 and 90 percent of the world trade, including the exports of developing countries. Some of these firms are integrated backwards into growing, ginning and warehousing and forwards into spinning and weaving, all possess highly sophisticated networks of economic and trading intelligence. These characteristics give them considerable advantages of speed and flexibility in dealing with national marketing organizations in developing cotton-exporting countries" (1987: 17).

The United States is the largest exporter of raw cotton, accounting for about 25 percent of the world total. Since colonial times, cotton has been a major export crop and an important source of income for most southern farmers. However, after the Great Depression, U.S. cotton farmers had to be buffered from world price movements by national policies. Although price supports were an incentive for domestic production, export promotion policies increased their international competitiveness irrespective of economic efficiency considerations. Currently there are three export programs in operation. The first is P.L. 480, which allows sales of cotton and unfinished textiles on long-term credits. The second, introduced in 1980, is the Export Credit Guarantee Program, which finances export sales and provides protection for exporters on nonpayment risks. The third, inaugurated in 1985, is the Immediate Export Credit Guarantee Program, which covers loans to finance cash purchases by less-developed countries (Morris 1988). In 1987, according to Palmeter (1989: 48), all U.S. cotton exports were benefiting from subsidies.

Also in Europe, from the end of World War II until the beginning of the 1980s, cotton consumption suffered a slow decline. Even so, the EC is still an important cotton market for Third World countries, despite the community's support mechanisms, investment modernization grants for agriculture and manufacturing, and production quotas favoring Greece and Spain (the main EC cotton producers) and the associated African, Caribbean, and Pacific (ACP) countries.

International trade in raw cotton remains relatively unhindered by tariff and nontariff barriers. Yet prices are basically manipulated by the speculative elements that predominate in the New York Cotton Exchange futures market. The price of synthetic substitutes often sets the price ceiling of the natural products (Maizels 1984).

Since 1961, the textile and clothing market has been governed by the Multifiber Agreements (MFA). The first agreement, which ran from 1974 to 1977, was drafted at the request of the United States as an exception to the GATT rules. While in principle a multilateral treaty, it was really a set of bilateral agreements allowing importing countries to negotiate quotas individually and to impose quantitative restrictions unilaterally and without penalties. The third MFA expired in 1991. It worked mainly as a market-sharing mechanism protecting the early entrants from the marginal suppliers of the Third World (IMF 1990; Khanna 1990). The mid-sized exporters of Latin America, Brazil and Peru in particular, oppose the extension of the agreement; however, the Asian newly industrializing countries (NICs), which have secured a market niche within the EC and the United States, are adamantly in favor of a fourth treaty.

In the early 1980s, a rapid buildup of stocks and output increases of Brazil, Pakistan and India led to a downward plunge in prices. However, by the mid-1980s cotton consumption recovered from its long downward trend, mainly as a result of the marketing strategies favoring the return to natural and healthy products as opposed to synthetic materials. The 1985–1986 collapse of prices, encouraged by the stockpiling and manipulations of the large international traders, was a reminder as to who really commands the market.

The Bitter Competition over the Sugar Market. Sugarcane, a tropical and subtropical herbaceous perennial, has experienced a wider geographical scenario, a lengthier cultivation history, and a more differentiated production pattern than any other plantation crop in Latin America. Since the early sixteenth century, slave-worked sugarcane plantations were the economic backbone of the Greater Antilles Spanish colonies and Portugal's Brazilian Northeast. During the early nineteenth century, a sugar price boom led to rapid expansion of cane plantations as far south as the Tucuman province in Argentina and as far north as Jalisco state in Mexico.

Between 1963 and 1974, the former Cuban quota in the United States market was redistributed to other Latin American countries and the Philippines, thus stimulating sugarcane booms in Central America, Colombia, Peru, and the Dominican Republic. However, since the 1970s persistent oversupply has depressed prices, thus eroding regional income from sugar exports.

The U.S. and EC import-substitution policies that protect their domestic producers, and in the case of the EC its subsidized exports too, are major factors behind structural oversupply and depressed prices in the international markets. Since 1789 the United States has imposed barriers on sugar imports to protect its domestic farmers. In 1934 a system of import quotas was enacted, which, except for a 1974–1981 interruption, has been in place thereafter (Maskus 1989). According to Gilbert, during the 1981–1983 period, "U.S. imports have been declining with the result that sugar exporters have found the largest import market declining by around 40 percent, from four million tons annually to a current figure of around 2.5 million tons" (1987: 609).

In 1968, the EC guaranteed domestic price supports to its sugar beet producers through a system of quotas, taxes, and subsidies, in spite of its high subsidy costs (Mahler 1966). As a result, "E.C. production rose 9 million tons in 1974 to 15.7 million tons in 1982, and the E.C. from being a net importer of 1.0 million tons of sugar in 1970 became a net exporter of 4.2 million tons in 1982" (GEPLACEA 1986: 55).

A largely unintended result of the quota system in the United States, besides the resulting high domestic prices, has been the development of alternative sweetener industries. Two types of sweeteners are currently on the market: the "natural" or caloric sweeteners, which not only include the sugars extracted from both sugarcane and sugar beet, but also the corn-based syrups and honey; and the "synthetic" sweeteners (saccharine, aspartame, etc.).

Particularly significant has been the growth in consumption of high-fructose corn syrup, a corn-based sweetener. Although it made its first appearance in the 1960s, consumption soared after the 1974–1975 rise in sugar prices. By 1986, corn sweeteners accounted for 53 percent of caloric-sweetener consumption in the United States, up from 32 percent in 1980. (Maskus 1989: 88). Meanwhile, sugar consumption had diminished from 83 percent of sweetener consumption in 1970 to less than 50 percent by 1985 (GEPLACEA 1986: 52).

There are two clear-cut international sugar markets. One is the substantial portion of trade moving along the lines drawn by the preferred market agreements of large trading powers (the EC and its related ACP countries, until 1974 the U.S. market, and the special relationship between Cuba and the USSR until recently). The other is the "free" or residual market, which represents less than 20 percent of world production. The residual nature of this sugar market has made it subject to disproportionately large shocks. To offset this instability, a first International Sugar Agreement (ISA) was signed in 1954 by consumer and producer countries alike. The ISA objectives were to stabilize prices in the residual market through a combination of export quotas and stocks. A major problem, as in all export-control agreements, is how to allocate quotas to member countries.

In 1960, the U.S. ban on sugar imports from Cuba was a severe blow to the first ISA. Cuba, already the single largest exporter with 38 percent of the overall quota, sought a substantial increase in this quota, which other countries were unwilling to concede. This contention led to the collapse of the agreement in 1982.

In 1984, again, the fourth ISA failed. This time, the cause of discontent came from the EC decision not to join the agreement. Export controls could hardly be successful if the second largest exporter was dumping its produce in the international markets. As a result, the "free-market" mechanism was restored in the international sugar market. Future contracts operate in conjunction with spot market quotations, whereas prices are influenced by the hedging and speculative activities by the large trading corporations (Maizels 1984). Thus it is not surprising that sugar prices are currently at a low (Galvan 1988), below the cost structure of even the most efficient producers.

Diversifying production and upgrading to value-added exports could be alternative strategies the less-developed exporters could use to recover their markets. Although the traditional use of sugarcane in the production of raw sugar, refined sugar, sugar in bags and cubes, candies, and preserves could be profitable alternatives, the convergence of the food and fuel crises has also led some countries to develop other sugarcane by-products. Cuba, for instance, produces yeast feedstuff from sugar molasses, whereas Brazil, Jamaica, and Belize produce ethanol, a fuel alcohol, from sugarcane (GEPLACEA 1986; Maskus 1989).

Since 1983, however, the imports of sugar-containing products have been banned by the U.S. government. The EC also established high tariffs for all sugar-added products. Also in the United States, since 1985, ethanol exports from Brazil have been subject to a high compound tariff after being hit by antidumping duties.

Nontraditional Agricultural Exports: A New Arena of Struggle

The shift toward outward-oriented growth strategies, particularly in Latin America, has meant an effort to build up comparative advantages in off-season fresh fruits and vegetables, fresh cut flowers, as well as "exotic" products such as ornamental tropical plants, live tropical fish, etc. These nontraditional exports are mainly oriented toward the high-income consumers and specialty market "niches" of affluent First World societies. These new Third World exports, although still not generating such big markets as the more traditional mass-consumed commodities, are usually generating high value, making their market value outweigh their relatively reduced export volume. Furthermore, the "fresh," perishable products in particular confront less restrictive tariff barriers than mass-consumed commodities (Garramon and De Obschatko 1990; Palmeter 1989).

Nevertheless, the development of nontraditional agricultural exports is not an easy task. Each activity demands not only the development of novel technical solutions but also highly sophisticated infrastructure facilities and marketing services. In the producer countries, domestic markets tend to be controlled by the oligopolistic power of a few transnational corporations, mainly through contract farming schemes. This control is sometimes reinforced further by vertical integration into trading or brokering in the consumer countries (Colaiacovo 1990; Sanderson 1986). Nontraditional agricultural exports provide interesting examples of the difficulties that arise when less-developed, and less-powerful, newcomers enter markets held and strongly defended by the powerful farm lobbies of the advanced capitalist world. Let's review some recent examples.

The U.S.-Mexico Tomato War

Since the early 1970s, Mexico has held a significant share of the U.S. winter vegetable market, especially tomatoes, because of its propitious climate, cheap wages, and low costs of land, credit, and water (cf. Sanderson 1989).

The 1937 U.S. Agricultural Marketing Agreement Act allowed farmer groups in any state to establish the internal quality standards and marketing regulations that would provide a "marketing order" for a particular commodity. However, in 1954 an amendment of the act extended the same regulations to imports.

In 1968, the Florida Tomato Committee signed a marketing order agreement setting up grade and size provisions for its domestic producers and attempted to extend it to all tomato imports. These provisions were promptly approved by the U.S. Department of Agriculture (USDA), without public hearings, thus establishing a de facto nontariff barrier on imports of Mexican tomatoes (Bredahl, Schmitz, and Hillman 1987; Schmitz et al. 1981).

The first to react against these restrictions were the vegetable importers located in Nogales, Arizona, who are supplied exclusively by Mexican producers. The West Mexico Vegetable Distributors of Arizona (WMVDA), a Nogales-based importer lobby with strong political support in the U.S. Congress, filed a restraining order to prevent the USDA from applying the marketing order. In March 1971, the WMVDA got a hearing before the USDA. But it was not until 1973, when the USDA relented in the face of legal and political pressure, that imported tomatoes were required to comply only with minimum grade and size requirements and did not have to be graded and sized like Florida tomatoes (Mares 1980, quoted in Bredahl, Schmitz, and Hillman 1987: 7). Meanwhile, after long bilateral negotiations, the Mexican government agreed to restrict production and exportation of tomatoes to the U.S. market, setting up an interesting case of a so-called voluntary export restraint in the international trade of nonprocessed agricultural products.

In 1978, a new skirmish occurred when various Florida grower associations, unhappy with the Mexican voluntary restraint, attempted to erect a new tariff barrier on imports through the administrative procedures of the U.S. antidumping legislation. However, the Florida growers were unable to mobilize enough political support to succeed in their protectionist attempts. Therefore, despite the assessment of variable, seasonally adjusted duties on fresh vegetables, the Mexico-U.S. winter vegetable market remains basically unhindered, and, in any case, the general upward trend in prices has significantly decreased the restrictive effect of tariffs. Following the peso devaluations of 1982–1983, Mexican producers have expanded exports, at the risk of provoking new trade wars with their U.S. competitors (Sanderson 1989).

The 1989 Chilean Grape Poisoning Incident

The demand for fresh fruit and vegetables has been steadily growing during the last few decades as a result of the health food and natural products ideology now predominant in the affluent societies of the First World. Increased profitability has allowed new preservation techniques to be developed, making long-distance transportation possible for highly perishable products and so creating new winter season markets. Since the mid-1970s, Chile became the world's largest supplier of fresh fruit and vegetables during the U.S. winter months. Table grapes accounted for about 60 percent of Chilean fresh fruit and vegetable exports to the United States.

On 13 March 1989, two poisoned grapes were found in the U.S. Food and Drug Administration laboratories as a result of a routine inspection. Who did it and how these two grapes got there is still unclear, but the immediate reaction of U.S. authorities was to bar all Chilean grape imports, resulting in a major crisis in the grape industry. Seven million boxes of Chilean grapes had to be collected and destroyed in the United States and Canada, and 200,000 in Japan. Not only were Chilean growers affected, but also the export service industries in general. The cost has been estimated at $349 million. But there are other indirect costs that are not so easily measured, such as the subsequent short-term drop in demand and prices of all Chilean fruit exports not only to the United States but to world markets in general, as well as the loss in market shares and benefits of all the agents involved (Brown 1989).

Chilean grape exports (and fruit exports in general) have now largely recovered from the crisis but other barriers still exist. Every year the U.S. government imposes a new marketing order on all fruit imports. The EC and Japan also establish quality and phytosanitary import controls. Chile has complied with all these controls, most of them through bilateral agreements. Yet, frequent norm shifts, working more as nontariff barriers than what they purport to be, are still a constant worry for this industry.

Chilean exporters have also been active in developing other market penetration strategies. In 1985, for instance, the Aconcagua Fruit Grower Association bought a warehouse in Philadelphia to market fruit in the United States and Canada (Rivera 1990). Chilean growers have joined Mexican fruit exporters in developing alliances with U.S. import lobbies, a strategy that will be effective as long as the U.S. growers remain relatively weak within their domestic market.

Conclusion

Latin America is trying to find a new place in the emerging world order, in which a new international division of labor in agriculture is appearing. Willingly or not, most Latin countries have been laying down a new growth strategy that closely follows the recommendations of the global "multilateral" agencies (International Monetary Fund, World Bank, and GATT) in which the rules of the emerging world order are implicit. This new recipe for growth calls for an across-the-board unilateral opening of the Latin American economies to the "benefits" of free-market forces and financial flows across borders. Given the current scenario, I think there are many reasons to be skeptical about the chances for success of this growth strategy as it stands, especially for agriculture.

Tropical Agricultural Exports

Most traditional tropical exports are declining in importance and are characterized by substantial oversupply. In most cases, demand is either stagnating or only growing slowly. In spite of concessions made by the consuming countries during the 1973–1979 Tokyo Round of multilateral negotiations at GATT, tariffs and tariff escalation are still the main brake in tropical commodity trade (cf. Cobban 1988). Large stocks and speculation in the futures markets in the consuming countries further deteriorate conditions.

Tropical exports, it is true, were discouraged by overvalued exchange rates, taxes, low regulated prices, and inefficient state marketing boards (cf. Thomas et al. 1990). Yet, with the failure of almost all international commodity agreements and producer cartels and the elimination of state marketing boards, both the governments and their domestic growers are more than ever at the mercy of the vagaries of the market and the power of transnational corporations.

Future prospects are bleak. One of the main advances of the biotechnological revolution is the reduction of biological specificities of crops and livestock. "Tropical" commodities will profitably be grown in temperate regions in the foreseeable future, thus eliminating the only remaining Third World natural comparative advantage. It seems highly unlikely that economic growth will come from traditional tropical exports, although diversification or upgrading might be viable.

Temperate Products

Under the umbrella of the Bretton Woods agreements most tropical Latin American countries became increasingly dependent for food and feed grain supplies, as First World suppliers achieved undisputed control; at the same time, Southern Cone meat, dairy, and wheat markets shrank. These damaging trends were the result of the combined effects of deliberate First World protectionist and import substitution-cum-export promotion policies. Subsidized First World dumping has further eroded Third World international competitiveness irrespective of comparative advantages. Brazil's soybean export success was basically achieved through temporary U.S. failures, backed by research in developing new strains.

Nontraditional Agricultural Exports

The dynamism of these agricultural markets is largely based on the whims of consumer tastes in affluent societies for exotic commodities. However, signs of saturation are appearing as First World competition is mounting (Sanderson 1986), encouraged by nontariff barriers. The U.S.-Mexican tomato trade war, the Chilean poison grape incident, and the antidumping legislation to curb flower imports from Costa Rica illustrate these neoprotectionist trends in First World consuming countries.

Chile's success in nontraditional agricultural exports is partly related to a deliberate policy in adjusting supply to the diversified needs and tastes of current global markets. Furthermore, Chile's success is linked to a demand-driven market penetration approach based on sending scouts all over the world in search of export opportunities, as well as developing products well suited to the various domestic weather and natural conditions. As a result, Chile is currently exporting salmon to Scandinavian countries during the low Northern Hemisphere season, exporting agar agar algae to Japan, and competing with New Zealand in kiwifruit production. Last but not least, Chile's success has resulted in the development of a sophisticated network of domestic marketing infrastructure and the establishment of permanent trading offices abroad.

Given the reduced size, and probably short-lived nature, of these markets, a national growth strategy could not be based on these export opportunities alone. Excessive specialization would only reinforce the current position of Latin American countries as food staple importers. Exporting value-added industrially processed agricultural products could be a solution. However, value-added agricultural exports are capital- and knowledge-intensive industries. Furthermore, these products also suffer frequent demand shifts and are protected by high tariffs and tariff escalation. According to Cobban, "There are duties on imports into developed countries of almost all semi-processed tropical products except tea, most essential oils and jute, and on all processed tropical products" (1988: 246).

It should be clear that comparative advantages have almost nothing to do with current trends in agricultural markets. Successful competition in rice, peanuts, vegetable oils, soybeans, wheat, meat and dairy products, to name only a few, is severely handicapped. Neither short-term nor long-term economic efficiency is going to be obtained through unilateral liberalization and opening of domestic markets. On the contrary, a biased outward-oriented strategy will only increase export vulnerability and import dependence. Paraphrasing Bhagwati (1988), the gloomy assessment must be that "free trade" will close markets once one has entered them. I am not suggesting that an outward-oriented growth strategy can't work, but that, at least in Latin America, its uncritical adoption is risky, especially at a time of generalized economic and political turmoil and of constant market closures.

Nevertheless, there seems no way back to former import-substitution schemes either. Latin American countries must search for a viable place in the emerging world order, in which international trade is essential for technical advance in an increasingly integrated world. In a world of strategic moves involving trade superpowers, multilateral agencies, and transnational corporations, the only realistic option is to achieve increased bargaining power in all economic and political arenas. Contrary to the laissez-faire ideology currently predominant in most of the world, in my opinion, the nation-state is the only defense for Latin Americans.

Bibliography

Bertrand, Jean-Pierre, Catherine Laurent, and Vincent Leclerq. 1984. *Le monde du soja*. Paris: Editions la Découverte.

Bhagwati, Jagdish. 1988. *Protectionism*. London and Cambridge, Mass.: MIT Press.

Bredahl, Maury, Andrew Schmitz, and Jimmye S. Hillman. 1987. "Rent seeking in international trade: The great tomato war." *American Journal of Agricultural Economics* 69, 1: 1–10.

Brown, Ronald. 1989. "La crisis de la fruta y su impacto en el sector frutífero en la temporada 1988/1989." Unpublished manuscript, Seminario Frutífero. Santiago: Fundación Chile.

Byerlee, Derek. 1987. "The political economy of Third World food imports: The case of wheat." *Economic Development and Cultural Change* 35, 2: 307–328.

Carles, Antonio. 1987. "Orígenes, desarrollo, crisis y perspectivas de la industria bananera." *Capitulos del SELA* 15: 81–86.

Clairmonte, F. F., and J. Cavanagh. 1984. "El poderio de las empresas transnacionales en algunos productos alimenticios." *Comercio Exterior* 34, 11: 1051–1064.

Cobban, Murray. 1988. "Tropical products in the Uruguay Round negotiations." *World Economy* 11, 2: 233–248.

Colaiacovo, Juan Luis. 1990. *Canales de comercializacion internacional*. Buenos Aires: Ediciones Macchi.

De Albuquerque, Rui. 1989. "Estrategia del complejo soja en el Brasil." Pp. 43–40 in República Argentina, *Estrategias de la Agroindustria Exportadora*.

Delpeuch, Bertrand. 1989. *Las interrelaciones alimentarias Norte-Sur*. Madrid: Editorial IEPALA.

Faminov, Merle D., and Jimmye S. Hillman. 1987. "Embargoes and the emergence of Brazil's soyabean industry." *World Economy* 10, 3: 351–366.

Friedmann, Harriet. 1989. "Agro-food complexes and export agriculture: Changes in the international division of labor." Unpublished manuscript.

―――. 1990. "Family wheat farms and Third World diets: A paradoxical relationship between unwaged and waged labor." Pp. 193–213 in Jane L. Collins and Martha Gimenez (eds.), *Labor and Self Employment within Capitalism*. Albany: State University of New York Press.

Friedmann, Harriet, and Philip McMichael. 1989. "Agriculture and the state system: The rise and decline of national agricultures, 1980 to the present." *Sociologia Ruralis* 19, 2: 93–117.

Galvan, Hector. 1988. "Políticas de ajuste en Costa Rica y República Dominicana." *Revista Ciencias Económicas* 8, 1: 67–81.

Gargiulo, Gerardo. 1989. "Estrategias de la agroindustria exportadora." Pp. 7–16 in República Argentina, Secretaría de Ciencia y Tecnología (ed.), *Estrategias de la Agroindustria Exportadora*. Buenos Aires.

Garramon, Carlos, and Edith S. De Obschatko. 1990. *La comercialización de granos en la Argentina*. Buenos Aires: Editorial LEGASA.

General Agreement on Tariffs and Trade. 1989. *Activities*. Geneva: GATT.

GEPLACEA. 1986. *La agroindustria de la caña de azúcar en América Latina y el Caribe*.

Gereffi, Gary. 1989. "Rethinking development theory: Insights from East Asia and Latin America." *Sociological Forum* 4, 4: 13–45.

Gilbert, Christofer. 1987. "International commodity agreements: Design and performance." *World Development* 15, 5: 591–616.

Gilpin, Robert. 1987. *The Political Economy of International Relations*. Princeton, N.J.: Princeton University Press.

Girvan, Norman. 1987. "Transnational corporations and non-fuel primary commodities in developing countries." *World Development* 15, 5: 713–740.

Gomes, Gerson, and Antonio Perez. 1979. "El proceso de la modernización de la agricultural latinoamericana." *Revista de la CEPAL* 8: 57–77.

Goodman, David., and Michael Redclift. 1989. *The International Farm Crisis*. London: Macmillan.

Gouveia, Lourdes. 1990. "Rural Crisis, North and South: The Role of Wheat in the US and Venezuela." Paper presented at the Twelfth World Congress of Sociology, Madrid, Spain, July.

Green, Raul. 1990. "La evolucion de la economia internacional y la estrategia de las multinacionales alimentarias." *Desarrollo Economico* 29, 116: 511–527.

Grigg, David B. 1974. *The Agricultural Systems of the World: An Evolutionary Approach*. Cambridge, Mass.: Cambridge University Press.

Hopkins, Terence K., and Immanuel Wallerstein. 1986. "Commodity chains in the world-economy prior to 1800." *Review* 10: 157–170.

Huekman, Bernard. 1989. "Agriculture and the Uruguay Round." *Journal of World Trade* 23, 1: 83–96.

International Monetary Fund. 1990. *World Economic Outlook: A Survey by the Staff of the IMF*. October. Washington: The Fund.

Kenney, Martin, J. Kloppenburg Jr., and J. T. Cowan. 1989. "Midwestern agriculture in U.S. Fordism." *Sociologia Ruralis* 29, 2: 131–198.

Khanna, Ram. 1990. "Market sharing under multifiber arrangement: Consequences of non-tariff barriers in the textiles trade." *Journal of World Trade* 24, 1: 71–94.

Kuttner, Robert. 1990. "Managed trade and economic sovereignty." *International Trade* 37, 4: 39–51.

Kuwayama, Mikio. 1988. "La comercialización internacional de productos básicos y América Latina." *Revista de la CEPAL* 34 (April): 81–118.

Lipietz, Alain. 1987. "Towards global Fordism?" *New Left Review* 132: 33–47.

Mahler, Vincent A. 1966. "Controlling international commodity prices and supply: The evolution of United States' sugar policy." Pp. 149–179 in F. Lamond Tullis and W. Ladd Hollis (eds.), *Food, State, and International Political Economy*. Lincoln: University of Nebraska Press.

Maizels, Alfred. 1984. "A conceptual framework for analysis of primary commodity markets." *World Development* 12, 1: 25–41.

_____. 1987. "Commodities in crisis: An overview of the main issues." *World Development* 15, 5: 537–549.

Maskus, Keith. 1989. "Large costs and small benefits of the American sugar programme." *World Economy* 12, 1: 85–104.

Morris, David. 1988. *Cotton to 1993: Fighting for the Fibre Market*. London: Economist Intelligence Unit.

Morrison, Thomas K. 1984. "Cereal imports by developing countries," *Food Policy* 9, 1: 13–26.

Ojala, Eric. 1985. "International relationships in the beef trade." Pp. 172–188 in Hartwig de Haen, Glenn L. Johnson, and Stefan Targermann (eds.), *Agriculture and International Relations*. Basingstoke and London: Macmillan.

Paarlberg, Philip L., and Philip C. Abbot. 1986. "Oligopolistic behavior by public agencies in international trade: The world wheat market." *American Journal of Agricultural Economics* 68: 528–542.

Palmeter, N. David. 1989. "Agriculture and trade regulation: Selected issues in the application of U.S. antidumping and countervailing duty laws." *Journal of World Trade* 23, 1: 47–68.

Pineiro, David. 1988. "La crisis en los mercados agrícolas y sus consecuencias económicas y sociales sobre un pequeño país agroexportador: El caso de Uruguay." Unpublished manuscript. Montevideo: CIESU.

Rama, Ruth, and Fernando Rello. 1979. "La internacionalización de la agricultura mexicana." *Estudios Rurales Latinoamericanos* 2, 2: 199–223.

Renard, Marie-Christine. 1989. *La comercialización internacional del café*. Chapingo, Mexico: Universidad Autónoma.

Rivera, Rigoberto A. 1990. "El desarrollo agroexportador chileno." Paper presented at the Third Latin American Congress of Rural Sociology, Neuque, Argentina.

Robinson, Kenneth L. 1985. "The use of agricultural export restrictions as an instrument in foreign policy." Pp. 214–228 in Hartwig de Haen, Glenn L. Johnson, and Stefan Targermann (eds.), *Agriculture and International Relations*. Basingstoke and London: Macmillan.

Ruhl, J. M. 1983. "La influencia de la estructura agraria en la estabilidad política de Honduras." *Estudios Sociales Centro Americanos* 36: 39–72.

Sanderson, Stephen. 1986. *The Transformation of Mexican Agriculture: International Structure and the Politics of Rural Change*. Princeton, N.J.: Princeton University Press.

_____. 1989. "Mexican agricultural policy in the shadow of the U.S. farm crisis." Pp. 205–233 in D. Goodman and M. Redclift (eds.), *The International Farm Crisis*. Hong Kong: Macmillan.

Schmitz, Andrew, Robert S. Firch, and Jimmye S. Hillman. 1981. "Export dumping and Mexican winter vegetables." *American Journal of Agricultural Economics* 63: 645–654.

Stander, Henricus J. and David G. Becker. 1990. "Postimperialism revisited: The Venezuelan wheat import controversy of 1986." *World Development* 18, 2: 197–293.

Thomas, Vinod, et al. 1990. *Lessons in Trade Policy Reform*. Washington: World Bank.

Tubiana, Laurence. 1989. "World trade in agricultural products: From global regulation to market fragmentation." Pp. 23–43 in D. Goodman and M. Redclift (eds.), *The International Farm Crisis*. Hong Kong: Macmillan.

UN Economic Commission for Latin America. 1989. "Ronda Uruguay: Hacia una posicion latino-americana sobre los productos agricolas." *Comercio Exterior* 39, 6: 458–484.

Vidali, Carlos. 1989. "La agricultura mexicana en el GATT: Experiencias para Centro-America." *Ciencias Economicas* 9, 1/2: 155–169.

Williamson, John. 1990. "On the Origins and Course of Latin America's Economic Crisis." Paper presented at the Senior Policy Seminar: Latin America Facing the Challenges of Adjustment and Growth. Caracas: World Bank/IESA.

10 The New Globalization: The Case of Fresh Produce

William H. Friedland

Something relatively new has developed in food consumption habits: In the past decade or so, the consumption of fresh—and pseudo-fresh—fruits and vegetables has become a notable pattern in advanced industrial societies. A product of a constellation of features resulting from processes to be discussed below, what perhaps might be referred to as a postmodern diet has begun to characterize the eating patterns of significant segments of populations in advanced capitalist societies.

Representing a shift from diets previously based on durable foods and meats, which characterized the predominant patterns of food consumption since before the First World War, this new dietary pattern has produced yet another form of globalization: integrated networks of agri-food chains that deliver fresh fruits and vegetables from all over the world to economically privileged strata in North America, Western Europe, and Japan, a set of areas that will be referred to summarily as the advanced capitalist West. Based on integrated systems of refrigeration, these networks link major consumption areas with old and new production areas. What is perhaps most remarkable about them is the integration of Third World production—locations characterized as "developing" or "underdeveloped"—with the consumption of fresh produce, a "privileged" set of commodities intended for distant markets with high living standards.

In this chapter I set out some of the global dimensions of this new food system.[1] My purposes are to provide data on the development of the new global system of production and distribution, explain the emergence of the new system, and explore the relationship of the new system to the forms of social stratification that characterize advanced capitalist—"post-Fordist"—societies.

First it would be useful to set out some preliminary arguments and definitions. It is necessary to clarify what is meant by fresh and pseudo-fresh commodities. These foods which are socially defined as being fresh as opposed to processed. In fact, all foods are processed in the sense that human mediation always occurs between food and the consumer. The "fresh" tomatoes or bananas that we consume are harvested prior to full maturity, chilled, and transported (usually over thousands of miles), warmed and/or gassed to produce the appearance of ripeness, and then placed on retail shelves. Such foods are termed fresh because of their relative perishability, which stands in contrast to the relative long life or durability of other foods that either store well (grains, sugar) or that because of some form of intervention (drying, canning, freezing) store for extended periods of time.

To put the argument simply, all foods consumed by human beings in advanced industrial societies are products of thousands of years of human intervention: through the breeding of plants and animals, through the development of myriad forms of intervention in the production process, through the ways in which the product is handled after actual production has been accomplished. Indeed, to talk of "nature" and "natural" with respect to any foods presently consumed in advanced industrial societies is to ignore the fantastic levels of intervention by human beings that have transformed those foods from their original forms found in nature.

Thus "fresh" represents a *socially defined* description of foods that ostensibly have not been processed in some form to extend their durability into the distant future. The various forms of processing—drying, canning, freezing—transform food from a state in which its longevity is relatively short[2] to those whose longevity is significantly longer, i.e., are more durable (Friedmann 1987: 252).

Other foods that tend to be regarded as fresh are already the product of extensive transformation. Good examples are frozen concentrated orange juice (FCOJ) and tofu. Recently, the U.S. Food and Drug Administration (FDA) required a firm making *reconstituted* orange juice from FCOJ to eliminate the word "fresh" from its label (*New York Times*, 27 April 1991: 1A). This legal "victory" has little to do with the fact that most orange juice consumed in North America and Western Europe is not freshly squeezed but is reconstituted. Truly fresh orange juice is rare in the advanced capitalist West. A somewhat different situation exists with tofu. Made from the fermentation of soybeans, tofu is still considered a fresh food by its many aficionados, perhaps because of its short longevity,[3] perhaps because it goes very well with fresh vegetables in stir-fry form, perhaps because it is a high-protein, low-cholesterol food.

My purpose in citing these examples of processed foods that are considered fresh is to indicate the somewhat arbitrary character of "fresh."[4] Nevertheless, the widespread popularity of "fresh" and the fact that regulatory agencies must regulate the use of the term indicates that "fresh" is a social category that must be grappled with in dealing with food. We will have to accept the fact that there are foods that are relatively less processed than so-called processed foods. More important, we have to acknowledge that there are now categories of foods, increasingly found in year-round consumption, that have relatively short longevity once removed from their cool chains, networks of refrigeration from the point of production to the point of consumption.

I have characterized the fresh food system as being global, which refers to the fact that fresh produce is now moving extensively between countries, regions, and continents, involving almost every major geographical area on earth except Antarctica. Until the end of the Second World War, the fresh system could be characterized as being either localized or national, with the exception of bananas.[5] The fresh system originated in the United States, where fresh produce could be shipped great distances through railroads and refrigeration from California to the East and Midwest. It was not until the 1970s and 1980s, however, that globally extensive cool chains were organized that delivered dozens of fresh commodities on a year-round basis to hundreds of millions of consumers.

Four critical and relatively new elements are notable about the fresh food system: (1) the development of counterseasonal production; (2) the creation of mass clienteles for fresh produce consumption; (3) the creation of market niches including the differentiation of existing products as well as new products such as "tropicals" (or "exotics") and "baby vegetables"; and (4) the search for value-adding, particularly at retail levels.

Counterseasonal production—sometimes referred to as "contraseasonal" (Drum 1990)—involves the integration of new regions of production to supply markets on a year-round or near year-round basis with seasonal commodities. This form of production was pioneered with lettuce in California where it was discovered that, by moving lettuce production sites through various locations in California (and later Arizona), it was possible to produce lettuce for delivery fifty-two weeks out of the year (Friedland, Barton, and Thomas 1981). Later, other products such as tomatoes moved into annual production even though the original season for tomatoes is naturally short. This was accomplished by developing production locations in Florida and in west central Mexico.

A major form of mass market counterseasonal production developed in the late 1970s when Chile began to ship table grapes to the United States and Western Europe during the winter. Because grapes ripen in Chile during Northern Hemisphere winter months, grapes, which disappeared from northern markets after November or December, became available on a year-round basis. The opening of other production areas in the Caribbean and Central America made melons and a variety of other seasonal fruits and vegetables available year round. In addition, extensive technical development in greenhouse production of vegetables in Holland has contributed to the availability of produce during nonnormal periods. Thus, the Dutch produce tomatoes, capsicum (peppers), aubergines (eggplant), and a variety of other vegetables for eight to ten months out of the year (CBT n.d.), contributing to counterseasonal availability.

The second unusual and new element in the fresh food system has been its Fordist or post-Fordist character.[6] Post-Fordist refers to the period in which mass production is replaced by the differentiation of markets and the creation of many market niches. In fact, the appropriate—and parallel—term that should be used instead of post-Fordist is "Sloanist,"[7] after Alfred P. Sloan, who headed General Motors for many years. It was Sloan who revitalized the automobile industry during the period in which Henry Ford made but a single model automobile (the Model T) in a single color (black). Sloan introduced a host of changes in General Motors production, including annual model changes, product diversification ("a car for every purse and pocket") while, in fact, minimizing "internal variety . . . with many hidden standardized parts." Thus, while providing a range of products with all sorts of options, Sloan differentiated a previously undifferentiated market and GM surpassed Ford in automobile manufacturing (Kuhn 1986: 19).

The development of Sloanist fresh foods—mass production, mass transportation, and mass consumption intended for mass and niche markets—is an artifact of the changing structure of employment and income in advanced capitalist countries: It is a post-Fordist phenomenon in which the segment of the labor force concerned with production has declined and the segment of the labor force dedicated to consumption, i.e., services production, has increased.[8] This phenomenon has been accompanied by a bimodalization of the population in terms of income, education, and other socioeconomic indicators. However, where only recently there was a limited market for fresh fruits and vegetables, these markets have grown significantly and massive consumption patterns have now become common.

Production of esoteric or exotic fresh foods for luxury markets has long existed. Chilean grapes, for example, were available at specialty greengrocers in the eastern United States (by air transport) long before there was a surface cool chain to handle these grapes in the Fordist mode. Similarly, produce grown in greenhouses by specialists aimed at a very wealthy but restricted consumption market was available long before the Dutch learned how to accomplish this on a mass production basis. What now characterizes the fresh system is the increase in the sheer number of commodities that were once exotic. Some, such as kiwifruit, were considered exotic less than five years ago (*Packer*, New Zealand kiwifruit insert, 28 May 1988: 6C). Because of massive plantings in Italy, Spain, France, the United States, and elsewhere, kiwifruit has shifted from exotic to quotidian, or commonplace, within the last decade. Other fruits—primarily tropicals such as atemoya, breadfruit, carambola (starfruit), chayote, cherimoya, lychee, papaya, and sapodilla, plus dozens of others whose names are unrecognizable to most consumers—have also begun to appear.

An important factor contributing to the spread of exotics has been the movement of populations. The migration of Jamaicans to London and New York, of North Africans to France and Italy, of Mexicans and Central Americans to the United States, etc., led to the gradual importation of fruits and vegetables from native lands intended for restricted ethnic markets. As ethnic food consumption has spread beyond the original client base to the broader population, everyday consumption of what were originally ethnic foods is becoming standardized. Jicama, a staple Mexican vegetable, is now routinely used by many non-Mexicans in California; plantains, originally a Caribbean exotic, are moving into the mainstream in some urban markets; other fruits and vegetables are following similar trajectories.

As the market for fresh products has expanded, the differentiation and elaboration of product lines has become notable. Thus, not only do some exotics such as kiwifruit become ordinary but each year new exotics are being introduced. Similarly, where once there were only tomatoes, now there are beefsteak tomatoes (referred to as beef tomatoes in Europe), cherry tomatoes, small round tomatoes, pear tomatoes, etc. The Dutch announce the shipment of eight different colors of capsicum (bell peppers) ʻᴖ the United States (*Packer*, 23 March 1991: 16A). Iceberg lettuce, once the emperor of lettuces in the United States and almost unknown in Europe, is being augmented by red leaf, oak, green leaf, radicchio, arugula, and other leaf lettuces in the United States and is moving toward royalty in some European markets (although still far from being king, let alone emperor).

Another development has been the tendency in the fresh industry to increase profit margins at retail through value-adding. This is a process in which value is added to a simple commodity, particularly in the form of labor, increasing its attractiveness to consumers (either visually or through ease of preparation or other means), which produces an increased profit. Examples of value-adding include wrapping of lettuce in plastic film, preparing mixed salads and presenting them in a plastic sack ready for the salad bowl, and washing and preparing of mushrooms and presenting them in a microwaveable tray ready for cooking. In some cases, producers seek to add value at the source rather than at the retail level (wrapping lettuce in plastic in the field rather than in the supermarket, for example).

The Growing Importance of Fresh

Statistical data on the increased global importance of fresh fruits and vegetables are difficult to develop. Macrodata on world trade in fresh produce (Table 10.1) and on the export value of fresh fruits and vegetables (Table

Table 10.1. World Trade by Commodity, 1984–1988 (US $000s)

	Imports				
	1984	1985	1986	1987	1988
Vegetables, fresh/simply preserved	8,649,258	8,481,294	10,570,800	12,737,427	13,259,007
Fruits and nuts, fresh and dried	11,459,019	12,338,090	14,632,407	17,474,403	16,245,520
	Exports				
	1984	1985	1986	1987	1988
Vegetables, fresh/simply preserved	7,225,198	6,855,730	9,124,911	10,365,498	12,932,842
Fruits and nuts, fresh and dried	9,485,469	10,014,852	12,596,807	14,608,240	17,487,199

Source: United Nations 1988, 2: 23, 25.

10.2) provide rough indicators of the growing importance of the fresh produce trade.

Other studies provide additional evidence. Cook (1990: 67), for example, reports that "fresh produce consumption in the United States expanded by 16 percent between 1978 and 1988." A trade industry publication reports that between 1970 and 1989 per capita vegetable consumption increased by 42.3 percent and fruit consumption increased by 21.7 percent (*Packer Focus*, "Fresh Trends '91": 24). Table 10.3 sets out the per capita consumption of fresh vegetables and fruits in the United States in selected years between 1970 and 1989.

Another measure can be found in fresh fruit exports from the United States. Between 1970 and 1988, these increased phenomenally by more than a factor of six (Table 10.4). Similar patterns can be found in the United

Table 10.2. Fresh Fruits and Vegetables, Three-Year Average Export Values, Worldwide, 1963–1985 (US $000s)

	1961–1963	1970–1972	1975–1977	1983–1985
Fruits	1,565,290	2,833,285	5,778,681	8,424,558
Vegetables	773,631	1,452,058	3,108,964	4,476,262

Source: Islam 1990, Table 40: 93 and Table 42: 99.

Table 10.3. Produce per Capita Consumption in the United States, 1970–1989 (in pounds per capita)

	Vegetables	Percentage Increase	Fruit	Percentage Increase
1970	71.7		79.4	
1975	75.0	4.6	85.0	12.6
1980	82.4	9.7	90.0	5.9
1985	90.5	9.8	89.0	− 1.1
1989[a]	102.0	12.7	96.6	8.5

Source: Packer Focus, "Fresh Trends '91," vol. 47, no. 54: 24.

[a]Preliminary.

Kingdom, where there have been steady increases in the volume and value of fresh fruits and vegetables marketed. Between 1978 and 1988, consumption increased 15.3 percent in volume and 109 percent in value (Table 10.5).

Holland is both a major producer of fresh vegetables for export and a vital entrepot for fresh fruits and vegetables. Its major port, Rotterdam, ties with Hamburg for receiving fresh fruit (after Antwerp), handling 17 percent of Western European imports (PGF 1990: B). Whether imported for the home market, imported for reexport, or simply in transit, fresh fruits and

Table 10.4. U.S. Fresh Fruit Exports (US $m)

Year	Value	Year	Value
1970	164	1985	743
1980	739	1986	851
1983	829	1987	939
1984	758	1988	1,093

Source: Bureau of the Census 1990, Table 1144: 657.

Table 10.5. Fresh Fruit and Vegetable Consumption, Volume and Value, United Kingdom, 1978–1988

	Volume (1,000 tons)	Percentage Increase	Value (£1m)	Percentage Increase
1978	11,181		2,378	
1980	11,323	1.27	2,953	24.2
1982	11,549	2.0	3,586	21.4
1984	11,665	1.0	4,397	22.6
1986	12,454	6.8	4,634	5.4
1988	12,892	3.5	4,962	7.1

Source: Geest, n.d.

vegetables have risen continuously in volume between 1970 and 1988. Fruit has more than doubled from 615,000 tons in 1970 to 1,674,000 tons in 1988; the volume for vegetables has gone from 171,000 tons to 546,000 tons in the same period (PGF 1990: C, D).

Imports of exotics (pineapples, avocados, coconuts, guavas) into West Germany show steady increases between 1980 and 1989 (*eurofruit*, May 1990: 5). A survey of thirty-two fruit and vegetable imports into Sweden between 1982 and 1989 shows that eighteen commodities have risen in volume, four have dropped, and ten have remained essentially stable. Among those that have increased are lemons, apples, melons, kiwifruit, leeks, mushrooms, and iceberg lettuce. Commodities dropping in volume include oranges, carrots, and brussel sprouts. Commodities remaining steady include grapes, cherries, peaches, plums, strawberries, cauliflower, and capsicum (*eurofruit*, November 1990: 50).

What is perhaps more compelling qualitatively, even if quantitative data are sparse, has been the rush to move into retail selling of fresh produce. In places as diverse as San Francisco and Chicago, London and Paris, The Hague and Cologne, supermarket chains have placed great emphasis on the sale of fresh produce, which has become notable in the trade as "high margin" (i.e., profitable). Thus, supermarket space dedicated to fresh produce has increased and the volume and variety of fresh commodities has elaborated.

Finally, although still constituting a limited market because of their shortage of hard or convertible currencies, the opening of Eastern European countries has unleashed a remarkable pent-up demand for produce, especially bananas. As the economies of these countries improve, they can be expected to seek increases in volumes and diversity of fresh produce.

The Changing Character of Agri-food Systems

The phenomenon of food systems is a product of the development of capitalism with its accompanying urbanization and proletarianization. Trade in agricultural products and food before the onset of capitalism was essentially limited. The trans-Saharan salt trade, the wine trade, the trade in olive oil, and the trade in eastern spices to Europe, while significant economic developments, represented an augmentation of agriculture and food production that was overwhelmingly localized. To talk of a global food system prior to the formation of basic capitalist economies exaggerates the importance of translocal trade. The lives of most individuals, except perhaps those at the top of the socioeconomic structure, were overwhelmingly enmeshed in local production, handling, transportation, and consumption. Indeed, most production was for self-sustenance.

The development of capitalism with its accompanying disruptions caused by urbanization and proletarianization laid the basis for the emergent global food system. The discovery of the Caribbean as a sugar-producing system (Mintz 1985) initiated a process whereby a stable, durable food could be produced cheaply in one location and transported in large volumes over great distances. But sugar by itself would hardly provide an adequate diet, and the grain trade, in turn, began to grow. Wheat, in particular, could be grown far from the centers of industrial populations such as Manchester or Lyons. This gave rise to wheat production in Eastern Europe and subsequently in the New World—in California, Argentina, Australia—and similar locations far from the growing centers of capitalist production (Friedmann 1978a, 1978b; Morgan 1980).

Over time, as urbanization and proletarianization continued and as urban working classes discovered their misery, self-organization and improvements in housing and diets became important. By the 1880s in the United States, scientific endeavors focused on nutrition, and the broader population gradually became more educated about diet (Levenstein 1988). Diets based on animal protein—milk, cheese, and meat—became important but brought about new problems in the handling of foods in the postagricultural phase. This represented a shift from durable foods, i.e., foods with long shelf life, to foods that required special handling if they were to reach populations distant from their agricultural origins. The technology of refrigeration for the handling of such foods took decades to develop.

At the same time, technological innovation permitted the conversion of short-lived foods such as fruits and vegetables into durable foods through canning. This form of preservation of dozens of vegetables and fruits permitted the elaboration of diets and the massive expansion of dietary inventories. New foods, including tropical products such as pineapple, were introduced to mass markets, and the global reach of the food system expanded. At a later stage, as refrigeration reached into private homes and the technology of freezing food and handling it over great distances improved, the durability of short-lived foods was maintained while their quality improved.

The combination of urbanization, proletarianization, and technological development in turn set the basis for mass consumption of fresh produce. Long-term experimentation and development established procedures that facilitated the elaboration of fresh produce consumption. In the United States, mobile refrigeration (icing insulated railway cars on a regular schedule) permitted the establishment of the Pacific Fruit Express, a regularly scheduled rail service from California to the Midwest and East, thereby opening major markets for fresh produce (Hofsommer 1986: 133–134). The development of storage procedures for fruits such as oranges and apples expanded their seasons of availability. The discovery that it was feasible to harvest green bananas and transport them over great distances, ultimately ripening them at locations close to their consumption markets, introduced the first fresh tropical fruits to urban populations. The fresh produce system began to expand beyond local production and consumption markets, although it remained largely regional (except for bananas and a few exotic items intended for the luxury trade) until after the Second World War.

The expansive postwar economies of the advanced capitalist West saw the emergence of new class structures in which a relatively privileged blue-collar proletariat was supplanted by a yet more privileged technical and managerial proletariat, a very large semiprivileged white-collar class, a largely underprivileged service stratum, and a variety of deprivileged groups (downwardly mobile and formerly privileged manual workers, service workers at minimum wage levels, the unemployed and the homeless, etc.).

From the viewpoint of the food system, a dual system of production/consumption has emerged.[9] This dual system, like any ideal type, has its overlaps but consists, essentially, of a stratum of relatively privileged, higher income, highly educated, well-traveled professionals increasingly concerned about food quality, safety, and variety. A second category consists of "all the others," relatively unprivileged strata less concerned and sophisticated about food variability, less educated, and only fitfully concerned about food safety. Both categories are involved with "productionist Fordist food categories," by which I mean that their foods are mass produced; the first, however, seeks greater variety and finds it in the new niche markets in which there is something of a handicraft character to production. To produce baby lettuce, for example, involves the production of many small lots of different varieties of lettuce that have to be planted and harvested on varying schedules. The goal of such producers is to "Fordize" the handicraft elements into standard production processes to reduce handicraft (i.e., labor) costs.

Whether baby vegetables, exotics, value-added produce, or produce treated in other special ways, the up-scale market for fresh fruits and vegetables is now a mass market presented in an artisanal handicraft guise. It should be distinguished from conventional Fordist food production systems embodied in the "ordinary" fruits and vegetables, in mass-produced snack food, and in the cheaply competitive fast food of McDonald's, Pizza Hut, and Taco Bell. What characterizes the new Fordist (or, more accurately, Sloanist) system of fresh fruit and vegetable production is standardization; mass consumption facilitated by higher incomes; the elaboration of food choices, i.e., great variety and possibilities in choosing foods to be consumed; and the differentiation of the market into a larger number of subsegments, contrasting with the tendency toward homogenization that characterizes the mass market of less privileged consumers.

Factors Producing Change in the Consumption of Fresh Fruits and Vegetables

Many social, economic, and technological factors have been producing the shift in dietary patterns toward the consumption of fresh fruits and vegetables. These social changes include the changing structure of employment and labor markets, which have produced a differentiated, bimodal pattern of income distribution; the aging of the population; and enhanced but intermittent concerns about health and longevity. The economic developments include the increased mobility of capital, which has facilitated the development of new production locations. The technological developments that have facilitated the emergence of the new food complex include the formation of global cool chains and technology transfer.

Social Trends

The changing structure of capitalist economies has led a number of social analysts to characterize the present state of modern capitalist economies as postmodern. Anticipated as early as the 1950s by perceptive analysts such as Daniel Bell (1953), the decline of the blue-collar industrial working class foreshadowed the emergence of a new class of workers who failed to fit the classical Marxian concept of the proletariat. Highly skilled, highly educated, and well paid, members of the so-called new working class (Gorz 1967; Mallet 1975a, 1975b) did not consider themselves to be proletarians despite their objective status in Marxian theory as employees and nonowners of the means of production. Other social commentators (Ehrenreich 1979) labeled the new class "professional-managerial." Still other commentators, focusing on cultural and life-style characteristics, evolved the term "yuppie" (young, upwardly mobile professionals), while a host of other terms, some favorable and some pejorative (e.g., DINKs—Double income, no kids) also were used.

Whatever the terminology, these conceptualizations seek to describe a significant new phenomenon. Whereas the numbers of technically qualified professionals originally had been relatively small in terms of percentage—as well as in numbers—in the total labor force of Western capitalist countries, the post-1950s transformation of the structure of employment required large numbers of technically qualified personnel. The necessarily higher levels of education were facilitated by the expansion of systems of higher education universally, albeit unevenly, in the advanced capitalist West.

With these developments came material changes—higher wages/salaries, greater material benefits, and the expansion of discretionary income—as well as changes in life-styles that expanded the horizons of this stratum. Travel brought them into contact with new foods and opened them to experimentation with dietary patterns. The presence of increased numbers of immigrants with different dietary habits also made available foods previously unknown to people in this stratum. Foods such as plantains and jicama, eaten by lower-income Jamaicans and Mexicans, became available. Media attention—not to speak of promotional materials explaining the use of esoteric food—plus a new willingness to experiment opened new markets to food distributors.

Another factor leading to expansion of the fresh fruit and vegetable system has to do with the aging of the population. In the advanced capitalist West, birthrates have dropped, and the segment of the population over forty-five years of age has increased. Older populations accumulate information over longer periods of time; have the leisure, especially after retirement, to inform themselves about issues that involve them (e.g., health and longevity); often have the resources to travel and expand their cultural horizons; and expend a greater proportion of income on food (versus housing). In the United States, for example, Americans between the ages of fifty-five and sixty-four consume 39 percent more fresh vegetables than the national average (Cook 1990: 67–68). Furthermore, by the year 2000, "the aging of the baby boomers will make the 45 to 64 year age group the single largest segment (23%) of the population" (Cooke 1990: 68). This situation is being duplicated elsewhere in the advanced capitalist West.

Both categories of population—the relatively privileged technical-professionals and the seniors—are particularly concerned with health and longevity. In a world that has become increasingly dangerous because of chemical contamination and carcinogens, there is more information available about such risks and greater access to health care information. It has become clear that some foods—red meat, dairy products, overly processed snack foods—are deleterious to health, whereas other foods—particularly fresh fruits and vegetable—are more healthful. As Cook has pointed out, "Fresh produce has benefitted from increasing health awareness. Per capita fresh vegetable consumption [in the United States] in 1988 was 100.3 pounds, up from 76.5 in 1978, and 1988 was the first year that fresh vegetable consumption equaled processed. The increase in fresh vegetable consumption partly came at the expense of canned vegetables, with canned consumption declining from 87 to 82.8 pounds. Per capita fresh fruit consumption in 1988 was 96.9 pounds, compared with 83.7 pounds in 1978, with total fruit consumption of 211.3 pounds" (1990: 69).

Economic Trends

A major factor contributing to the evolution of the global fresh fruit and vegetable system has been the increased mobility of capital. Although this has generally been the case in industries such as automobiles, steel, electronics, and computers, it has been a more recent phenomenon in fresh fruits and vegetables. Growers of fruits and vegetables for the fresh market were, until relatively recently, locally or regionally oriented. The notion of "going abroad" to establish new production locations began with several experiments during the 1960s when some California growers explored production arrangements with Mexican counterparts on the west coast of Mexico. Initially intended to expand the U.S. market, the success of the Mexican experiments led one Belgian entrepreneur to develop a joint venture with the U.S. vegetable firm Bud Antle, to produce vegetables in Senegal for the winter market in Europe (Mackintosh 1989). Israel intensified agricultural production aiming at the European market. The Israelis were following in the footsteps of the South Africans who had earlier taken advantage of being in the Southern Hemisphere to experiment with counterseasonal production to Europe, particularly to the United Kingdom. The boycott of South Africa opened opportunities for Israel and other counterseasonal producers to expand into Europe.

Despite the failure of the House of Bud experiment in Senegal, other entrepreneurs in a host of countries have been willing to explore similar approaches. The Chileans had long shipped small amounts of table grapes to the Northern Hemisphere for the luxury trade. During the late 1970s, the Chileans developed refrigerated ship services to transport table grapes to the Northern Hemisphere during its winter months. The success of winter grape sales encouraged northern capital investment in Chilean grape and soft fruit development (Goldfrank 1990). Today, of the four largest fruit shippers, only one firm remains in Chilean ownership, the other three being owned by U.S., Italian, and Arab interests (*eurofruit*, January 1991: 34).

The infusion of nonindigenous capital, often in joint ventures with indigenous entrepreneurs, has led to the expansion of production locations that would have been inconceivable a decade ago. Kenyan mangetout (snow peas), Zimbabwean and Jordanian green beans, Malaysian carambola (starfruit), Egyptian garlic, Colombian apple bananas, Zambian baby corn, Brazilian papayas all would have been impossible to find except, perhaps, in highly select luxury greengrocers. Yet all of these were found in London supermarkets in August 1990, in addition to the more "normal" fruits and vegetables from the United Kingdom, the United States, France, Italy, Holland, and elsewhere.

Technological Trends

As new production locations have opened, two technological preconditions have had to be satisfied: the establishment of global cool chains and the transfer of production technologies. The preconditions for the new fresh fruit and vegetable system are the cool chains that integrate production with consumption. A cool chain is an integrated system of refrigeration that chills a product within hours of harvest and maintains controlled cool temperatures, often varying between commodities, from the original place of chilling to the delivery to consumers who, in turn, can store the product under chilled conditions (Carter and Turner 1988). Without such integrated chains, the present fresh fruit and vegetable system would be impossible.

The establishment of such chains is a complex undertaking that involves not only the establishment of the chain itself but also the integration of production practices in anticipation of market needs several years in advance. The prototype of these complex systems can be found in California's lettuce industry (Friedland, Barton, and Thomas 1981) where planning and integration of year-round production of lettuce is undertaken by several dozen firms. Anticipating market needs a year in advance, these firms use different seed varieties in different locations to fit geophysical requirements. Production is planned to fit harvesting schedules, chill the product, and integrate its movement over thousands of miles to supermarkets, terminal markets, jobbers, wholesalers, and retailers who, in turn, move the product to consumers.

Since lettuce, table grapes, carrots, tomatoes, etc., have individual optimal temperatures for storage, the analysis of the transportation of each under optimal conditions has become a significant research topic. Some commodities can be optimally chilled by air, others by water, and still others by creating a vacuum. To ensure that temperature control is maintained effectively, a small industry has been created producing temperature recorders (which are inserted in shipments and record variations in temperature during transit).

The cool chains—requiring enormous capital investments in ships, trains, and trucks with refrigeration capacity; loading and unloading facilities and equipment; storage capacity with refrigeration, etc.—are necessary but not sufficient for the establishment of a global system. In each production location, local geophysical and biological circumstances must be assessed, transformed, and adapted; it is not possible to take iceberg lettuce seeds appropriate for the Salinas valley and simply plant them in Spain or Morocco; melon seeds appropriate to the San Joaquin valley in California may develop new diseases when planted in Costa Rica.

To establish successful production facilities in a multitude of geophysical and biological circumstances requires research and development to deal with diseases, insects, soil conditions, and the many particularized circumstances that characterize agricultural production. In advanced capitalist nations such as the United States, the United Kingdom, France, Italy, Holland, Germany, etc., a research and development infrastructure has been developed through state investment over decades. The U.S. land grant system of colleges of agriculture, experiment stations, and extension services is prototypical of such infrastructural developments. Whether through the Ministry of Agriculture, Food, and Fisheries in the United Kingdom, or through France's Institut National de la Recherche Agronomique, most advanced capitalist nations have created complex scientific networks to handle agricultural research and development problems.

This is not the case in developing and underdeveloped locations where infrastructure is thin or nonexistent. In these cases, private investors—whether indigenous or foreign—undertake the major research and development activities. While state assistance may be forthcoming either through the international agricultural research institutes or through governmental agencies such as the U.S. Agency for International Development or similar structures, it is essential to transfer technological know-how to new sites to adapt seed varieties to new conditions and to the different biological challenges they will meet. All of this requires capital since the employment of such technical capabilities in "exotic" (i.e., foreign) circumstances is expensive. Thus, the necessary investments can only be made by firms with substantial capital resources; this is not a business for the small investor or entrepreneur.

The Thorny Issue of Food Safety

Health concerns, as has been indicated, are a significant issue driving increased consumption of fresh fruit and vegetables. The growing body of information on the ill effects on health and longevity of overconsumption of cholesterol-rich meats, fats, and oils, and information on the pernicious effects of sugars and many snack foods has encouraged alert consumers to deemphasize these foods and consume more fruits and vegetables. Concerns about animal hormones in meats, as well as concerns about the potential effects of irradiated foods and of milk produced by BST (hormone)-injected cows, have also contributed to worries about food safety. Indeed, the entire issue of food safety poses significant dilemmas for consumers assailed by news about Alar on apples, cyanide in grapes, listeria, and salmonella, not to speak of other kinds of food problems.

The fresh fruit and vegetable industries confront similar problems because of the systems of chemical agriculture that predominate in world production. Whether in the massive agribusiness fields of California or the tiny intensive industrial glasshouses of Holland,[10] the prevailing system of agriculture is chemical based. In Holland this may entail using a growing medium such as rockwool, a product similar to fiberglass, in which plants are fed appropriate nutrient chemicals through drip irrigation systems. In California, west Mexico, and Spain, extensive agri-industry uses sophisticated spraying techniques to control insects and weeds.

Although government agencies continually assert the purity—and the lack of chemical residues—of fresh fruits and vegetables, there is a fundamental lack of public trust in these reassurances. Whether because of the United Farm Workers Union's continual reminders about pesticide residues on California crops or because the public remembers the scientific reassurances given about nematicides such as DBCP, which subsequently were found to produce sterility in men and proved to be carcinogenic as well (Murray 1983), there now exists a fundamental skepticism about the scientific integrity of the agricultural system.

The events of the spring of 1989 exemplify these tendencies.[11] Three significant environmental events, two involving fresh foods, came to a climax in March 1989 in the United States: the Alar scare, the two Chilean grapes laced with cyanide, and the *Exxon Valdez* disaster. Although unrelated, these three events dominated the news for the better part of a month, producing a major shift by consumers toward organic produce. In the United States, the *Packer* (25 March 1989), a weekly trade newspaper of the produce industry, headlined the story, "At Issue: Product Safety; Organics: Hot Demand, Short Supply." The director of produce operations at a Seattle supermarket said, "We went from selling 600 to 700 pounds a week (of organics) to selling 6,500 pounds." And in Santa Cruz, California, the office of the California Certified Organic Farmers reported that their telephone was "ringing off the hook" with calls from growers seeking information about conversion to organic production. In Holland, as yet another sign of changing times, the land dedicated to organic production has gone from 500 to 35,000 hectaves between 1984 and 1989 (*eurofruit*, May 1990: 26). The uneven and unsteady character of the shift toward organics was noted shortly thereafter by the *Packer* (2 September 1989) with the headline, "Organics, Strength Wanes at Retail; Look, Price Blamed."

The retail industry does not yet trust organics because of inconsistent demand and uncertain supply. Organic production has been dogged by uncertainties and legal complications. Many states have yet to come up with a legal—and enforceable—definition of organic production. Consumers therefore respond to a crisis such as that of spring 1989 by a significant—but temporary—shift to organics, which is then partially abandoned when the crisis abates and comparisons are made about price and appearance with conventional produce.

Still, there is a long-term trend toward organics. In the United States, sales of organics have risen from $175 million in 1980 to $1.5 billion in 1990.[12] Similar developments can be found in Western Europe. Yet organics still constitute only a minuscule percentage of the sales of conventional produce. Consumers want safe fruit and vegetables but remain uncertain as to whether the industry can supply them. On its part, the industry cannot quite make up its mind about how to handle the food safety issue. For a long time, the primary response of the food industries—growers, agricultural organizations, the scientific apparati associated with agriculture, and retailers—was to reject the criticism and contend that there was little or nothing to worry about. Over time, however, what was once a solid coalition has begun to unravel.

In this respect the example of Alar is enlightening. The use of Alar in the apple industry was initially defended by its manufacturer, Uniroyal, and major segments of the apple-growing community. As criticism of Alar increased, many growers voluntarily stopped using Alar; some retailers also required that their apple suppliers certify that their apples were Alar-free. At the time of the spring 1989 crisis, the apple growers, confronting a disaster in the form of a spontaneous boycott of apples, called on Uniroyal to stop manufacturing Alar. Under this pressure, Uniroyal agreed to stop selling it in the United States. This was unsatisfactory because Uniroyal stated its intention to continue to sell Alar outside the United States, which meant that Alar residues might be reimported with juice concentrate, applesauce, and other apple products. The pressures from growers on Uniroyal continued to the point that the company agreed to stop manufacturing Alar entirely.

A development related to organics has been the mushrooming growth of various forms of direct marketing in which the lengthy chain between producer and consumer is short-circuited[13] by direct purchase of produce from the growers. Taking a variety of forms—pick your own, farmers' markets, roadside stands, community-supported agriculture groups—this type of marketing, while still constituting a negligible percentage of produce sales, is growing substantially.

The food safety issue is very much a part of the fresh fruit and vegetable trade; thus the various industries involved in this trade cannot ignore the issue. At the same time, the industry is heterogeneous and broad, and its clienteles are at various levels of sophistication and interest, so that no coherent or consistent approaches have developed. With environmentally conscious consumers in Germany, the United Kingdom, and the United States on the one hand, and less conscious consumers in Italy and Spain on the other, and with varying degrees of consciousness in between, this remains an area of opportunity—or vulnerability—for the fresh produce industries.

Conclusion

The global fresh produce system is still very much in the process of development. The product of the global maldistribution of resources, it increasingly draws Third World nations and regions into production of new, nontraditional commodities. It also instigates the shipment of commodities indigenous to these areas, but exotic to the advanced capitalist West, to privileged consumption areas.

A variety of consequences will probably develop as more sectors of the Third World are drawn into production for the privileged First World. First, as Barkin and DeWalt (1988) have shown, when areas such as Mexico begin production aimed at a First World market—in this case the United States—domestic food supplies suffer.[14] The development of a very large complex of vegetable and fruit production in Mexico aimed at the United States has contributed to the shortage of staple foods such as corn and beans, which are now being imported from the United States. As areas in Central and South America are drawn into production for export, similar developments may occur in which production for local food systems becomes disrupted.

A second consequence may see the expansion of environmental problems as new acreages are brought into modern export production. Such production usually requires substantial use of chemical fertilizers. In addition, the exotic conditions in which some commodities are produced often require extensive use of pesticides, herbicides, nematicides, and other chemicals necessary to produce commodities in adequate volume and of satisfactory quality for the global market. Many Third World countries have begun to experience serious environmental problems as well as negative effects on the local labor force employed in agriculture (Wright 1990).

The fact that "healthy food"—food low in cholesterol, saturated fats, and other unhealthy food substances—will increasingly be coming from the Third World represents another form of North-South tension. Even leaving aside the effects of agricultural chemicals on farmworkers, populations, and environments, the reorientation of domestic food supply systems toward export, in the drive to earn necessary hard currencies, will have significant effects on Third World economies, polities, and populations. The new global food system, in other words, will be exacerbating the already existing exploitative factors in the North-South division.

The consumers of the advanced capitalist West can hardly be expected to exercise self-restraint in their demands for an increasing selection of foods, available on a year-round basis. Under these circumstances, the global fresh produce system can be expected to expand and perhaps even accelerate in its development. The social, political, economic, and environmental consequences of such an expansion have yet to be determined. Events in the next decade should permit a better understanding of the consequences of the new system.

Notes

1. The developments in food discussed here could also be applied, on a somewhat smaller scale, to flowers since flower production has expanded to sites in South America and Africa intended for consumers in Europe and North America. I will not discuss developments in flowers despite many similarities.

2. "Sell it or smell it" is the expression used by agricultural producers to emphasize the short life of many agricultural commodities.

3. New aseptic processing now extends the shelf life of tofu. Manufactured in the United States by a Japanese firm, this form of tofu is still treated sociologically as a fresh food.

4. The complex legality of "fresh" was recognized in the fresh produce trade newspaper the *Packer*, which asked (15 February 1992) in its banner headline on page 1, "What Is Fresh?" This issue has to do, among other things, with the irradiation of fresh produce, which extends its shelf life. Is such produce still "fresh?" Further, when unprocessed produce is prepared in a supermarket for immediate consumption through what the industry calls "pre-cut," can such produce be referred to as fresh or does it require the designation "freshly prepared?" As the *Packer* article points out, it is unclear that anyone has a solution to these problems.

5. Bananas were the first of the fresh fruits to move significantly between regions and continents. While massive food movements became global with the initiation of urban capitalism, i.e., sugar from the Caribbean to Europe and grains from eastern Europe, California, Argentina, and Australia, bananas were the first fresh commodity to be produced in one region (Central America or the Caribbean) for consumption fresh in another region (the United States or Western Europe).

6. Fordism is a term used by social scientists to describe the creation of mass consumption to accompany mass production. The origin of the term rests on the fact

that Henry Ford, by introducing the $5 a day wage, a level much higher than that then existing in industry, established the basis for higher levels of consumption by workers including enabling them to purchase automobiles. Fordism, as the term is now used, describes the conditions under which mass markets are created.

7. I am grateful to Larry Busch who suggested this term.

8. A concomitant development to the Fordist/Sloanist distinction in consumption can be found, at least incipiently, in production. Much of the standardized production of fresh fruits and vegetables takes place in *extensive* agribusiness production, in such locations as California. This contrasts to the *intensive* agribusiness production that is found in the glasshouses of Holland and elsewhere. The former form of production reaches enormous numbers of consumers; the latter form is intended for upscale niche markets. In addition to both forms, there is also what can be characterized as artisanal production, very often (but not always) organic in character intended for more restricted quality conscious consumers.

9. This dual system ignores the continued existence of the small luxury trade in food. Embodied in the expensive food boutiques such as Bloomingdales in New York, Harrods in London, and Fauchon in Paris, the foods available for the luxury trade are within occasional reach of some segments of the professional-technical class but are not intended primarily for them. I will not deal with this segment of the food system, which is characterized by highly specialized handicraft production.

10. A measure of the intensivity of production in Holland, as compared to the extensivity in California, can be found in the comparison of yields of tomatoes. In Holland, average production in glasshouses of tomatoes was 39.8 kilos per square meter (Verwegen 1991: 2), equivalent to 177.5 tons per acre. This compares with California production of tomatoes for processing in 1990 of 30.02 tons per acre, the highest yields in the United States (*California Tomato Grower*, March 1991: 18). The distinction between tomatoes for the fresh market (Holland) and for processing (California) is profound; what is far more profound, however, is the staggering difference between the capital-intensive system in California and the labor-intensive system in Holland. The Dutch yields are not unusual. Glasshouse hydroponic production in British Columbia has yields of 140–180 pounds per plant, with plants growing 30 feet high (*Produce Business*, June 1991: 17), compared with 8 meters (26.2 feet) reported in an interview with a glasshouse producer in Holland.

11. I present a more detailed analysis of the spring 1989 events in Friedland 1991.

12. Figures for the intervening years were $435 million (1985), $893 million (1988), and $1,250 million (1989). *Packer*, 23 March 1991: 1A.

13. I am grateful to Terry Marsden for this suggestion.

14. It may not be, as in the case of Mexico, that basic foodstuff production suffers in order to benefit export agriculture; rather, as Barkin and DeWalt (1988) have shown, limited government resources get allocated to supporting export agriculture at the expense of domestically oriented production.

Bibliography

Barkin, David, and Billie DeWalt. 1988. "Sorghum and the Mexican food crisis." *Latin American Research Review* 20, 3 (Fall): 30–59.

Bell, Daniel. 1953. "The next American labor movement." *Fortune* (April): 120–123, 201–206.

Carter, David, and David Turner. 1988. *Cool Chain Developments*. Watford, Eng.: Institute of Grocery Distribution/National Farmers Union.

CBT (Central Bureau of Dutch Auctions). n.d. *Rich Harvest: Fruit and Vegetables from Holland*. The Hague, The Netherlands: CBT.

Cook, Roberta L. 1990. "Challenges and opportunities in the U.S. fresh produce industry." *Journal of Food Distribution Research*, (February): 67–74.

Drum, David. 1990. "Wave goodbye to contra-seasonal doldrums." *Produce Business* 6, 1 (January): 29–30, 32, 34–36.

Ehrenreich, Barbara, and John Ehrenreich. 1979. "The professional-managerial class." Pp. 5–45 in Pat Walker (ed.), *Between Labor and Capital*. Boston: South End Press.

Friedland, William H. 1991. "Global Awareness and Social Action for the Sustainability Movement." Paper presented at the conference on Varieties of Sustainability: Reflecting on Ethics, Environment, and Economic Equity, Asilomar Conference Center, Pacific Grove, Calif., 10–12 May 1991.

Friedland, William H., Amy E. Barton, and Robert J. Thomas. 1981. *Manufacturing Green Gold: Capital, Labor, and Technology in the Lettuce Industry*. New York: Cambridge University Press.

Friedmann, Harriet. 1978a. "Simple commodity production and wage labour in the American plains." *Journal of Peasant Studies* 6, 1: 71–100.

———. 1978b. "World market, state, and family farm: Social bases of household production in an era of wage labour." *Comparative Studies in Society and History* 20, 4: 545–586.

———. 1987. "The family farm and the international food regimes." In Teodor Shanin (ed.), *Peasants and Peasant Societies*. Oxford: Basil Blackwell.

Geest. n.d.. *The Fresh Produce Report 2*. London: Geest and the Fresh Fruit and Vegetable Information Bureau.

Goldfrank, Walter L. 1990. "State, market, and agriculture in Pinochet's Chile." Pp. 69–77 in W. Martin (ed.), *Semi-Peripheral States in the World Economy*. Westport, Conn.: Greenwood Press.

Gorz, Andre. 1967. *Strategy for Labor*. Boston: Beacon.

Hofsommer, Don L. 1986. *The Southern Pacific, 1901-1985*. College Station: Texas A&M University Press.

Islam, Nurul. 1990. *Horticultural Exports of Developing Countries: Past Performances, Future Prospects, and Policy Issues*. Research Report 80. Washington, D.C.: International Food Policy Research Institute.

Kuhn, Arthur J. 1986. *GM Passes Ford, 1918-1938: Designing the General Motors Performance-Control System*. University Park: Pennsylvania State University Press.

Levenstein, Harvey A. 1988. *Revolution at the Table: The Transformation of the American Diet*. New York: Oxford University Press.

Mackintosh, Maureen. 1989. *Gender, Class, and Rural Transition: Agribusiness and the Food Crisis in Senegal*. London: Zed Books.

Mallet, Serge. 1975a. *The New Working Class*. Nottingham, Eng.: Spokesman Books.

———. 1975b. *Essays on the New Working Class*. St. Louis: Telos Press.

Mintz, Sidney W. 1985. *Sweetness and Power: The Place of Sugar in Modern History*. New York: Viking.

Morgan, Dan. 1980. *Merchants of Grain*. New York: Penguin.

Murray, Douglas L. 1983. "The Politics of Pesticides: Corporate Power and Popular

Struggle over the Regulatory Process." Ph.D. diss. University of California, Santa Cruz.

PGF (Produktschap voor Groenten en Fruit) Market Research Department. 1990. *Trends in Import of Fresh Fruit and Vegetables in the Netherlands*. The Hague, The Netherlands: PGF.

United Nations. 1988. *1988 International Trade Statistics Yearbook*. New York: United Nations.

United States Bureau of the Census. 1990. *Statistical Abstract of the U.S. 1990*. 110th ed. Washington, D.C.: Government Printing Office.

Verwegen, Hans. 1991. "Development Dutch Alimentary Horticulture." Dutch Golden Tomato Club, 8 August 1991.

Wright, Angus. 1990. *The Death of Ramon Gonzalez: The Modern Agricultural Dilemma*. Austin: University of Texas Press.

11 New Fruits and Vanity: Symbolic Production in the Global Food Economy

Ian Cook

In the penultimate chapter of *The Sociology of Agriculture*, Buttel, Larson, and Gillespie (1990) identify nine trends and six gaps in the contemporary sociology of agriculture. Among these are the trend of commodity systems analysis (Friedland 1990) and the gap to be filled by critical ethnographic fieldwork. A number of writers have attempted to apply the latter in their work on the former to assess how the distinctive industrial structures of the global food economy are produced, reproduced, and transformed by the day-to-day actions of those people who work within them.

Like these writers, I believe that a deeper understanding of agricultural change can come through ethnographic fieldwork and the development of theory that engages local with global, agency with structure, and the symbolic with the material. In this paper I begin to explore these engagements through an analysis of interviews with a number of executives working for J. Sainsbury, Tesco, and Safeway, the three largest food retailing chains in the United Kingdom. An examination of the work that goes into the introduction of new—or "exotic"—fruits to customers suggests that the meanings that companies attempt to ascribe to these fruits play a crucial role in the articulation of commodity systems. Put differently, just because they are produced and packed in one place and shipped, ripened, and delivered fresh to a store in another, it does not necessarily follow that anyone will buy them. In short, there is a symbiotic relationship between the "material" production of a fruit or vegetable and the "symbolic" production of its meaning(s).

The major link between a fruit's material and symbolic production are its specifications. These include its acceptable shape, size, weight, internal pressure, blemishes, seasonal sourcing, and price as defined by the retailers. Day by day—albeit through highly asymmetrical power relations—these are negotiated through both symbolic and material labor processes. Here we will explore this link between the symbolic and the material.

Contract Farming

The main reason that I have chosen to discuss contract farming—as opposed to other forms of agricultural production—is that, here, explicit attention has been paid to the day-to-day negotiation of specifications by growers.[1]

The Nature of Contracts

In the underdeveloped world, where many exotic or new (to Westerners) fruits are grown, contract farming has emerged for two major reasons: First, in many places, agribusiness corporations have been forced to give up their rights to land as a result of nationalist pressures and the attendant threats of expropriation and local regulation (Watts 1992). Second, independent peasant households have been institutionally captured by contract farming with its promises of modernization and credit (Clapp 1988).

Perhaps the most important features of contract farming are that its labor force consists of peasants who work their own land and that it is usually promoted as a "dynamic partnership" between the rural poor and private capital. This partnership, to quote Watts (1992: 15) "promises rapid market integration, economic growth and technical innovation while protecting the rights and autonomy of the grower via the contract." It legitimates the continued activities of agribusiness corporations, organizations such as the World Bank and the U.S. Agency for International Development (USAID), and ruling classes in the underdeveloped world. Through contracts, smallholding peasants become tied to local merchants, the state, agribusiness corporations, or joint enterprises that buy, process, and/or export their produce. However, whatever the nature of these enterprises, they demand produce that satisfies the retailers' specifications. This, in turn, means that peasants must follow a detailed checklist of instructions concerning the methods and dates of soil preparation, pesticide and fertilizer application, planting and harvesting established in the contract. Furthermore, even when this has been done, the contractor's inspectors can reject the crop on the grounds of "quality" standards, which they also specify (Clapp 1988). Only when all of these conditions have been satisfied can the crop enter the processing and transportation networks that make up its commodity system and the grower be paid for his or her work.

Meaning for Growers

From the contractor's perspective, this form of production is extremely efficient: It allows the programming of produce in advance at a predictable price, quality, and schedule of supply. At the same time, it insulates contractors against the risks of weather, insect attack, disease, and labor bottlenecks because they pay based on results, not by the hour. These risks are further minimized through multiple sourcing.

Though the contractor cannot avoid acts of God, the suppression of labor unrest is a key strategy of risk avoidance. Contract farming is extremely labor intensive, as great care has to be taken to produce fruit that is the right color, texture, shape, size, and ripeness on the supermarket shelf. So, for instance, one study of snow pea cultivation in Central America found that it was six times more labor intensive than the local staple, maize (Watts 1992).[2] To provide this labor, growers draw on family and other social networks in times of need. At the same time, the specialized knowledge required to successfully produce contracted fruit is usually in the hands of the contractor's outreach workers. Thus, while they own their own land, growers are effectively deskilled agricultural laborers working for a piecework wage for the contractor.

Behind the image of a dynamic partnership between the parties concerned, then, lies a mode of production in which contractors can obtain a continuous supply of high-quality produce by placing the risks of production almost entirely in the hands of growers and their families. Having entered into a legal agreement with growers, companies effectively absolve themselves of any welfare responsibilities. A newspaper article about Margaret Thatcher's visit to, and praise of, the South African farming sector in mid-1991, for instance, pointed out that its 1.5 million black laborers "enjoy no statutory protection on minimum wages, conditions of service, health and safety standards, unemployment insurance, working hours, overtime pay, maternity leave, [or] holidays" (Beresford 1991: 26). Although South Africa may be an extreme example, it is fair to say that contracts do not promote the "rights and autonomy" of growers but exploit their poverty and procure the grower's "self-exploitation" (Clapp 1988: 10). Thus, struggles over the production process are often fought not against the contractor but within the household. As a result these struggles become conjugal and/or generational and are often over "the customary rights, responsibilities and obligations linking [the] labor claims and property relations" of household members (Watts 1989: 18; cf. Thomas 1985).

Symbolic Production

At the other end of the chain in the U.K., there have been two major developments in the sale of fresh fruit in recent years. First, the market has grown quite considerably: Between 1983 and 1989 imports of fresh fruit into the U.K. grew by about 25 percent (Commonwealth Secretariat 1990). In the retail industry, this has been explained largely in terms of an increased consumer interest in healthy diets and a breakdown of traditional meal patterns. Consequently, more fruit is being consumed both in regular meals and as snacks (MSI 1988).

Second, during this same period, unusual and exotic produce has become increasingly important. This is illustrated by the fact that between 1983 and 1989, although the percentage of U.K. fruit imports by weight changed very little, by value the "other" fruit category (in which the exotics have been placed) registered a significant increase (Commonwealth Secretariat 1990). This pattern can be explained largely as the result of changes made by the major supermarket chains (or multiples) both at the point of sale and in terms of their buying strategies. At the point of sale, self-selection is the key issue, as it allows customers to handle the produce, select the particular pieces of fruit they want, and thereby to "discover" new varieties rather than by having to ask for them by name. Moreover, the chains have organized their suppliers to provide more and more produce year round, allowing formerly exotic fruits to become a regular part of their customers' diets.

In this arena, the supermarket chains have been able to carve out an increasingly large slice of fresh fruit sales. For instance, their share of the market grew by 2 percent per year between 1985 and 1987, when it stood at 46 percent (MST 1988). Furthermore, this growth happened at a time when the largest of them were undergoing a long-term expansion in terms of selling area, turnover, and profits and has continued even through the current recession (Thornhill and Urry 1991; annual reports).

From the perspective of the supermarket chains, the symbolic production of exotic produce can be seen as rooted in the daily lives of a small number of trading managers and technologists working in their headquarters. At Tesco, for example, the exotic fruit team established in December of 1990 consists of just one technologist and one trading manager. For the other supermarket chains, exotic produce usually falls within the purview of much larger soft and hard fruit teams.

Trading managers and technologists work very closely with the representatives of a small number of suppliers (e.g., Geest, Del Monte, Brooks Brothers, and Worldfresh) to set the specifications for their chosen range of fruit. They do this with two major corporate obligations in mind: to increase turnover by getting the best quality fruit year round; and to set their prices to meet the budgetary targets set by their senior management. Here, struggles ensue as to which new fruits to sell and how to promote them. Interestingly, however, immediate profits are not the sole determinant of whether the introduction of an exotic fruit can be termed "successful." These struggles and successes can both be seen to take place in a circuit of cultural forms.

Struggles

Struggles over the introduction of new fruits involve a blend of meanings and money, neither of which can be entirely separated from the other. A key problem, as a senior manager at Sainsbury's told me, is that trading managers have to deal with the fact that "one of the problems with exotic fruits is they're a bit like armadillos—you can't get into the damn things! You've got to have an instruction manual on how to eat it and what to do with it." But, given their budgets, the trading teams often cannot ordinarily provide these for customers because, as a Safeway trading manager explained:

They are very low volume, they are very high price and, to try to get things off the ground, you've got to spend a lot of money on them—and there isn't much money available. We've just launched a new exotic called the Pitahaya. . . . On average, we're looking for 35, 36 percent gross profit—somewhere round there—on the exotics. And, for the Pitahaya, we're talking about less than 10 percent. So, by the time the store, inevitably, has thrown one out of the box of ten away, you haven't got any profit—and they're more likely to throw four or five out of the box of ten away. So, there's no profit in it, but it's just trying to establish that product. Now, because the sales are so low, you can't go out and get a glossy brochure.

Faced with this situation, the stores have experimented with a wide variety of manuals to get their message across. All appear to be designed to draw new fruits into consumers' "maps of meaning" (Burgess 1990; Hall 1980; Jackson 1989) through associating them with popular notions of class, place, healthy living, and sensual experience. The latter includes, but is by no means limited to, that involved in tasting other more mainstream fruits. To illustrate these associations, consider three of the many types of manuals that were available on supermarket shelves in the U.K. in 1990 and 1991.

First, supermarket chains have produced wide-ranging manuals for sale. Take, for instance, the exotic fruit and vegetable manual available in early 1991 at the checkouts of Asda—the fourth largest chain—for twenty pence. For instance, on the page that promotes limes, mangoes, lychees, and papayas, all are described in terms of their origins, properties and brief suggestions for their preparation (Illustration 2). Finally, the back of the manual

FOOD-RETAILING still offers enormous growth potential – potential which can be realised by developing attractive new products of the highest quality, and by satisfying new customer values such as health, the environment, and the source and methods of manufacture.

During 1989, we introduced 1,000 new products, more than 400 of which were fresh foods. We now offer our customers a total of 14,000 food products – a massive increase from the 5,000 that we stocked just seven years ago, and we continue to lead the industry in providing on-pack nutritional information.

Cosmetics without cruelty

'Healthy Eating' range

*F*ourteen thousand food products...

The pick of the world's crops

Our Healthy Eating range was extended during the year. We now offer over 50 products with this branding. Most are short-life provisions such as salads, yoghurts, desserts and non-dairy spreads. The Healthy Eating brand is unique to Tesco and is now worth nearly £50 million a year in sales. Our Healthy Eating yoghurt won the *Quality Food Award* for the supplier of the year. We won more quality awards for both our foods and our wines than did any other retailer.

Other new food products introduced during the year included a highly successful range of fresh cream cakes, which opens up a large new sector of added-value convenience foods. No other national retailer, we believe, could market such a range on such a scale, for it demands very close temperature control and absolute integrity of the chill chain. 1989 also saw the introduction of free-range chickens and turkeys, which are reared in the Landes forest in France, as well as our *Nature's Choice* range – the only cosmetic products currently available which satisfy the 'Cruelty Free' criteria of the British Union for the Abolition of Vivisection.

I would like to thank all our suppliers for their cooperation during the year. Dedicated, cost-efficient suppliers are essential to our strategy, and many have set up factories or special facilities to manufacture products exclusively for Tesco.

Tesco is now undoubtedly in the forefront of food retailing in the UK. In terms of variety, absolute quality, value for money, product integrity and new product development, we set and consistently achieve exceptionally high standards.

JOHN GILDERSLEEVE
Buying and Marketing Director

Illustration 1

EXOTIC FRUIT

1 LIMES

ORIGIN: Brazil, West Indies, South Africa, USA.

A green skinned citrus fruit, shaped like a lemon, but smaller. The flesh is very juicy and highly scented.

PREPARATION: Use as a lemon. Can be substituted in any dish which calls for lemon. It is particularly refreshing when used in drinks and cocktails.

LYCHEES (NOT ILLUSTRATED)

ORIGIN: The Far East, Madagascar, USA, South Africa.

A small fruit with a rough reddish-brown shell. The flesh inside is translucent white and very juicy, with a delicate rose scent. Originates in China, and is used in a variety of Chinese dishes — sweet and savoury.

PREPARATION: Shell and eat raw, discarding the stone in the centre.
Can be poached lightly in sugar syrup and served chilled with cream. Or use in savoury Chinese dishes, such as stir-frys.

2 MANGO

ORIGIN: The Caribbean, Africa, South America, Asia.

A large stone fruit which varies in size and shape according to variety. It has a delicate green/orange skin and bright yellow flesh inside. When ready to eat, the mango will feel soft to the touch. It is rich in Vitamin A and is an important part of the diet of many tropical countries. Its taste resembles a mixture of apricot and pineapple.

PREPARATION: Slit round the fruit horizontally and carefully remove the flesh from the centre stone. Peel, slice and use in fruit salads, mousses and sorbets, or eat by itself. It is best to prepare the mango just before serving — this way the delicate aroma is preserved.

3 PAPAYA (PAW PAW)

ORIGIN: South America, West Indies.

A green skinned fruit resembling a large pear. It is ready to eat when the skin turns yellow/orange. The flesh is pinky orange in colour and the taste resembles a peach or apricot.

PREPARATION: Cut in half lengthways and scoop out seeds. Serve like a melon, cutting the flesh into wedges. Or pulp the flesh to make mousses and fools. Makes delicious jam.

Illustration 2

contains a number of recipes including "kumquats in honey butter" and "fluffy mango fool" (Illustration 3).

Another type to be found on supermarket shelves is the single fruit manual put together by its suppliers. Consider, for instance, the one provided free by Morris, sole producers of the Kiwano melon (Illustration 4). Turning this over, one of the recipes provided here is for the "Kiwano smoothie" (Illustration 5).

The rather outlandish approach to the marketing of this exotic fruit can be better understood by taking into account the motives of its producer. In November 1990, in an article in the *Sunday Times* color supplement, John Morris described why he had paid $25,000 to register "Kiwano" as a trademark: "There is an advantage in brand names . . . because we are in an age when people buy labels. What we're after for the horned melon is a Pierre Cardin image" (Martin 1990: 27). A photograph (Illustration 6) taken from the December 1990 edition of *Expressions* (p. 70)—the magazine for American Express cardholders—features another glamorous fruit and can be seen as part of this process. The man shown is Sir Terence Conran; the fruit he is holding is variously named carambola, starfruit or Chinese vegetable, and the theme of the text is setting the table for a dinner party: "Ever watchful of excessive detailing or effect, Sir Terence gives attention to dramatic color combinations like purple and gold, offset by elegant simple cutlery and glass. Decoration is bold and inventive—unusual ceramics with bursts of orange and yellow berries as spot color on either side of a display of Chinese vegetables." Conran is then quoted as saying: "Chinese vegetables are so intriguing. I first thought of using them as decoration when I was wandering around Chinatown—they all look so wonderfully sculptural and surprising."

My final example is a brochure that was available free in Safeway produce departments in the fall of 1990. It begins by describing how they are able to provide "the widest possible choice of fresh fruit and vegetables—throughout the year" and, among the pages devoted to their grapes, apples, aubergines, beansprouts, tomatoes, potatoes, and oranges is one on carambolas (Illustration 7). Interestingly, unlike the other manuals I have seen, this paints an image of their material production.

Rather than being the sole source of information on new fruits, trading managers see the production and distribution of these manuals as part of a wider circuit of cultural forms in which, as one at Safeway put it,

> The people who buy exotics . . . are looking for them basically. . . . . You get a sort of gourmet person—they don't necessarily have to be on a high income, but . . . they'll go out and buy the Pitahaya. What we've got to

FLUFFY MANGO FOOL

METHOD

Serves: 4-6

1 Gently heat the milk in a saucepan.
Add the beaten egg yolks and sugar away
from the heat. Warm the mixture gently,
stirring continuously, until the custard begins
to thicken and coat the back of a spoon.
Chill thoroughly.

2 Peel the mangoes, and cut 4-6 slices from
the flesh to reserve for decoration.
Remove the remaining flesh from the stones
and puree it.

3 Mix the mango puree with the chilled
custard. Fold in the whipped cream.

4 Whisk the egg whites until they form soft
peaks and fold them into the mango
mixture.

5 Divide the fool between sundae glasses.
Decorate with the reserved mango slices.
Serve with brandy snaps.

INGREDIENTS

125ml (¼pt) Milk
2 size 2 Eggs, separated
25g (1oz) Caster Sugar
2 Mangoes
125ml (¼pt) Double Cream,
    lightly whipped

KUMQUATS IN HONEY BUTTER

METHOD

Serves: 4
Cooking Time: 10 minutes

1 Melt the butter in a saucepan. Add the
honey and orange juice and bring to the
boil.

2 Place the sliced kumquats into the honey
butter mixture and simmer gently for
10 minutes. Remove any pips that rise to the
surface. Stir in the Cointreau.

3 Serve with cream or use as a filling for a
sponge flan case.

INGREDIENTS

50g (2oz) Butter
4x15ml sp (4 tbsp) Honey
150ml (¼ pint) unsweetened
    Orange Juice
200g (8oz) Kumquats, sliced
15ml (1 tbsp) Cointreau,
    if desired

Illustration 3

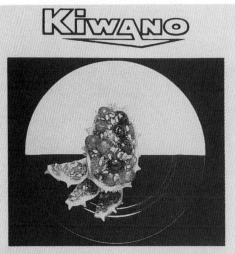

This unique fruit has a delightfully refreshing flavour, with the subtle taste of banana, limes and passionfruit. A natural thirst quencher. The Kiwano is golden orange when ripe with the pulp dark green and full of flavour.

Ce fruit unique en son genre, délicatement parfumé, surprend par son goût subtil de banane, de citron vert et de fruit de la passion. Un goût frais, naturellement désaltérant. Bien mûr, le kiwano se présente sous l'aspect d'une orange dorée, à la pulpe vert foncé très parfumée.

Diese einzigartige Frucht hat einen köstlichen, erfischenden Geschmark, an eiene Aroma – Kombination aus Banane, Limone und Passionsfrucht erinnernd. Ein natürlicher Durstlöscher. Wenn die Schale golden orange ist und das Fruchtmark dunkelgrün, ist die Kiwano voll ausgereift. Dann bietet sie ein Höchstmaß an Aroma.

TRY THIS VERSATILE FRUIT

★ On its own consumed straight from the shell as a refreshing drink.
★ Combined with other fruit or juices to produce exotic tasting combinations.
★ As a dessert or topping for cheese cakes, souffles, mousses, flans, sundaes and pavlova.
★ As a serving vessel, the attractive shell adds originality to all dinner occasions.
★ Its decorative quality will enhance fruit, flower and ornamental arrangements.
★ A must in the cocktail bar.

Illustration 4.

do is then convince some of the people who don't like trying things, but might have a lot of money. . . . . What we've got to try and do is break some of them into eating that product. It's a slow process. Gradually, . . . they may see recipes in . . . women's magazines or television, or recipe leaflets that we produce as well. It's a very slow process.

KIWANO SMOOTHIE

pulp of 1 Kiwano   1 tablespoon honey
1 cup (8 fl. oz) plain yoghurt   2 scoops vanilla ice cream
   Place all ingredients in a blender or food processor and blend until smooth.
Serve in long glasses or in Kiwanos which have had one end removed and have
been hollowed out. Serves 1-2.

Illustration 5.

He continued by explaining that the information available in these circuits
was not always complimentary and referred specifically to the media:

> They will phone our public relations department and say, "We're going to
> do a programme", or, "We're going to do an article on so-and-so. Can we
> have some?" and "Can we have your comments?" . . . . So then we will
> supply them—with some wariness because they don't always give particu-
> larly good comments about it. We could do a lot of work—there are one
> or two in particular where we do a lot of background work—and then all
> . . . we get is just slagged off about how bad it is. Obviously they've got to
> be truthful, but . . . we can't bend over backwards to help someone who's
> just got an axe out.

Illustration 6

Success

After having listened to my contacts talking about the difficulties of introducing new fruits to the British public and the long periods of making little or no profit on them, I wondered what purpose is served by these exotic fruits. I put this question to the man at Safeway and he provided an explana-

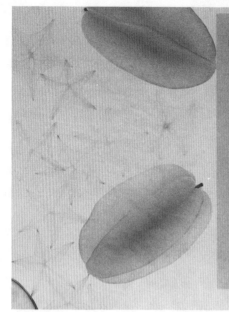

CARAMBOLAS

The best Carambolas are grown for Safeway in Malaya. They are ripe when they have a rich yellow colour with the edges just turning brown. They have a sharp, refreshing flavour and melon-like texture. Best eaten raw, you can slice them to liven up a fruit salad, garnish a cheesecake or even eat them with a spicy meat dish.

The care taken to grow Carambolas for Safeway is really something special. The Malayan farmers wrap each budding fruit in its own paper bag. This protects the fruit from pests and extreme weather conditions while it is growing. The special bags also make sure that all Carambolas grow to the correct size and shape – ensuring the best quality Carambolas time after time. Once grown and harvested, each Carambola is individually hand-washed in pure warm water, before being hand-dried and carefully wrapped to seal in the freshness. Sponge-lined boxes protect the fruit while they are air-freighted to Britain. Here they are all checked once more to guarantee freshness and quality before being brought to your store.

Illustration 7

tion: "First of all, it's a point of difference for Safeway. There's a lot of products that are exactly the same, any supermarket you go in. People won't come to you because you sell Heinz Beans, because everybody sells Heinz Beans. But, people may just do their 75, £100s worth of shopping a week with you because you sell the Pitahaya and . . . Safeway's the only place you can get it. So, you could actually attract customers by making the shopping interesting." In the U.K., as in the United States, supermarkets are commonly designed so that customers enter directly into the fresh produce department. With their colors and smells, and, through a European Community (EC) directive, the place of origin of all produce is clearly displayed on the shelf alongside the price. Sainsbury's marketing director described entering the store as a geography lesson or a trip around the world.

Moving back to Safeway, my contact gave a second reason for selling exotic fruit: "For any new product to take off, you've got to work at it for ten years. Avocados came in, first, into Safeway and . . . they were an exotic item for ten years and suddenly they're a major item for us now." As well as avocados, he could have mentioned kiwifruit and mangoes—both of which have shed their exotic image to become everyday fruits available, like apples and oranges, throughout the year.[3] In a relatively short time, both have grown into approximately £20 million markets in the U.K.[4] Therefore, trading managers, technologists, and suppliers are all searching for the kiwi or mango of the future.

Critical Ethnographies
in the Modern World System

Having argued that symbolic production is a key process in the articulation of commodity systems, I would like to conclude with some notes on the prospect of a broader critical ethnography of the modern world system. Perhaps the most important insights that ethnographic research can provide for us are found in the "maps of meaning" drawn upon and contested within and between groups of people working at different stages in a commodity system. Looked at critically, these are not "merely subjective." Rather, growers, outreach workers, trading managers, technologists, and consumers—as well as other related groups—conceptualize the horizons of their power and future fortunes with these maps. Thus, it is interesting to note Clapp's observation that in many rural areas in Latin America,

> The Coca-Cola sign on the local *bodega* may be ten years old and its glow filtered by a coat of dust, but the Dow poster in the extension agent's office has the aura of the new and successful in a town where not much does. These advertisements may not persuade a farmer to buy one brand rather than another, but the cluster of them together, reinforced by the urging of state and company promoters, may define what it is to be a modern and "progressive" farmer. It should not surprise us that [in one Guatemalan study] . . . personal crop sprayers had become a sign of status and that farmers with access to credit through the contract had gone deeply into debt to buy them.

This imaging of the Other is also a key component drawn on by supermarket executives. My main goal in talking with them was to trace connections between their work and that of the people who grow the fruit that they sell. In their companies' annual reports, claims are often made that they "care" about the production process. Consider, for example, one page from Tesco's 1990 report. It begins: "Food retailing still offers enormous growth potential—potential which can be realized by developing attractive new products of the highest quality, and by satisfying new consumer values such as health, the environment, and the *source and methods of manufacture*." It ends by noting that, "in terms of variety, absolute quality, value for money, *product integrity* and new product development, we set and achieve exceptionally high standards" (emphases added).

Yet, when challenged about sourcing and methods, they responded with rather limited conceptions of "product integrity" that had little or nothing to do with labor processes. The trading director of Sainsbury's explained:

I think we would assume that anybody we dealt with . . . would be fulfilling any criteria that we set down as a bona fide supplier—which would mean having clean factories, and standards, and all the rest of it. And the factories would be vetted, and they're vetted . . . often on unannounced audits. Now, all of our Kenya dwarf beans packed in Kenya—you will note that they all point the same way. We had a customer letter about it two weeks ago asking, "Why do they all point the same way?" The simple reason is that there's . . . lots of black ladies out there who put them in all facing the same way. Now, that's not forced labor. They just choose to do it.

This, of course, is by no means a free or simple "choice." Yet, thinking so allows those involved in symbolic production to quite sincerely peddle their caring approach in an exotic, rather than systematically exploited, world. At a general level, much of this would seem to be embroiled in British culture with its colonial legacy and, more generally, a disassociation of exotic or holiday locations from the widespread poverty and hunger of many of those who live there. Moreover, those executives who do trot the globe visiting sites of material production do not spend any great length of time sharing experiences with their growers. They are unlikely even to speak the same language (Hannerz 1990).

In sum, the articulation of commodity systems in space and time is not just a technical matter. It necessarily involves the production and consumption of the commodity's meaning(s) within, as well as between, all stages of its existence (Burgess 1990; Johnson 1986). As such, the "struggles" shaping the course(s) of agricultural change are by no means confined to growers and their families negotiating new relations of production that have resulted from their incorporation into the capitalist world system. Rather, as Marcus and Fischer (1986: 91) argue, we should see this system as being produced, reproduced, and transformed more broadly by "the activities of dispersed groups of individuals whose actions have mutual, often unintended, consequences for each other, as they are connected by markets and other major institutions that make the world a system."

Thus, a key component of critical ethnography—particularly with respect to the exploration of power relations—is that its fieldwork should take place in more than one locale (Marcus 1986) within a given commodity system in order that the local and the global, agency and structure, and the symbolic and the material can be more directly engaged.

Notes

This research has been funded through an assistantship from the Economic and Social Research Council of the United Kingdom.
1. This choice can also be justified by virtue of the fact that some have seen this mode of production as the agricultural component of the new regime of "flexible accumulation" in global capitalism; see Friedland (1990) and Watts (1992).
2. Snow peas are known as "mangetout" in the U.K.
3. One contact at Tesco noted that exotic fruits are given the name "queer gear" by market traders. One of his tasks was to change this image.
4. Martin (1990) and MSI (1988) report data on kiwis and mangoes, respectively. However, caution should be used in that my contacts described mangoes as being "the kiwifruit of the future." Yet, the figures reported suggest that the mango market had risen to £22m by 1987, whereas the kiwifruit market had risen to just £20m three years after. In 1987, were kiwis the mangoes of the future?

Bibliography

Beresford, David. 1991. "Adoring South African farmers name a fruit after Thatcher, bearer of unworthy praise." *Guardian*, May 17.

Burgess, Jacqueline. 1990. "The production and consumption of environmental meanings in the mass media: A research agenda for the 1990s." *Transactions, Institute of British Geographers* new series 15: 139–161.

Buttel, F. H., Olaf Larson, and Gilbert W. Gillespie. 1990. *The Sociology of Agriculture*. Westport, Conn.: Greenwood Press.

Clapp, Roger A. J. 1988. "Representing reciprocity, reproducing domination: Ideology and the labor process in Latin American contract farming." *Journal of Peasant Studies* 16, 1: 5–39.

Commonwealth Secretariat. 1990. *Fruit and Tropical Products*. London.

_____. 1987. *Fruit and Tropical Products*. London.

_____. 1984. *Fruit and Tropical Products*. London.

Friedland, William H. 1990. The Transnationalization of Production and Consumption of Food and Fibre: Challenges for Rural Research. Paper presented at the seminar on Rural Futures in an International World, University of Trondheim, 17–18 September.

Hall, Stuart. 1980. "Encoding/decoding." Pp. 128–138 in S. Hall et al. (eds.), *Culture, Media, Language*. London: Croom Helm.

Hannerz, Ulf. 1990. "Cosmopolitans and locals in world culture." *Theory, Culture and Society* 7: 237–251.

Jackson, Peter. 1989 . *Maps of Meaning*. London: Unwin Hyman.

Johnson, Richard. 1986. "The story so far, and further transformations?" Pp. 277–313 in D. Punter (ed.), *Introduction to Contemporary Cultural Studies*. Harlow, Eng.: Longman.

Marcus, George E. 1986. "Contemporary problems of ethnography in the modern world system." Pp. 165–193 in J. Clifford and G. E. Marcus (eds.), *Writing Culture: The Poetics and Politics of Ethnography*. Los Angeles and Berkeley: University of California Press.

Marcus, George E., and Michael M. J. Fischer. 1986. *Anthropology as Cultural Critique: An Experimental Moment in the Human Sciences*. Chicago: University of Chicago Press.

Marketing Strategies for Industry (MSI). 1988. *Fruit UK: Marketing Database*. Surrey, Eng.: Marketing Strategies for Industry.

Martin, Peter. 1990. "Trolley fodder." *Sunday Times Magazine*, 4 November, 24–36.

Thomas, Robert J. 1985. *Citizenship, Gender and Work: Social Organization of Industrial Agriculture*. Los Angeles and Berkeley: University of California Press.

Thornhill, John, and Maggie Urry. 1991. "Where growth is the food of life." *Financial Times*, 30 January, 2.

Watts, Michael J. 1989. "The agrarian question in Africa: Debating the crisis." *Progress in Human Geography* 13, 1: 1–41.

———. 1992. "Living under contract: Work, production, politics and the manufacture of discontent in a peasant society." Pp. 65–105 in Allan Pred and Michael Watts (eds.), *Reworking Modernity: Capitalism and Symbolic Discontent*. New Brunswick, N.J.: Rutgers University Press.

Part 3

Current Theoretical Issues of Globalization

12 The Locus of Polity Action
in a Global Setting

Alessandro Bonanno

My objective in this chapter is to analyze the complex relationship between the new global agricultural and food order and fundamental political institutions such as the state.[1] The basic focus is to illustrate some of the implications of the globalization of the agriculture and food order for the capacity of the domestic state to perform its role in society.

I open with a discussion of the changes that the increasingly globalized nature of agricultural and food production and distribution has brought about. Particular emphasis is placed on emerging new issues and their differences from issues that have traditionally occupied center stage in the scientific debate in the substantive areas of agriculture and food. In this context, it is recognized that the traditional agrarian question has been replaced by that of the food and natural resource question, particularly in advanced Western societies. To be sure, a number of themes typical of the agrarian question are still present in some regions of the advanced West and in developing countries. However, the complex multisectorial integration characterizing the agricultural and food sector, the fragmentation of traditional interests associated with the agrarian question, and the growing relevance of urban masses have generated a setting that differs from that of the old agrarian question.

In the second portion of the chapter I discuss some specific implications of the emergence of a global agricultural and food system for the domestic state. It is argued that the transnationalization of the economic sphere has hampered the ability of the political sphere (the state) to assist actors in the processes of accumulation of capital and social legitimation. Though in recent years transnational companies have operated so as to bypass state action, state action remains as the principal consolidated locus of political regulation and mediation of conflicting interests. Transnational corporations have interests in maintaining some form of state assistance to their operations. However, these interests are paralleled by similar demands stemming from a heterogenous mix of groups that also require state assistance. The interest in maintaining some form of state assistance, though mutual, is also contradictory as these groups demand intervention for opposing reasons and objectives. Furthermore, the limitations of domestic state action at the transnational level shift the locus of political action at the international level. This situation opens up a new set of questions concerning the relationship between locally generated social demands and internationally located arenas available for their resolution.

The Global Dimension of the Agricultural and Food Sector and the New Agrarian Question

The traditional terms of the agrarian question (Kautsky 1987) were still relevant in the advanced West at the end of World War II. The crucial importance that land reforms and agrarian movements had in Japan and Eastern and Western Europe are all cases in point. More recently, the issues characterizing the traditional agrarian question, such as the presence of a relatively large agricultural labor force, the primary developmental role assigned to the agricultural sector, and the prominence of agricultural issues in the political arena, have been replaced by other, "new" issues. These new issues constitute the so-called food and natural resource question or the new agrarian question. Agricultural overproduction, food abundance accompanied by unavailability of food to some segments of the population, and the protection of the environment constitute some of the most relevant issues of the new agrarian question. In fact, in recent years, domestic and multinational policies[2] of advanced societies have been directed toward these new problems (Bonanno 1990a).

To a great extent, the shift from the agrarian question to the food and natural resource question appears evident only if advanced Western societies are taken into consideration. Moreover, it becomes theoretically plausible only if a *domestically centered, sectorial analysis* is carried out. Indeed, the latter have been fundamental elements in research on the agrarian question. An alternative account, however, can be developed if the analysis is extended to the global level and if a transnational and intersectorial posture is adopted. From this perspective it becomes evident that the agrarian question and the food and natural resource question coexist at the world level, as the former still characterizes the agriculture of developing countries and both questions are systemically interconnected at the global level. A number of factors account for the support of a posture that reunifies the traditional and new agrarian questions at the global level. Following are some constitutive elements of this alternative approach.

Internationally, the socioeconomic problems associated with the agrarian question are still dominant in developing countries and some underdeveloped regions within advanced countries. In these areas issues such as the presence of a large farm-dependent population and a large number of farms, the primacy of the agricultural sector in the economic panorama, and the lack of food products for local consumption are all central problems to be resolved (Barkin 1990; Bonanno 1987a).

Recent research has pointed out the connection between the emergence of the food and natural resource question in the advanced West and the concentration of the traditional terms of the agrarian question in developing regions. In this respect, two items are important to mention for the discussion at hand.

First, capitalist development has abandoned its multinational phase to enter a transnational phase. In the multinational phase it was possible to identify corporations with countries of origin (Bonanno 1991; Sassen 1988). In this context, international operations were treated as extensions of entrepreneurial activities designed and engineered in the home country and supported by the home state apparatus. In the transnational phase the association of economic activities, identity, and loyalty of conglomerates with a particular country are decreasingly visible. The large number of acquisitions of companies by other international conglomerates, the decentralization of production across national borders and the transnationalization of the financial sector are all cases in point (Bluestone and Harrison 1982; Bonanno 1991; Friedmann and McMichael 1989; Heffernan 1990).[3]

Second, the transnationalization phase of capitalism has affected the internal organization of productive sectors, including the agricultural and food sector. Today it is no longer possible to equate the notion of agriculture with that of farming. In the classic debate on the agrarian question the two concepts were synonymous, as they reflected the status of a productive apparatus in which the production of food was almost entirely contained within the farm. Currently, the concept of agriculture refers to a productive structure in which the production of food largely transcends the farming sector. Accordingly, the concept of agriculture as originally adopted in the discussion of the agrarian question is qualitatively different from that adopted in the modern debate.

The agricultural and food sector is integrated into a transnational and transectoral network. In other words, integration develops at the *spatial* and *sectoral* levels. Spatially, transnationalization indicates an intensification of agricultural specialization at both the regional and productive-unit levels. At the sectoral level, it implies the increasing transformation of agricultural products from items destined for immediate consumption to inputs for the greater food manufacture system. This situation has been described in various manners. Friedmann and McMichael (1989, 1988) and McMichael (1991) have analyzed it in terms of food regimes. According to these authors, the first food regime (circa 1870–1945) was characterized by the emergence of national economies, which governed the development of national agricultural sectors and state apparati. In this context, agricultural production had a national character. On an international level it was concentrated in both nonsettler colonies, which traded agricultural products for manufactured goods, labor, and capital from the European metropole, and settler colonies, which were distinct forms of economies (Bonanno 1991). The early second food regime (1945–1973) was characterized by "an intensive accumulation process geared, not to cheapening consumption, but rather to incorporating consumption relations into the accumulation process itself as required by the Fordist model of rising wage/productivity contract" (McMichael 1991: 7). The post-1973 phase of the second food regime is characterized by the crisis of the Fordist model (Kenney et al. 1989) and the increasing transnationalization of the sector. Transnationalization indicates "(i) intensification of agricultural specialization (for both enterprises and regions) and integration of specific crops and livestock into agro-food chains dominated at both ends by increasingly large industrial capital and (ii) a shift in agricultural products from final use to industrial inputs for manufactured foods" (Friedmann and McMichael 1989: 105).

Similar issues are discussed by William D. Heffernan and his associates (Constance and Heffernan 1989, 1991; Heffernan 1990, 1984). According to these authors, the evolution of the food sector has transcended the national arena, since there has been a concentration of the food sector orchestrated by a few global conglomerates. The global dimension of the concentration of food production is based on these conglomerates' actions to increase economic returns and reduce economic uncertainties by shifting production from one location to another and to avoid state regulations (such as environmental and health regulations, etc.) that have added to production costs.

These and other authors (Friedland 1991; McMichael and Buttel 1990) underscore the integration of the agriculture and food sector with other economic sectors from a number of viewpoints. From the productive point of view, food production is increasingly integrated into a network that involves a number of other economic sectors. Goodman and his associates (Goodman, Sorj, and Wilkinson 1987), for example, indicate that technological innovations in agriculture have generated two relevant processes: appropriationism and substitutionism. Appropriationism indicates the development of new items to be produced by agriculture, such as new crops and new varieties of animals for breeding. As a result, agriculture is increasingly integrated with the chemical, pharmaceutical, and financial sectors. Substitutionism indicates that through the use of new technologies it is possible to replace agricultural production with manufactured products. In this latter case, there is a tendency to shift production from the farm to the factory.

From the point of view of the use of labor in farming, it is evident that full-time farmers and/or farmworkers are no longer the dominant agricultural workers. In fact, in recent years the separation between work in farming and in other economic sectors has become increasingly tenuous, resulting in the emergence of the new social figure of the multiple job holder (Pugliese 1991). Furthermore, the restructuring of the traditional manufacturing sector has paralleled transformations occurring in the farming sector. In this respect, in many productive areas the traditional "Fordist" full-time employed worker has been replaced with workers whose employment is increasingly flexible, whose pay is lower than in the past, and whose fringe benefits have been largely eliminated (Bluestone and Harrison 1982; Calasanti and Bonanno 1992).

The production of cheap and abundant food has been paralleled by economic crises in developing countries and in some regions within developed countries and by an increasing differentiation of the link between production and consumption. As research has indicated (Barkin 1990; Goméz and Goldfrank 1991; McMichael 1991; Morett 1991; Renard 1990), the production of abundant and inexpensive food for the West would be impossible under present conditions without the contribution of developing countries to global production. Moreover, the same research indicates that the process of integration generates regional inequalities as the global terms of production and trade make economic growth in these regions increasingly difficult. More specifically, the development of monocrop production for the global integrated market has often resulted in a decrease in food self-sufficiency for producing regions and an increase in foreign debt.

In terms of the production–consumption linkage, the transnational chains of production create an increasing divergence between local food demand and local production aimed at entering international circuits. In this context, farm-generated products become constitutive parts of a process that responds to economic demands of affluent consumption centers. Although it is possible that agriculturalists benefit from situations based on a stable economic demand, it is often the case that even minimal fluctuations in the international market, productive restructuring in a situation of inelasticity of demand, and limitations in the practice of subsistence farming (production of food for direct consumption by producers) generate economically and socially regressive outcomes.

Regional economic problems have emerged in advanced countries, as well. In this case farm-dependent regions are affected by price fluctuations as well as by changes in the international financial market. Though in advanced societies employment alternatives and resources are available to counter economic crisis, the farm crisis as experienced in North America and in Western Europe in the 1980s has had lasting consequences.

In synthesis, recent research has stressed the global dimension of food and agricultural production in both its transnational and transectorial aspects and in terms of developed and developing countries. Some of the implications of this new situation in regard to agricultural policies are discussed in the following section.

Agricultural Policies in the Global Agricultural and Food System

The emergence of a new organization of food production in which the agrarian question and the food and natural resource question are unified at the global level invites the reexamination of the parameters of policy objectives.

In general terms, the global agricultural and food system contains a fundamental contradiction. On the one hand, it produces cheap and abundant food for the West. On the other, it creates a situation of regional socioeconomic dependence that touches large segments of the population of developing countries and some segments of the population of developed countries. This contradictory situation has sparked a debate on the characteristics and functioning of the system itself, as well as generating a number of proposed alternatives to the current situation (Friedland 1991; Friedmann and McMichael 1989; Goodman, Sorj, and Wilkinson 1987; Heffernan 1990). However, relatively little attention has been paid to the characteristics of the social setting within which the process of social restructuring is taking place and, more specifically, to the locus where new social and political demands are to be addressed. In terms of patterns of development in the agricultural and food sector, the above research clearly indicates that if the sector is left to evolve according to current patterns, the contradictions characterizing the system are more likely to grow than to fade. In fact, food abundance will continue to be a phenomenon limited to affluent regions and social groups. In this case the commodified nature of food (i.e., the fact that food must be purchased) is largely irrelevant to consumption, since the cost of food represents a relatively small portion of the disposable income of this segment of the world population. For other segments of the world population, the commodified nature of food will continue to create a problem of accessibility, since they cannot afford food. Put in a different manner, the satisfaction of the world food demand will be only partially addressed because only some segments of the world population, concentrated in the North, can afford food, while a significant portion of the world population, concentrated in the South, cannot afford food. Accordingly, and despite its physical availability, food will remain economically unavailable.[4]

From the productive point of view, the consolidation of a transnational agricultural and food sector will reinforce social and economic dislocation within producing regions. More specifically, production for the globalized system will be increasingly detached from local economic expansion and local food needs. Food self-sufficiency in developing countries will continue to decline (Barkin 1990; Gómez and Goldfrank 1991), and existing economic difficulties of family farm producers in the developed world will not improve.

Following this analysis, the issues of desired patterns of development in the agricultural and food sector must be addressed in a context in which intervention is sought regardless of its direction. In this case the emerging central issue is the locus of political action.

The Locus of Political Action
in the Globalized System

The emergence of a global agricultural and food system and the qualitative changes introduced by the transnational phase of economic development have brought about a reconstruction of the arenas within which production takes place. This process, ultimately, mandates the transcendence of the domestic-centered production process (Bonanno 1991).

A fundamental aspect of this situation is to the development of a set of limits for national political institutions, such as the domestic state apparatus. As indicated elsewhere (see Bonanno 1991: 21–27), the globalization of the agricultural and food system generates a dislocation between the transnationalization of the accumulation process and the national dimension of state action. More specifically, the national state is increasingly unable to perform its historical societal "functions," i.e., fostering economic development (accumulation) and guaranteeing mediation between social groups and social organization (legitimation).

The state has been concerned historically with fostering the conditions necessary for the accumulation of capital in society. Moreover, in order to accumulate, there must be a certain degree of harmony in society. This situation, which Block (1980) called "business confidence," involves two related issues. The first refers to the creation of harmony between the ruling class and subordinate classes. The second refers to the harmonizing of competition and conflict among the various segments of the ruling class. The shifting of production at the transnational level has produced a situation in which competing segments of the ruling class do not seem to have an organizing entity such as the state at the domestic level. Put differently, the transnational bourgeoisie does not have an organizing state that mediates its action vis-à-vis opposing classes. These organizing and mediating actions are necessary as segments of the bourgeoisie compete among themselves in the pursuit of profit.

Paradoxically, the globalization of capital accumulation has developed as a partial response to the increasingly interventionist role of the state at the domestic level (Bonanno 1987b; Friedmann and McMichael 1989; Sassen 1988). However, limiting the intervention of the state in the process of accumulation carried on by transnational corporations has hampered its ability to organize economic activities in a situation in which the transnationalization of the economy demands more (state) coordination[5] (Sassen 1988: 135). After all, historically the state played a fundamental role in earlier phases of the international expansion of capital (Murray 1971; Rowthorn 1971). In essence, the state is increasingly unable to assist the process of accumulation of capital in the redefined economic arena, as the bourgeoisie's need for organization finds its limits in the global range of its economic action and in its concomitant desire to avoid state action.

It can be argued that transnational corporations actually attempt to coordinate their action and, thus, overcome the lack of a coordinating state. In fact, the reduced action of the state is not a relevant problem for transnational companies since they can substitute state action with other forms of organizational and mediating entities. Furthermore, these attempts are not new, as indicated by the case of the Trilateral Commission, which was established more than two decades ago.

It should be stressed, in response to this point, that organizations such as the Trilateral Commission can never obtain all the various powers associated with a state apparatus. Corporations do not have the monopoly of power that the state has and cannot directly legislate and/or execute legislation. They can influence legislation and political action in general, but they are not the state (see Poulantzas 1978: 179–185). While it is undeniable that attempts to organize at the global level are undertaken by the transnational bourgeoisie, these attempts have not historically replaced the mediating and organizing functions of the state. Nevertheless, empirical tendencies toward the emergence of a multinational state are found in the expansion and consolidation of the European Community (EC), the creation of the North American Free Trade Agreement (NAFTA); political attempts by Japan to organize a multistate organization of countries of the Orient, the Organization for Economic Co-ordination and Development (OECD) regulatory patterns in the agricultural and food area and in other productive sectors, etc. Among these attempts, the EC is the most advanced with its thirty years of history and proposed schedule for economic and, eventually, political unification (Bonanno 1990c: 3). However, even in the EC case the attempt to create a multination state is still embryonic and is limited from the outset. It is embryonic because the EC is still an organization of nations without a unifying political authority. In fact, decisions are negotiated in institutional settings in which national rather than communitarian interests are represented (Bonanno, Fernández, and Gilles 1990: 231–239). It is limited from its inception because the dislocation between state power and the arena of capital accumulation might well continue to exist since the EC incorporates only a limited number of nations and does not constitute a global political entity.

Problems associated with the lack of a political institution addressing social and economic interests are not confined to the transnational bourgeoisie. The national state's apparent inability to extend its action to the new transnational arena affects the interests of subordinate classes, as well.[6] Scholarship on the role of the state in society (Block 1980; Bonanno and Calasanti 1988; Offe 1985; Poulantzas 1978) underscores the fact that, along with a repressive role, the state can in some circumstances perform a progressive role (i.e., that through political action subordinate classes force the state to protect some of their interests). However, the interests of subordinate classes are protected only in so far as the state maintains normative control over the production process. As this control is reduced or eliminated, so is the protection of the interests of subordinate classes. Accordingly, legislation passed to establish wage levels, safety and health regulations, and regional and community development programs has been partially voided through economic maneuvers such as the migration of capital and production outfits across national borders and other forms of bypassing state authority (Calasanti and Bonanno 1992; Constance and Heffernan 1991; Sassen 1988).

State action in favor of the transnational bourgeoisie and the simultaneous state protection of the interests of subordinate classes point to a convergence of interests on the part of these two groups in preserving the existence of a state that could effectively intervene in socioeconomic affairs. However, this convergence of action is contradictory. The interests of transnational companies and subordinate classes in maintaining state action are motivated by opposing reasons, and, more importantly, they tend to undermine the objectives of the other group.

Transnational capital is interested in state action that fosters accumulation. If this action is opposed, counteractions are taken. In recent years such counteraction has assumed the form of bypassing the coordinating and mediating role of the state. This solution, in turn, undermines the state's ability to assist corporations in the process of accumulation. Subordinate classes are interested in state action that protects their economic and social well being. The transnational restructuring of the economy has severely limited the national state's action to protect the social and economic gains that subordinate classes have obtained in previous periods (Bonanno 1988, 1987a).

Attempts to dismantle interventionist state policies do not imply the actual elimination of state intervention. Rather, they mandate a reorganization of such intervention in favor of one or more groups involved in the process. In this context, for instance, interpretations of General Agreement on Tariffs and Trade negotiations as attempts to end the distorting intervention of the state[7] overlook the fact that a normative intervention of the state is still required and that previous normative patterns are replaced by new ones that still require some form of state intervention. For instance, in the case of the EC (Bonanno 1990b), protectionist regulatory patterns aimed at enhancing the value of food security within a given territory are challenged in the name of other accepted values such as fair and unrestricted economic competition. A decision to uphold either of these two sets of values will result in advantages for some groups over others that, ultimately, require state intervention to maintain them and to legitimize their outcomes to the general population. The contradictory convergence of interests in establishing a transnational state indicates that the terrain of crucial confrontations between opposing social forces is shifting to the international arena. More specifically, the void generated by the nonexistence of a transnational state opens up the possibility of creating such a state based on a democratic, rather than totalitarian, model.

To be sure, it would be inaccurate to argue that this void is experienced with the same degree and quality by the transnational bourgeoisie and subordinate classes alike. The transnational bourgeoisie has shown some ability to address some of the functions performed by the State at the international level. This phenomenon is empirically traceable to the ability of this class to use its own economic structures (i.e., its ability to organize and control economic systems [Constance and Heffernan 1991]), to its ability to influence emerging transnational political entities such as the EC, OECD, etc., and to its attempts to create and maintain transnational coordinating entities such as the Trilateral Commission. Subordinate classes have established a presence in some of the emerging transnational political institutions (i.e., the EC). However, their presence, though occasionally quite significant politically, reflects their status as a political minority at the domestic level.

Despite their unequal presence at the transnational level, it is fundamental to stress that neither group has direct and total control of the international political arena. The limited ability of environmental movements to limit and/or alter production patterns engineered by transnational companies, consumer movements that have prompted the rejection of transnationally supported new products such as the biotechnologically generated bovine growth hormone, and the ability of transnational corporations to effectively respond to these challenges have testified to the unresolved character of the political situation at the transnational level.

Increased attention to the international arena should not be confused with disregard for action at the local level, which has provided the context within which subordinate class demands have emerged. More importantly, the local level will remain the context within which labor participates in the productive process. In other words, while other aspects of production have been transnationalized and can be moved more easily across national borders, issues involving labor remain local. The local level, then, remains the forum within which needs emerge and demands for their satisfaction are developed (e.g., employment opportunities, availability of consumption items, social services). However, it is increasingly difficult for the domestic state to address these locally originated needs and related social demands, because processes that affect them are increasingly shifted to the transnational arena (reallocation of employment opportunity across national boundaries, global production, disarticulation of local production and immediate consumption, globally oriented investments, and so on.).

If this scenario is correct, three basic issues emerge in the new transnational system. First is the issue of the formation of a transnational state. In a context in which no social force has gained total control of the transnational arena and in which the restructuring of existing state intervention does not imply its elimination, the actual organization of such a political entity assumes paramount importance if the objective of the creation of equitable social arrangements is to be achieved. Second, the transnationalization of the economic process shifts to the international level the terrain in which socially generated needs are addressed. However, social needs will continue to emerge at the local level. This situation implies a gap between the locus of origin and the locus of possible resolution of these needs. Third, and related to the above, if there is a gap between the loci of origin and resolution of social needs, what are the instruments available to connect the two? Moreover, provided the limited range of action of the national state and the absence of a transnational state, what is the immediate institutional counterpart available to address the demands emerging from the social context?

In an increasingly transnational society the form of the evolving relationship between economic and political institutions will be key to the establishment of equitable social arrangements. In this respect, the relationship between the polity and the economy in the transnational setting should occupy central stage in the democratic debate on the social, economic, and political institutions and trends that characterize the new global order.

Notes

1. The concept of the state employed in this analysis refers to the country's government, its national and local agencies, local governments and their agencies, and local and national government agents. Moreover, it includes agents who operate on behalf of the state.

2. See the case of the European Community as an example of multinational agricultural policies. For a detailed account of the evolution of such policies see Bonanno (1990a) and the articles in the special issue of the journal *Agriculture and Human Values* on the "Crisis of European Agriculture," 6, 1/2, 1989.

3. A report in the specialized media describes this process as follows: "As cross-border trade and investment flows reach new highs, big global companies are effectively making decisions with little regard to national boundaries. Though few companies are totally untethered from their home countries, the trend toward a form of "stateless corporation is unmistakable" (*Business Week* 14 May 1990: 98). Moreover, this trend involves not only the largest corporations but medium and some small companies as well (Filippello 1991).

4. This situation can be corrected both domestically and internationally through welfare programs. For the present discussion welfare programs are considered political rather than economic mechanisms. In fact, the adoption of domestic and international welfare programs, including international aid programs, is often motivated by political reasons rather than strict economic considerations.

5. This analysis runs counter to accounts that view transnational corporations as able to organize their economic activities independently and to control increasingly the economic arena. In this view transnational corporations are seen as entities in control of socioeconomic relations.

6. The concept of subordinate classes is employed here in its most general sense. It refers to social and economic groups that do not occupy a dominant position in society. Moreover, the concept of subordinate class does not imply homogeneity in terms of political goals or actions. On the contrary, it refers to heterogeneous groups that have been and can be at odds in the political arena.

7. A corollary of this position is that issues involving the role of the state become secondary once its role is subordinated to pure economic forces emerging from an unrestricted market.

Bibliography

Barkin, David. 1990. *Distorted Development*. Boulder, Colo.: Westview Press.

Block, Fred. 1980. "Beyond relative autonomy: State managers as historical subjects." Pp. 227–240 in R. Miliband and J. Seville (eds.), *Socialist Register*. London: Merlin Press.

Bluestone, Barry, and Bennett Harrison. 1982. *The Deindustrialization of America:*

Plant Closing, Community Abandonment, and the Dismantling of Basic Industry. New York: Basic Books.

Bonanno, Alessandro. 1991. "The globalization of the agricultural and food system and theories of the state." *International Journal of Sociology of Agriculture and Food* 1: 15–30.

————. 1990a. "The Agrarian Question and the Food and Natural Resource Question: Some Reflections on the Case of the EC." Paper presented at the annual meeting of the Rural Sociological Society, Norfolk, Va., August.

———— (ed.). 1990b. *Agrarian Policies and Agricultural Systems.* Boulder, Colo.: Westview Press.

————. 1990c. "Introduction." Pp. 1–8 in A. Bonanno (ed.), *Agrarian Policies and Agricultural Systems.* Boulder, Colo.: Westview Press.

————. 1988. "Theories of the state: The case of the land reform in Italy, 1944–1961." *Sociological Quarterly* 29, 1: 131–147.

————. 1987a. *Small Farms: Persistence with Legitimation.* Boulder, Colo.: Westview Press.

————. 1987b. "Agricultural policies and the capitalist state." *Agriculture and Human Values* 4, 2/3: 40–46.

Bonanno, Alessandro, and Toni M. Calasanti. 1988. "Laissez-faire, welfare strategies and the elderly." *Sociological Focus* 21, 3: 245–264.

Bonanno, Alessandro, Donato Fernández, and Jere L. Gilles. 1990. "Agrarian policies in the US and EC: A comparative analysis." Pp. 227–251 in A. Bonanno (ed.), *Agrarian Policies and Agricultural Systems.* Boulder, Colo.: Westview Press.

Calasanti, Toni M., and Alessandro Bonanno. 1992. "Working 'over-time': Economic restructuring and retirement of a class." *Sociological Quarterly* 33, 1: 135–152.

Constance, Douglas H., and William D. Heffernan. 1991. "The global poultry agro/food complex." *International Journal of Sociology of Agriculture and Food* 1: 126–142.

————. 1989. "The rise of Oligopoly in Agricultural Markets: The Demise of Family Farms." Paper presented at the Agriculture, Food, and Human Values Society meeting, Little Rock, Ark., November.

Filippello, Frank. 1991. "The Role of U.S. Firms in the Globalization Process." Paper presented at the seminar New Trends in Socio-Economic Development, University of Missouri, Columbia. March.

Friedland, William H. 1991. "The transnationalization of agricultural production: Palimpsest of the transnational state." *International Journal of Sociology of Agriculture and Food* 1: 48–58.

Friedmann, Harriet, and Philip McMichael. 1989. "Agriculture and the state system." *Sociologia Ruralis* 29, 2: 93–117.

————. 1988. *The World Historical Development of Agriculture: Western Agriculture in Comparative Perspective.* Sociology of Agriculture Working Paper Series. London: Rural Studies Research Centre.

Gómez, Sergio, and Walter Goldfrank. 1991. "World market and agricultural transformation: The case of neo-liberal Chile." *International Journal of Sociology of Agriculture and Food* 1: 143–150.

Goodman, David, Bernardo Sorj, and John Wilkinson. 1987. *From Farming to Biotechnology: A Theory of Agro-Industrial Development.* Oxford: Basil Blackwell.

Heffernan, William D. 1990. "Internationalization of the Poultry Industry." Paper presented at the Twelfth World Congress of Sociology, Madrid, Spain, July.

————. 1984. "Constraints in the U.S. poultry industry." Pp. 237–260 in H.

Schwarzweller (ed.), *Research in Rural Sociology and Development*. Greenwich, Conn.: JAI Press.

Kautsky, Karl. 1987. *The Agrarian Question*. Manchester: Manchester University Press.

Kenney, Martin, Linda M. Lobao, James Curry, and Richard Coe. 1989. "Midwest agriculture and US Fordism." *Sociologia Ruralis* 29, 2: 131–148.

McMichael, Philip. 1991. "Food, the state and the world economy." *International Journal of Sociology of Agriculture and Food* 1: 71–85.

McMichael, Philip, and Frederick H. Buttel. 1990. "New directions in the political economy of agriculture." *Sociological Perspectives* 33, 1: 89–109.

Morett, Jorge. 1991. "Nuevas modalidades de control de las empresa transnacionales en la agricultura Mexicana: El caso de la fresa." *Agricultura y Sociedad* 60, 3: 29–47.

Murray, Robin. 1971. "The internationalization of capital and the nation state." *New Left Review* 67: 84–109.

Offe, Claus. 1985. *Disorganized Capitalism*. Cambridge, Mass.: MIT Press.

Poulantzas, Nicos. 1978. *State, Power, Socialism*. London: New Left Books.

Pugliese, Enrico. 1991. "Agriculture and the new division of labor." Pp. 137–150 in William H. Friedland, Lawrence Busch, Frederick H. Buttel, and Alan P. Rudy (eds.), *Towards a New Political Economy of Agriculture*. Boulder, Colo.: Westview Press.

Renard, Marie-Christine. 1990. "The World Market and the Production of Coffee in the Soconusco, Chiapas, Mexico." Paper presented at the Twelfth World Congress of Sociology, Madrid, Spain, July.

Rowthorn, Bob. 1971. "Imperialism in the 1970's—unity or rivalry." *New Left Review* 69: 31–54.

Sassen, Saskia. 1988. *The Mobility of Labor and Capital*. New York: Cambridge University Press.

13 Globalization as a Discourse

Mustafa Koc

In recent years globalization has become a fashionable concept, used unsparingly by academics, politicians, and the media. "The Globalization Thing," as the title of an article in *Cornell Hotel & Restaurant Administration Quarterly* put it, has captured its place in public imagery of "reality." Referring to "the intensification of world wide social relations which link distant localities in such a way that local happenings are shaped by events occurring many miles away" (Giddens 1990: 64), globalization has described and explained global linkages and interdependencies (Campanella 1990: 4). People living in different localities have come to realize that the social and economic conditions affecting them have something to do with events taking place elsewhere. In this new era of global consciousness, external causality is being used as a reason or excuse for social and economic problems and justification for unpopular austerity measures and structural changes by various governments. Unemployment, inflation, and recession are blamed on global economic conditions, and high interest rates, cuts in welfare, layoffs, and restrictions on democracy are presented as measures for coping with the global challenges.

The word "globalization," which first appeared in *Webster's* in 1961, has quickly entered into the global Esperanto of popular English notions that have been adopted by various other languages. Rather than signaling an increasing public awareness of the globalization process, the recent popularity of this concept has a lot to do with the neoconservative discourse that has come to define government programs in different parts of the world since the 1970s (Carroll 1990; Gamble 1988; Hall 1988; Jessop, Bonnett, and Bromley 1990; Overbeek 1989; Warnock 1988; Whitaker 1987). Emphasizing the discursive character of "globalization" does not imply that it is simply an imaginary construct, a rhetorical package.[1] Globalization as discourse means that it involves both concrete historical processes and a selective ideological interpretation of those processes.

Globalization as a Process

Despite its recent appearance in the popular vocabulary globalization is not a new phenomenon. It has been an ongoing process since the inception of the capitalist world economy. Globalization has manifested itself most notably as a process of expansion of commodity relations, integration of domestic markets, and emergence of an international division of labor. The internal dynamics of capitalism have created unbounded tendencies for the geographic expansion of the accumulation process. Also, accumulation on a world scale implied a social and economic system that went beyond nation-states. Capitalism itself, in Schumpeter's words, has been a global phenomenon "both in the economic and sociological sense, essentially one process, with the whole earth as its stage" (quoted in Bornschier and Stamm 1990: 203).[2]

Phases of Global Expansion

The dynamics of accumulation, the agents of expansion, and their opponents have not always been the same. In each phase of the development of capitalism different "regimes of accumulation" and "modes of regulation" have shaped the patterns of expansion (Aglietta 1979; Lipietz 1987, 1988).[3] The dynamics of different stages of capitalist development or regimes of accumulation have not been determined simply by the specific laws of motion of the accumulation process itself. Rather, the conditions of accumulation have been continuously redefined and renegotiated by various sociopolitical actors at the national or international levels (Bryan 1987; Cox 1987; Van der Pijl 1984, 1989).

During the mercantilist phase (1500–1800) merchant capital began to expand on a global scale through state-chartered companies. Primitive accumulation of capital in Western Europe was made possible through commerce, colonial plunder, the slave trade, and depeasantization. Colonized territories began specializing in the production of consumer items such as sugar, coffee, spices, and fabrics or staples such as salted fish, fur, and later wheat and timber. While the production of consumer items expanded in the colonies, subsistence economies in Europe and the rest of the world were being destroyed.

In the industrial phase (1800–1890), the engine of global expansion was the industrial capital of Western Europe. A particularly important feature of this phase of capitalist development was a change in the dominant economic discourse from protectionism to free trade and competition. The victory of the manufacturing class over the landowners and mercantile bourgeoisie in repealing restrictive trade practices, such as the corn laws in Britain (which meant lower costs of production), marked the victory of the free traders.

Another important characteristic of this era was the emergence of nation-states and nationalism. Bringing together different regions and localities "in one nation, with one government, one code of laws, one national class-interest, one frontier and one customs-tariff" (Marx 1913: 18), the nation-state has become an institution shaping conditions of accumulation and class conflict within its boundaries. At the international level, nation-states secure sovereignty and class rule of the hegemonic/dominant classes against others.

The nation-state system has also played a contradictory role in the globalization of the world economy. Through "universal" regulation, the nation-state system introduced standardizations (such as institutionalization of time and calendar) and enforced the application of laws and regulations within its geographic borders (Robertson 1990). The nation-state has created a new platform of legitimacy for negotiations among dominant social classes/groups in different geographic areas. Despite some major failures (i.e., the world wars), the international platform has resulted in the creation of some global rules of conduct through international agreements (i.e., the General Agreement on Tariffs and Trade [GATT]) and the operations of supranational institutions (i.e., International Monetary Fund [IMF]).[4] The desire to create a new, "fictitious" identity out of various past ethnicities has also led the state to introduce a "universalistic" notion of "nation," which has had a strong ideological influence in redefining social differences. While nationalism has played a harmonizing role within nation-states, it has also created a contradictory tendency of particularism, which has contributed to the compartmentalization of the global economy.

Expansion of global trade during the industrial phase led to the establishment of new linkages outside the boundaries of imperial/nation-states. In this environment, settler farming and plantation agriculture in the colonies and postcolonial states further specialized in export crops. In cases such as the United States, where agricultural expansion was paralleled by cheap immigrant labor, domestic industry flourished. With the destruction of the subsistence economy, urban and rural populations created an expanding market for the emerging food manufacturers.

The first Great Depression between 1873 and 1890 marked the end of the competitive industrial stage of capitalism. In the monopoly phase that followed, concentration and centralization of capital led to the emergence of monopolies and cartels. Financial oligarchies were born out of the merger of industrial and financial capital. This period was characterized by a new wave of imperialist expansion to secure cheap raw materials and foodstuffs.[5] Imperialist expansion involved large-scale military and administrative operations maintained by the imperial states and their colonial satellites, as well as export of capital in the form of portfolio investment and interest-bearing loans.

The contradictory tendencies of the globalization of the market and forces of production and nationalization of the interests of capital went hand in hand. As national blocs of capital became concentrated and central-ized, they "fused" more closely with the state, using military power to com-pete against other national blocs of capital (McNally 1991: 236). The in-creasing territorial division of the world among imperial powers and the resulting compartmentalization of the world markets ultimately led to two world wars during the twentieth century.

Out of the First World War came the first socialist state excluded from the capitalist world economy. However, the socialist state's ideological challenge and the demands of the working people for economic justice (and of capital-ists for the regulation of the markets following the crisis of the 1930s) con-tributed to the emergence of the liberal welfare state.[6] The welfare state, which first appeared as a temporary response to the accumulation and legiti-macy crises of the capitalist state, has become common in advanced coun-tries. Its persistence has been due, in part, to its ability to offer an alternative to socialism by creating an image of prosperity and equality within the capi-talist societies. Supplemented with institutions of collective bargaining, sub-sidies, and government contracts, it has created relative peace among social classes.

The welfare state also fits well with the dominant Fordist regime of accu-mulation based on mass production for mass consumption. Well-paid seg-ments of unionized labor in the manufacturing sector, farmers, the state bu-reaucracy, and the military offered a very appealing market for Fordist industry within the advanced capitalist world. Moreover, once institutional-ized, dismantling the welfare state required either extrapolitical intervention (i.e., military regimes) or the creation of a new hegemonic discourse. Until the crisis of the 1970s neither an economic necessity nor a political possibil-ity for the former have arisen within the advanced capitalist countries. In the following decades, however, dismantling of the welfare state has become one of the tenets of the neoconservative discourse.

The Cold War International Order

The end of World War II marked the end of the colonial empires and the di-vision of the world into two blocs: the West, under the economic and ideo-logical domination of the United States, and the East, under the domination of the USSR.[7] In the West there were a series of attempts driven by the United States to set the rules of the new economic order. The Bretton Woods agreement of 1944, which led to the emergence of the IMF and the World Bank, were the first products of this attempt. The U.S. initiatives also in-cluded the establishment of an International Trade Organization within the

United Nations system. The Havana Charter introduced regulative measures against restrictive trade practices and introduced provisions for trade in staples, services, and capital movements. Failure of the ratification of the Havana Charter led to the adoption of a revised version of its chapter IV, creating the GATT in 1948. In general terms, GATT required members to agree to not discriminate against others in trade by applying most favored nation status multilaterally and automatically to all members. The GATT agreement also included the principle that there should be a general and gradual reduction in tariffs. Once negotiated, tariffs should not be modified without the consent of the trading partners, and quantitative restrictions on imports and exports should be eliminated.

While these institutions were setting the rules for international economic conduct, an aggressive economic aid plan was introduced for the reconstruction of Europe and Japan. The Marshall Plan and following aid packages for Taiwan and South Korea were mostly driven by the expansionist concerns of the U.S. state and corporate capital. These political and ideological concerns were aimed at weakening socialist opposition in Europe and Asia and strengthening the chain around the USSR and China. The idea of a European Common Market was also partly influenced by Cold War security concerns. European integration was seen as necessary for economic recovery; European capital had to fit well with the interests of U.S.-based transnationals (Cocks 1991).

Political and ideological motives also resulted in the emergence of the North Atlantic Treaty Organization (NATO), which played an important role in the prolonging of the Cold War order. The military wing of NATO initially created the desired, but dangerous, security chain against the East. Increasing military spending led to the emergence of a military-industrial complex, the vitality of which was tied to prolongation of the Cold War and armament sales to the Third World. Ideological war against an "external threat" was also used to weaken left opposition and radical labor unionism within the West.

Generally respecting each other's spheres of interests, the Eastern and Western blocs also competed for expansion of their ideological and economic domains in other parts of the world. Actions such as foreign aid were tied not only to economic and humanitarian concerns but also to geopolitical and strategic interests. Tensions of postcolonial social and economic restructuring in many Third World countries were inflamed by the strategic interests of the superpowers, leading to civil wars, insurgency, military interventions, and regional wars. While the superpowers had manipulated these national and regional conflicts for their own interests, Third World regimes have also used the Cold War conflict to secure their rules, to resolve border conflicts with neighboring states, and to receive foreign military and economic assistance and preferential trade practices.

Ironically, the Cold War created a spiral of increasing military spending in the USSR and the United States, hampering their economic development to a certain extent. While Germany and Japan were building their economies with the help of U.S. aid and avoiding costly military expenditures, some of the most dynamics sectors of U.S. industry (concentrated in the armament sector) were gradually losing markets to European and Japanese manufacturers.

If the monopoly phase of capitalism could be characterized by portfolio investment, the post–World War II phase could be identified with direct investment through transnational corporations (TNCs). Extending their investments to more than one country, transnational corporations have enjoyed the freedom of mobility in various markets. Their ownership and control of knowledge, including financial, marketing, and organizational systems and production technologies have allowed them to expand their investments all around the world in the post–World War II era, making transnational corporations one of the most dynamic actors of globalization.

TNCs' global operations have often created tension between the domestic development policies of nation-states and corporate accumulation strategies. TNCs have had a rather ambiguous relationship with the nation-state. Despite their economic power and political influence, TNCs have never possessed the legitimacy of the state to coordinate domestic economic and social programs, to engage in politics, or to use force at the national and international levels. TNCs, like other corporate entities, have demanded the state's involvement in creating a stable environment for accumulation, defined as probusiness regulations; preferential treatment in the form of subsidies or tax breaks; supply of the necessary infrastructure; and defense of the corporate interests domestically and internationally. For this reason, support of the parent state (often an economic power) and cooperation of the branches have become necessary. Given the conflictual nature of national and international politics, however, TNCs have preferred minimum state intervention. This rather ambiguous position toward the nation-state has led corporate leadership to become one of the main participants of the neoconservative alliance; defending a deregulated, privatized, lean and mean state that has been stripped of its "excessive" welfare policies and nationalism.

The agriculture and food sector constitutes an interesting case for studying the patterns and contradictions of the globalization process. Shaped earlier by the global expansion of commodity relations, first by merchant capital, then by colonial and imperialist expansionism and international division of labor, agriculture in the post–World War II era has been globalized in a highly uneven manner by the TNCs. This process, however, has not been completely structured by accumulation concerns. Other factors have played a major role in the restructuring of the agriculture and food sector: geopolitics of the Cold War international regime; the fear of hunger; the desire to have some degree of authority in foodstuff; the political influence of the farm sector and/or urban consumers in the electoral politics in democratic regimes. Food and farm subsidies have continued despite their enormous fiscal burden on the state. Agriculture has remained one of the most heavily regulated branches of the economy.

In line with global discourse, one of the main proposals at the Uruguay Round GATT negotiations was removal of all barriers to trade in agricultural commodities. Even though there appeared to be a unanimous agreement on these provisions, agriculture still continues to be the main stumbling block in these negotiations. Bargaining at the international level reflects the complexity of differing class interests in this sector. While globally integrated capital (branches of agriculture specializing in export crops) tends to prefer free trade and unilateral removal of subsidies, food processors and farmers (those producing for the domestic market under supply management) oppose GATT. This is reflected in the often contradictory proposals of national representatives at GATT who defend free trade for certain products while at the same time defending trade restrictions and subsidies for others.

Limitations on the Globalization of Labor

Despite an increasing tendency toward globalization of financial and commodity markets, this process has largely excluded labor (Amin et al. 1990: 15). Tied to the notion of citizenship rights, full and free mobility of labor has become a privilege that citizens can enjoy only within the geographic boundaries of their nation-states. Except for population movements during wars and other armed conflict, mobility of labor at a global level is limited to illegal migration[8] (e.g.,Central American labor in the United States), temporary migrant labor regimes *regulated* by the states (e.g., Southeast Asian labor in the Middle East, Caribbean farmworkers in Canada, and Mediterranean workers in Western Europe), and to a limited number of high-flying professionals and technical personnel. The most significant step toward globalization of the labor market has been the recent removal of restrictions on labor mobility in European communities. Even this move, however, was restricted to the citizens of member states. Certain European Community (EC) members are still trying to regulate migration across their national boundaries (Widgren 1990).

The fact that certain rights and privileges of labor are tied to citizenship appears to create new political tensions in a global economy (Gamble 1988; Miles 1991). While globalization as a universalizing tendency can reduce some aspects of nationalism, it can also intensify such sentiments. The effects of globalization on the definitions of identity (ethnic or national) have varied widely. Among the unemployed and underemployed victims of economic "restructuring" and "rationalization" in the industrialized countries globalization has strengthened populist and nationalist movements tainted with antiimmigrant and racist overtones. Similarly, attempts to capture a better location in the global economy have led to nationalist or regionalist separatist movements within the borders of already existing nation-states. Discussing the rise of nationalism and fundamentalism in many parts of the world, Hall argues that these movements should not be seen simply as "revivals of the past but reworkings of it in the circumstances of the present," as resistance to the homogenizing "indifference of globalization" (1991b: 18–19).

Globalization as a Discourse

As the crisis of the 1970s began to shake the foundations of the post–World War II (or more correctly the post-Depression) order in the West, the merits of the Fordist regime of accumulation, the national mode of market regulation, and the Keynesian welfare state have come into question (Clarke 1990a and 1990b; Lipietz 1988). Although it is still too early to talk about a clearly defined "post-Fordist" regime of accumulation, most observers agree that the recent attempts at restructuring present a divergence from classical Fordism (Hall 1991a; Harvey 1989; Murray 1991; Rustin 1989). Restructuring includes

> a shift to the new "information technologies"; more flexible, decentralized forms of labor process and work organization; the decline of the old manufacturing base and the growth of the "sunrise," computer-based industries; the hiring off, or contracting out, of functions and services; a greater emphasis on choice and product differentiation, on marketing, packaging, and design; the "targeting" of consumers by lifestyle, taste, and culture rather than by the categories of social class; the rise of the service and white-collar classes; the "feminization" of the work force; an economy dominated by the multinationals, with their new international division of labor and their greater autonomy from nation-state control;

and the "globalization" of the new financial markets, linked by the communications revolution (Hall 1991a: 58).

Responses to the economic crisis found echoes among the globally integrated segments of corporate capital and other classes. The neoconservative leadership, notably Reagan in the United States and Thatcher in United Kingdom, offered a reform package involving privatization, deregulation, economic restructuring, and the dismantling of the welfare state. Neoconservative discourse has found supporters among a number of politicians, business leaders, academics, and even religious figures, all agreeing that globalization was inevitable and that the restructuring of the economy and renegotiation of the social charter were necessary. Pointing out the global challenges as an excuse in their attack against the welfare state, the new right defended tight monetary measures, regressive taxation, reduction in social services, deregulation, and privatization with antiunion policies and practices. These national-level policies paralleled international connections aiming to liberalize trade and the movement of capital and services through supranational institutions, bilateral and multilateral agreements, customs-free zones, and free-trade areas.

According to the new right ideologists, global sensitivity has required increasing economic connections but has also necessitated measures for the protection and implementation of "global" rules of conduct. Thus, in the midst of economic decline, spending millions of dollars for military ventures in the Falklands, Grenada, Panama, and the Persian Gulf met with almost no opposition. The rhetorical justification behind all these events was that "we" had to adjust ourselves to the challenges of global competition and at the same time set global economic and political principles and assure their implementation. Although these two perceptions included contradictory attitudes of fatalism and voluntarism about the inevitability of globalization, lack of counterhegemonic alternatives (due to the crisis of socialism and social democracy) allowed the neoconservative interpretation of globalization to become a hegemonic discourse.[9]

The discursive character of globalization does not mean that it is simply an imaginary construct of global capital and the neoconservative right. As a discourse, globalization has been more than a rhetorical package. Although the process of globalization has been ongoing since the inception of the capitalist world economy, since the mid-1970s its public image has been reconstructed by neoconservative ideology. In this environment, globalization emerged as a discourse involving both concrete historical processes and a selective ideological interpretation of these processes.

The process of globalization has been presenting itself in the form of uneven distribution of conditions of wealth and poverty among different social classes, ethnic groups, regions, and nations around the world; by the emergence of dependencies and interdependencies; and by the integration of regional and national economies to the world economy through the expansion of capitalism on a world scale. What the new right provided was a new interpretation about the inevitability of this process and a package of solutions to the crises of the welfare state, Fordist accumulation, and the Cold War international order. Neoconservative discourse defends not only free movement of goods and services (and restricted mobility of labor) across national borders but also the redefinition at the global level of the social agenda and conditions of work, production, and consumption within national boundaries. Behind the rhetoric of getting rid of state interventionism lies the desire to dismantle all forms of "unfavorable" interventions, as well as public policies, programs, and institutions that try to regulate factor markets at the national levels: for example, minimum wage laws, trade unions, environmental protection acts, unemployment insurance, public medicine, marketing boards, supply management, and cooperative structures.

Mediation of conflicts arising within the global economy and the definition of the social agenda have been provided and negotiated by the nation-states and supranational bodies within the boundaries of national political struggles and international negotiations (depending on the strengths of the participants). For this reason, globalization has been far from smooth. It has been tainted with contradictions, reflecting the conflicting demands of different classes (or fractions of classes) and states. It has been no surprise to see that in international negotiations some of the participants defend multilateral free trade while attempting to use protectionist measures for certain branches of the economy.

Although the nation-state is still an important actor in the international arena, the pressures of the global economy and international rules and regulations have increasingly limited its sovereignty, set restrictions on withdrawing from world markets without major economic sacrifices and political turmoil, and led to its gradual weakening. The gradual weakening of the nation-state does not imply a categorical crisis of the capitalist state. In fact, Gamble (1988) points out that Thatcherism, while liberalizing the economy, at the same time was attempting to restore the authority of the state.

Furthermore, Murray (1991) argues that Tory policy in Great Britain was aiming to reform the British state into a full-fledged Fordist state with commitments to standard products, scale, Tayloristic labor practices, and centralized information administration. The new right agenda, in fact, aims to change and redirect the state rather than dismantle it. "Social ministries shrink while trade and finance ministries grow. The enhanced economic ministries are tied to capitals and outside agencies, and the reduced ones to civil (national) society" (Friedmann 1991: 35). The state envisioned by the neoconservatives aims to enhance the power of global capital while compelling the underprivileged classes, ethnic groups, and regions to live under globally structured local rule.

Rather than seeing the disappearance of the nation-state, we see decentralization of regulation at suprastate, nation-state, and substate levels. At the global level, suprastate institutions such as IMF, the World Bank, the EC, and multilateral or bilateral agreements such as the North American Free Trade Agreement or GATT define and determine the global rules of conduct. These decisions have increasingly been made outside the confines of national politics, in a highly elitist fashion with a group of experts and negotiators, often in ideological congruity with transnational corporate interests. At the local level, substate formations such as provincial or municipal governments' attempts to grab a better market share have led to the emergence of local- and regional-level deregulation through bylaws, incentives, and concessions to transnational capital. As Soja (1989) argues, one result of increasing competition for investment among cities, regions, and nations is that the unevenness of development has become even more pronounced.

As the complex division of labor created by the globalization of production and distribution has opened both capital and producers to the influences of world commodity markets, the more vulnerable regions and social groups (i.e., women, minorities, working class, poor) have called for intervention by the nation-state. This tendency indicates antagonistic responses toward globalization. While certain fractions of capital, such as financial and transnational capital and export-oriented branches of agriculture, defend further integration, nation-based industrialists, the petite bourgeoisie, branches of agriculture under the protection of supply management, small family farmers, and labor in general tend to defend protectionist measures and nationally based accumulation strategies.

Public awareness of globalization has not simply been shaped by the neoconservative discourse. Increasing mobility of transnational capital, emerging multinational and supranational alliances, treaties, and negotiations have made the public in every country aware of global linkages. Improvements in information and communication technology have facilitated the dissemination of information (fact/interpretation). Images of war, hunger, starvation, and environmental problems have raised a new form of global consciousness and the desire to do something about it. Despite their limitations, attempts of nongovernmental agencies such as Amnesty International and Green Peace, donations to supranational agencies such as the Red Cross and UNICEF, and activities of religious and secular foreign aid projects reflect this new sensitivity. Unfortunately, while carrying the seeds of discontent, this sensitivity has been far from creating a counterhegemony. Nationalism of labor movements, class reductionism of the traditional left and its slowness in incorporating the concerns of new social movements (i.e., feminist, environmentalist, etc.) into its agenda, as well as the single issue politics of the latter groups have created obstacles to the success of alternative discourse. Instead of responding to the challenges of globalization, alternatives remain to be restricted to autarchic models of development and/ or "state interventionism" (Clarke 1990b; Geddes 1988; McNally 1991).

Conclusion

Globalization, as a contradictory tendency toward both universalism and particularism, has been an outcome of the expansion of capitalist relations of production around the world. On the one hand, it has been destroying particularisms and creating universal standards in production, consumption, and in social and political processes. On the other hand, because of the uneven nature of this process, it has also created new particularisms in addition to the ones that already existed. The inevitability of this process has been determined not by its own laws of motion but by sociopolitical historical moments. In other words, neither globalization, compartmentalization, nor their consequences are predetermined, unavoidable destinies. For this reason, the neoconservative definition of globalization as inevitable, requiring the renegotiation of the "social charter," and its insistence on a new international division of labor according to market principles has to be challenged.

Such a challenge requires a global response, not a national one. Whether we like it or not "the world economy is now so thoroughly integrated across national boundaries that an autonomous national capitalist strategy is no longer possible" (Radice 1984: 113). Instead of defending the welfare state by disregarding its class character, we need to search for a "new world order," international hegemonic rules of social, political, and economic conduct (by respecting particularisms) that would challenge the uneven nature of development. Rather than being a painful destiny that people all around the world should follow under the leadership of global capital, globalization needs to be envisioned as the recognition of global sensitivity. The knowledge that we are sharing the same world and the same resources calls for a responsible and caring relationship among the members of the world community.

"The capitalist world is no longer just a 'world economy': it is also a space of 'unified' and monopolized world communications in which, potentially, all populations are somehow, immediately 'visible' and in contact with one another. Such a world has never before existed" (Balibar 1991: 14). The emergence of formations larger than nation-states and the expansion of international communication and interaction add to the awareness that we are living on a small planet. From our interdependence we may be able to create new possibilities and tools for an alternative vision of the global society.

Notes

I am grateful to Enzo Mingione for his valuable suggestions.

1. Discourse is defined here as the articulation of language, practices and institutions (Laclau and Mouffe 1987).

2. Universalistic characteristics of this process are taken to their logical extreme in Wallerstein's analysis of the world system where all particularisms are explained with the logic of the whole. As Wallerstein points out, "The modern world comprises a single capitalist world economy, which has emerged since the sixteenth century and which still exists today. . . . National states are not societies that have separate, parallel histories, but parts of a whole. . . . To understand the internal class contradictions and political struggles of a particular state, we must first situate it in the world-economy" (1979: 53).

3. In their critique of the regulationist school, Brenner and Glick (1991) argue that the regulationists do not adequately take into account the general and distinctive features of the capitalist mode of production. Although their warnings are justified to a certain extent, one should avoid falling into an economistic trap. Capital does not follow an inner logic independent of social and political struggles.

4. There is a tendency among mercantilist (Krasner 1985) and regulationist (Aglietta 1979) scholars to overemphasize the national dimension by regarding the world economy as "a system of interacting national social formations" (Aglietta 1982: 6). Although the role of the nation-state in modern societies has been very important, "treating nation states as actors having connections with each other and with other organizations in the international arena makes it difficult to deal with social relations that are not between or outside states, but simply crosscut state divisions" (Giddens 1990: 67). As some of the twentieth-century nation-states are torn apart by ethnic and religious conflicts, and as new social identities organized around religion or regionalism are emerging, insistence on the nation-state as the unit of analysis will significantly limit in our understanding of the political and ideological dimensions of globalization.

5. Historians question the original hypothesis of Lenin that the shortage of raw materials was one of the reasons for imperialist expansion. Fieldhouse (1972), for example, points out the role of psychological necessity in leading to imperialism, implying that the reasons might not necessarily be real in structural terms, but real because the proponents of imperialism believed that they were real. As W. I. Thomas once argued, "If men define situations as real, they are real in their consequences" (Merton 1967: 19).

6. The authoritarian conservative alternative to the welfare state was the fascist state.

7. Cox (1987) and Van der Pijl's (1984, 1989) attempts to apply the Gramscian no-

tion of hegemony to international relations are problematic. Hegemony in the Gramscian sense implies consensual politics and class compromise. Pax Americana was a "power bloc" under U.S. domination. Consensus as support of governments does not imply hegemony. The Iranian regime under the shah was a strong ally of the United States, yet the United States was far from being a hegemonic power for the people of Iran. Similar examples could be found during the Gulf War in the Arab world.

8. Even when the state tolerates or even encourages it, illegal immigration has to be seen as a special case of restricted labor mobility. Lack of citizenship rights turns these workers into subproletarians, stealing from them the right to enter into free contracts with capital.

9. There is no doubt that the new-right politics (Thatcherism, Reaganism) has not been very popular among the working classes and the poor. However, as Leys (1990: 127) argues, "For an ideology to be hegemonic, it is not necessary that it be loved. It is merely necessary that it have no serious rival."

Bibliography

Aglietta, Michel. 1982. "World capitalism in the eighties." *New Left Review* 136: 25–35.

———. 1979. *A Theory of Capitalist Regulation*. London: New Left Books.

Amin, Samir, G. Arrighi, A. G. Frank, and I. Wallerstein. 1990. *Transforming the Revolution: Social Movements and the World-System*. New York: Monthly Review Press.

Balibar, Etienne. 1991. "Es gibt keinen staat in Europa: Racism and politics in Europe today." *New Left Review* 186: 5–19.

Bornschier, Volker, and Hanspeter Stamm. 1990. "Transnational corporations." *Current Sociology* 38, 2/3: 203–229.

Brenner, Robert, and Mark Glick. 1991. "The regulation approach: Theory and history." *New Left Review* 188: 45–70.

Bryan, Richard. 1987. "The state and the internationalization of capital: An approach to analysis." *Journal of Contemporary Asia* 17, 3: 253–275.

Campanella, M. L. 1990. "Globalization: Process and interpretations." *World Futures* 30: 1–16.

Carroll, William K. 1990. "Restructuring capital, reorganizing consent: Gramsci, political economy, and Canada." *Canadian Review of Sociology and Anthropology* 27, 3: 81–112.

Clarke, Simon. 1990a. "New utopias for old: Fordist dreams and post-Fordist fantasies." *Capital and Class* 42: 131–155.

———. 1990b. "The crisis of Fordism or the crisis of social democracy." *Telos* 83: 71–98.

Cocks, Peter. 1991. "Towards a Marxist theory of European integration." Pp. 34–48 in Jeffry A. Frieden and David A. Lake (eds.), *International Political Economy*. New York: St. Martin's Press.

Cox, Robert W. 1987. *Production, Power, and World Order*. New York: Columbia University Press.

Crookel, Harold, and Allen Morrison. 1990. "Subsidiary strategy in a free trade environment." *Business Quarterly* 55, 2: 33–39.

Fair, Milton. 1991. "Doing business in agriculture." *Business Quarterly* 56, 1: 119–123.

Fieldhouse, D. K. 1972. "Imperialism: An historiographic revision." Pp. 95–123 in K. E. Boulding and T. Mukerjee (eds.), *Economic Imperialism*. Ann Arbor: University of Michigan Press.

Friedmann, Harriet. 1991. "New wines, new bottles: Regulation of capital on a world scale." *Studies in Political Economy* 36: 9–42.

Gamble, Andrew. 1988. *The Free Economy and the Strong State: The Politics of Thatcherism*. Basingstoke, Eng.: Macmillan.

Geddes, Mike. 1988. "The capitalist state and the local economy: 'Restructuring for labour' and beyond." *Capital and Class* 35: 85–120.

Giddens, Anthony. 1990. *The Consequences of Modernity*. Stanford, Calif.: Stanford University Press.

Hall, Stuart. 1991a. "Brave new world." *Socialist Review* 21, 1: 57–64.

———. 1991b. "Europe's other self." *Marxism Today* August: 18–19.

———. 1988. *The Hard Road to Renewal: Thatcherism and the Crisis of the Left*. London: Verso.

Harvey, David. 1989. *The Condition of Postmodernity*. Cambridge, Mass.: Basil Blackwell.

Jessop, Bob, Kevin Bonnett, and Simon Bromley. 1990. "Farewell to Thatcherism? Neo-liberalism and 'new times.' " *New Left Review* 179: 81–102.

Krasner, Stephen D. 1985. *Structural Conflict: The Third World against Global Liberalism*. Berkeley: University of California Press.

Laclau, Ernesto, and Chantal Mouffe. 1987. "Post-Marxism without apologies." *New Left Review* 166: 73–106.

Leys, Colin. 1990. "Still a question of hegemony." *New Left Review* 181: 119–128.

Lipietz, Alain. 1988. "Accumulation, crises, and ways out: Some methodological reflections on the concept of 'regulation.' " *International Journal of Political Economy* 18, 2: 10–41.

———. 1987. *Miracles and Mirages: The Crises of Global Fordism*. London: Verso.

Marx, Karl. 1913. *The Communist Manifesto*. Chicago: Charles H. Kerr and Company.

McCarthy, Shawn. 1991. "Adapt or die, Canadian branch plants warned," *Toronto Star*, 8 October 1991.

McNally, David. 1991. "Beyond nationalism, beyond protectionism: Labour and Canada-US free trade agreement." *Capital and Class* 43: 233–252.

Merton, Robert K. 1967. *On Theoretical Sociology*. New York: Free Press.

Miles, Robert. 1991. "Immigration, Racism and the Nation State." Keynote address at a conference on Immigration, Racism, and Multiculturalism: The 1990s and Beyond, at the University of Saskatchewan, Saskatoon, Canada, 22–23 March 1991.

Murray, Robin. 1991. "The state after Henry." *Marxism Today* May: 22–27.

Overbeek, Henk. 1989. *Global Capitalism and National Decline*. London: Unwin and Hyman.

Radice, Hugo. 1984. "The national economy: A Keynesian myth?" *Capital and Class* 22: 111–140.

Robertson, Roland. 1990. "After nostalgia? Willful nostalgia and the phases of globalization." Pp. 45–61 in Bryan S. Turner (ed.), *Theories of Modernity and Postmodernity*. Newbury Park, Calif.: Sage.

Rustin, Michael. 1989. "The politics of post-Fordism: Or the trouble with 'new times.' " *New Left Review* 175: 54–77.

Soja, Edward. 1989. *Postmodern Geographics*. London: Verso.

Van der Pijl, Kees. 1989. "Ruling classes, hegemony, and the state system." *International Journal of Political Economy* 19, 3: 7–35.

_____. 1984. *The Making of an Atlantic Ruling Class*. London: Verso.

Wallerstein, Immanuel. 1979. *The Capitalist World-Economy*. Cambridge: Cambridge University Press.

Warnock, John W. 1988. *Free Trade and the New Right Agenda*. Vancouver: New Star Books.

Whitaker, Reg. 1987. "Neo-conservatism and the state." Pp. 1–31 in Ralph Miliband, Leo Panitch, and John Saville (eds.), *Socialist Register 1987*. London: Merlin Press.

Widgren, Jonas. 1990. "International migration and regional stability." *International Affairs* 66, 4: 749–766.

Contributors

Alessandro Bonanno is associate professor of rural sociology at the University of Missouri, Columbia.

Lawrence Busch is professor of sociology at Michigan State University.

Doug Constance is a research associate in the Department of Rural Sociology at the University of Missouri, Columbia.

Ian Cook is a doctoral candidate in geography at the University of Bristol.

Andrew Flynn is professor of geography at the University of Hull.

William H. Friedland is professor emeritus of community studies and sociology at the University of California, Santa Cruz.

Lourdes Gouveia is assistant professor of sociology at the University of Nebraska, Omaha.

William Heffernan is professor of rural sociology at the University of Missouri, Columbia.

Raymond Jussaume is assistant professor of rural sociology at Washington State University, Pullman.

Mustafa Koc is assistant professor of sociology at Ryerson Polytechnic University, Toronto.

Luis Llambi is professor of sociology at the Venezuela Institute for Scientific Investigation, Caracas.

Mary Marchant is assistant professor of agricultural economics at the University of Kentucky, Lexington.

Terry Marsden is professor of geography and earth resources at the University of Hull.

Enzo Mingione is professor of sociology at the University of Messina.

Enrico Pugliese is professor of sociology at the University of Naples.

Michael Reed is professor of agricultural economics at the University of Kentucky, Lexington.

Bernardo Sorj is professor of sociology at the Federal University of Rio de Janeiro.

Neil Ward is professor of geography and earth resources at the University of Hull.

John Wilkinson is professor of sociology at the Federal University of Rio de Janeiro.

Index